"Where Traditions Meet"

"In the 21st-century, baseball has become a truly international game. Global interest and participation continue to grow. That includes the against all odds Israeli squad, whose adventures are recounted here."
- **Bob Costas**

"As a former Baseball Commissioner with more than 45 years of experience in the game, I am pleased to endorse Peter Kurz on his work in producing 'Where Traditions Meet', an outstanding book that describes how baseball and the World Baseball Classic contributed to bringing the people of Israel together in times of crisis, turmoil and uncertainty."
- **Allan H. (Bud) Selig, Commissioner Emeritus of Baseball**

"Baseball invites us to dream. Peter Kurz's new book describes the good that happens when we do. 'Where Traditions Meet' explains how the game has helped a people learn more about themselves — while inspiring others who might never have played catch before. Kurz helps us realize that pride in one's identity transcends the greatest trophies in sport."
– **Jon Paul Morosi, MLB Network**

"What Peter Kurz has accomplished in this book is to capture a one-of-a-kind sports story. In 'Where Traditions Meet', he shows how any dream is possible."
 - **Ken Belson, NY Times**

"Peter Kurz has done something one would think is impossible...taken his two great loves, Baseball and Israel, and joined them together into what is now Israel Baseball.   "WHERE TRADITIONS MEET" is a warm and heartfelt account of how this happened and how he made his dream, and the dreams of young Jewish men, come true!"
 - **Suzyn Waldman, NY Yankees Radio Broadcaster**

ISBN # 978-965-597-794-3 Print version

ISBN # 978-965-597-795-0 eBook version

A special thanks to JP Michaels

Dedication

This book is dedicated to Ronit whose love and support in life made this odyssey possible; to Maya and Adi, who humored me through the years with smiles and sighs; and Amit, who started as my protégé but quickly aced me and gave his dad all the reason in the world to love baseball.

May my grandchildren grow up having the same love for life that I have for baseball.

Contents

Prologue

Gocheok Skydome, Seoul, South Korea, March 6, 2017

As Josh Zeid toed the rubber and looked in to catcher Ryan Lavarnway for the sign, I couldn't completely process all that was riding on this next pitch.

For one thing, we were a strike away from winning the first game of the 2017 World Baseball Classic, a tournament no one but us thought Israel would make. Launched by Major League Baseball in 2005, the WBC was, and remains, one of the biggest baseball tournaments in the world.

For another, it would be Josh's 49th pitch, and the rules dictated that 50 by a pitcher in an outing required four days' rest before stepping back out onto the mound. This meant that if he didn't retire Dae Ho Lee with this forthcoming pitch, our best bullpen arm would be unavailable for the next two games against Chinese Taipei and the Netherlands. Since we would have to win at least one of those two contests to make it to the next round in Japan, the rest of our tournament could conceivably have been riding on this very pitch.

That may seem like an exaggeration to some, but this was pool play and it had taken us 10 innings just to scratch out two runs, while South Korea, also a top ten country, had only scored once in nine and two thirds. With Game One already going into extra innings, pitching was at even more of a premium than offense.

Not holding a pitch counter in my hand or keeping score, I was unaware that Josh was on the brink and it wouldn't have mattered if I had. It obviously didn't matter to our manager, Jerry Weinstein, whose first priority was to win this game. So, it was live or die with Josh.

The irony was that we had died with him on the mound in the quali-fiers in 2012, when he gave up two runs to Spain in extra innings, keeping us out of the 2013 iteration of the WBC. Josh is one of the best human beings in the world, which is one of many reasons why it hurt so much when we lost that night, and a primary reason why Jerry still wanted him out there that night.

Josh had already redeemed himself in the qualifiers the previous year in Brooklyn, leading us to an unbeaten record and punching our ticket to South Korea for Pool A. Brazil, managed by Hall of Fame shortstop Barry Larkin, had been the favorite to advance out of Brooklyn, be-ing that it had gone 3-0 under him in the 2012 qualifiers to reach the main draw in the spring 2013 tournament and in so doing shocking the international baseball community. Despite being eliminated early in 2013, Brazil had performed admirably, leading or being tied in the eighth inning of its three games, including against top - ranked Japan. With Larkin still calling the shots in 2016, all of the analysts and odds makers were betting on Brazil.

They would all lose and so would Brazil – to us - one to nothing, before getting ousted by an upstart Great Britain team that relied heavily on Bahamian players. We almost no-hit the mostly commonwealth Brits the next night and breezed into the 2017 World Baseball Classic with a rare blowout victory. Josh led that qualifier with nine strikeouts in relief and had unburdened himself of a heavy load he had been carrying for four years.

That, however, was already ancient history and none of the players, coaches or I were ready to rest on our laurels. Going into this fourth WBC- which was our first- we were decidedly the underdogs. The seem-ing absurdity of Israel, from the Middle East, competing in a major baseball tournament had ESPN comparing us to the Jamaican bobsled team that reached the 1988 Winter Olympics. But a victory on South Korea's home turf would silence the critics, put Israel on the interna-tional baseball map and set the course for our future in the greatest of all sports. (Yes, I know that's biased, but it's my book and baseball will always be king.)

TV sets south of the 38th Parallel were largely tuned in and the more astute fans might have noticed that the director of the country's ministry of sports was sitting directly behind home plate, giving himself a manicure with his front teeth. Lee, a first baseman and a power threat, was his country's last hope and our last hurdle.

We'd broken the 1-1 tie in the top of the 10th with an infield single from shortstop Scotty Burcham. Scotty had just made a sensational diving catch to deprive South Korea of a hit that would have made Lee the potential winning run at bat.

A small but formidable Jewish crowd watched from the stands, predominantly Israeli diplomats working at the embassy in Seoul and players' and coaches' relatives. Back in Israel, baseball lovers — primarily natives of the United States and Canada who grew up with the sport — tuned in at bars and on laptop screens to watch the game. Many more American Jews, mostly on the East Coast, where it was now nearly 8:30 a.m., watched on the MLB Network and were probably just as surprised as ESPN to find us on the precipice of victory. Even Brad Ausmus was watching on TV from the clubhouse of the Detroit Tigers' spring training site. Brad was now the manager of the Tigers. His first managing job of any kind was Team Israel at the 2012 WBC qualifiers. Clearly, we got Brad on his way up by providing valuable experience.

About 3,000 miles west, where the sun still hadn't risen, a gentile fan of Team Israel watched, too, on a computer at the front desk of the Menlo Park, California, hotel, where he worked. He knew more about our team than many of our players. He prayed that Lee would strike out to end the game. He was also hoping it would happen before a hotel guest called down for room service and prevented him from seeing the climax. I didn't know the man then, but he later told me about it. He became a fixture of our fan base and a personal friend.

So, it had all come down to this one pitch. A pitch not only for victory, but for legitimacy in a sport where we were known, if at all, for being fans rather than players.

Josh stood up straight after getting the sign from Ryan, went into his windup and delivered the fastball that would ultimately ... Wait! I'm getting way ahead of myself.

I didn't even mention the formation of the Israeli Association of Baseball, my being their secretary general and president, and the summer of the professional Israel Baseball League. Nor our Olympic run, our fundraising efforts, two documentary films and the building of new fields in the Holy Land.

There is so much more to this story that I really should start at the beginning.

First Inning

The Stage is set: The Six-Day War and the Miracle Mets

"Baseball is, was, and always will be the best game in the world to me."
– Babe Ruth

Whenever asked what brought me to where I am today, I point to two events from my youth that shaped my later path in life: The Six-Day War and the Miracle Mets.

I guess I was your typical kid born in America in the Fifties and raised in the Sixties during the cultural revolution of that time. In retrospect, maybe I wasn't so typical.

My parents were Holocaust survivors, and that alone made me different from many of my peers growing up. Jews were only 2.7 percent of the U.S. population in 1956, although in New York City they were over 15%. I was the first generation "American" in my family, while my best friend growing up could date his heritage back to the Revolutionary war. Baseball became the great equalizer.

I was aware of where and what my mother and father had come from, but like so many others who made that tragic journey, it was something rarely spoken about. Growing up as I did in the 60's, the Holocaust was too horrific for my parents to recount, and they lived life in the here and now.

It was only years later when I was able to pry some of the details out of them that I learned about their experiences which had to influence me as their son. A few months before she passed away, my mother wrote three pages about her early life in Hungary, the horrors of World War II and her escape from the Nazi occupation. It was a harrowing story, even for only three pages, and to read it some 50 years later, coming from the woman who raised and nurtured me, was very emotional.

"Only 20 years old, I had already learned that the only irreplaceable things in life were people and their love. Material possessions had no meaning," she wrote.

My father had the typical Eastern Europe background: born in Czernowitz which was once part of the Austro-Hungarian Empire, occupied by Romania (when he was born), and is now part of Ukraine. He grew up speaking Romanian, Yiddish, Hebrew, Russian and German (Don't ask me how he kept them all apart). He was raised as an orthodox Jew but belonged to a Zionist youth group. During the war he found himself in Uzbekistan, as part of the Russian army.

My parents met in Italy after the Axis powers were defeated - la dolce vita - and were married three weeks later, with no common language between them. My mother, having been raised in an assimilated Hungarian home, did not know Yiddish, although she would learn it very quickly.

Both had grown up in liberal, traditional, Jewish homes in Eastern Europe after the War to End All Wars. My dad became a member of the Youth Gordonia, a Zionist outgrowth of Shomer Hatzair that saw itself as the pioneering youth movement, rejecting theoretical ideals in favor of the practical pioneering advocated by A.D. Gordon.

In their teens, they were subjected to the horrors of leaving their families behind, seeking refuge, changing identities, and running from and escaping the Nazis. After the war, my dad worked in Italy for the Jewish Agency. His job was to accompany Jewish refugees and Israeli VIPs to the port of Brindisi, where they would set sail for what would soon become the State of Israel.

An avid opera lover, Dad told me he once took Moshe Dayan, later the Israeli minister of defense, to the Rome Opera. But the most important person he would encounter while working for the agency was the woman who became his wife and the mother of his children. She was with her girlfriends, all set to sail from Brindisi to what then was called Palestine to join a kibbutz, when they met. Something sparked between them and they were married after just three weeks. Those 21 days of bliss became 53 years of marriage, ending only when my mother passed away. My father would go on alone for 15 years before joining her.

Most of their families were murdered in the concentration camps: Mom's mother and two sisters, in Auschwitz; Dad's father and brother. Even with no one to return to, they decided to stay in Rome while the rest of their families left for the Land of Israel. Life was better in Italy than Israel in the Fifties, hence their decision not to make the perilous voyage to yet another land where many of their neighbors would not welcome them with open arms. My father often regaled me with stories of the Italian immigrant visiting his sisters in Israel who took two crates of apples: one for the family and one to sell to finance his journey.

My sister, Ester, was born in Italy and even played the main character in a movie in which she was an orphan involved in a court case between the two families. She still has a few photos from the film.

At about four years old, the story goes, she walked past a church and made the sign of the cross as many of her friends did. It was at that moment when my parents knew it was time to leave Italy for the Holy Land. So, after 10 years in Rome as state-less refugees with no passports or money, they left for the great Zionist dream – New York City.

They relocated with assistance from the American Jewish JOINT Distribution Committee, based in New York City, one of the few places in America where an effective Jewish relief organization existed.

While recently going through my parent's paperwork, it was unsettling to discover that when they arrived in NY in 1956 – as did the immigrants in all those grainy black and white photographs - they carried with them only two suitcases and had no citizenship. They were categorized as stateless immigrants. What they possessed was an immense desire to succeed and integrate in their new lives in the United States.

New York housed thousands of Italian-speaking immigrants in many neighborhoods. Ester, though, constantly rebuked my parents by saying, "English, English! We are in America!" She eventually forgot all of her Italian.

After a few stops, my family arrived in the Upper West Side of Manhattan, the happiest home they would ever know. I was their newborn American son, and they raised my sister and me to be independent, self-sufficient and responsible. Like all immigrants to New York in the Fifties who wanted to get ahead, my parents worked hard to make a living and raise their children. We didn't always have the most of everything, but we always had the best. They became naturalized American citizens and were very proud of that. My mother's sister, Agi, lived in the same apartment building, and in later years they opened a dress shop together, "Sister's Creations." Her sons, Richard and Tommy, were always my closest cousins, and still live in NY today.

My sister, who graduated high school in 1969, was the valedictorian of her class and gave a firebrand speech at the ceremony. NASA that summer sent men to the moon. My parents sent Ester to the Hebrew University in Jerusalem, with the intent of her avoiding radical American college campuses of the early 1970s.

Growing up in a liberal Zionist home, with my grandparents, aunts and cousins residing in Israel, I was reminded daily about our commitment to the Jewish nation and to the country I would later move to and call my true home. In June of 1967, my parents made the fateful decision to take us on a visit to Israel, a few weeks after the country had defeated six Arab armies and tripled its size in the Six-Day War.

It was a fateful visit for me. I found a nation in drunken exultation, not believing the dimensions of its victory, overwhelmed by the responsibility and unsure of the steps forward. I fell in love with Israel and the walls of my room at home would soon be covered by posters touting the country's military, the Israel Defense Forces. I was enamored by my cousins who fought in the war and knew then that I, too, one day would make Aliyah and live here. That two-month visit cemented those feelings forever.

That same year, the New York Mets were well on their way to another 100-loss season and could scarcely defeat two teams in six days. The running joke among New York sports fans then went something like this:

"A man walks into a bar and orders a drink. The bartender says, "Did you hear the Mets scored 18 runs today?" The man replies, "Really? Did they win?"

I wasn't aware of this at the time. The Mets wouldn't capture my heart until they won the World Series championship two years later, but 1967 was the summer the seed was planted for me. That's when Tom Seaver, nicknamed "Tom Terrific" and still the greatest Met of all time, was fashioning a stellar rookie season, earning 16 of their 61 victories and being selected for the National League's All-Star team. The franchise built around the boyishly handsome power pitcher, and he became the cornerstone of one of the most storied seasons in the history of baseball.

The Miracle of '69 was a huge thrill for me as a budding baseball fan. That summer, I witnessed the crazy sight of a black cat on the Shea Stadium field crossing past the Chicago Cubs' dugout in front of 50,000 fans. I saw the Mets win both ends of a doubleheader, 1-0, with the starting pitchers getting the only RBIs. And I celebrated as I watched leftfielder Cleon Jones going down to a knee as he caught the final out of the World Series. My Mets had won the World Series! Babe Ruth was a Yankee, but he was damned right when he said, "Baseball is, was and always will be the best game in the world." The final row of the upper deck at Shea Stadium became a second home to me and my buddies that season and onward.

I grew up on Israel and baseball. I gave blood as a 16-year-old, after lying about my age, to help during the Yom Kippur War; smoked joints in that same upper deck; and went to two- and three-day rock and roll festivals. I listened to The Beatles, not because they were the most popular band in the world, but because they deserved to be (I didn't get to see them at Shea but my sister did, though like everyone else, she couldn't hear them). I listened to heavy rock, smoked pot and other indulgences, and argued Marx and Lenin (and McCartney or Lennon).

I went to anti-war rallies in Washington, visited Israel again in 1973 (where I met Ronit for the second time – first was when we were 4 years old) and was so bored in high school, I left after my junior year for SUNY Purchase, an alternate educational experience in the 70's (yes, although I hold a master's degree, I don't actually have a high school diploma). I majored in political science, wrote papers about Israel and played on our college intramural softball squad, the Burnouts (named after our suite), locking down home plate as the catcher (and aptly called, Smiling Buddha). It was the closest I would ever come to actual baseball, beyond watching from that upper deck with a joint in one hand and a hot dog in the other. Purchase broadened my horizons, although growing up in Manhattan in the 60's, they were quite broad already. I spent my junior year in London, focusing on urban studies and the British political process, which was in total upheaval in this pre-Thatcher period when England quickly lost its preeminent position in the world.

I travelled throughout Europe that summer with my "friend/cousin" Andy Sandor (because our parents were close friends, we knew one another from infancy – he is 10 months older than me – he once said we were practically "cousins"). We learned about "Iron Curtain Europe" prior to the fall of communism and also had our share of adventures that I cannot begin to cover here.

After her army service, Ronit came over to the US for a month, to spend time with me as we travelled down to Florida together. That visit paved a relationship which lasts till this day, as she got to better understand my background and where I was coming from. I hoped to complete my master's degree in Israel, to better appreciate her background and determine if I could settle there.

But first, it was off to the Great Asian Odyssey.

Michael Powell was not only my next-door neighbor growing up in NY, but also my baseball comrade-in-arms. We went to Met games together, watched them on TV, even emulated them, with Michael pretending to be Tom Seaver pitching to me as catcher Jerry Grote in Riverside Park. We'd talk baseball all the time — and, 50-plus years later, we still do. Michael and I attended some of the same schools, and he was my campaign manager when, in fifth grade, I ran for school president. His sisters, Julie and Mary, were in the fourth and second grades, respectively, so we cornered those votes. (The girl I defeated then, also named Julie, would end up marrying Andy Sandor!) Michael and I published a newspaper together in fifth grade and were co-news editors of the SUNY–Purchase *Load*. (yes, that was the original name of that newspaper from which at least five present-day journalists got their starts, including Michael. Heck of a name, I know.) I don't remember whose idea that was, but as soon as college was over and we made some money, it was off to our year's journey through Asia, something quite unheard of in those days (1978).

Asia began, actually, when we drove west in a five-speed manual Volvo that someone hired us to deliver in San Diego in eight days. We made it to Colorado in 48 hours and spent the next six days meandering through-out the southwest, almost getting stuck in a snowstorm in Arizona. After a few days in Los Angeles, we flew to Fiji and began an eight-month adventure that is worthy of its own book. We witnessed the amazing natural beauty of New Zealand; the Bali culture of Indonesia; the bustling city of

Bangkok and imbibed in the Golden Triangle of northern Thailand; the surf of Sri Lanka; the blown-away culture of India; the highs of Nepal, both physical and spiritual; the legalities of Pakistan and Turkey. We almost set foot in Iran, were refused entry into Singapore and ended up in Israel for a few days. Michael continued on through Europe and I stayed in Israel, where my life would change dramatically, as you shall read about in the next inning.

That journey was a milestone by opening my consciousness to a large part of the world and shifting my attention to Asia and the Far East, which I would visit often in later years.

But, when people ask me today what motivated me to do what I do, I point to that 10-year-old kid who saw Israel just after the Six Day war, and the 12-year-old kid who watched those Amazin' Mets win their first World Series. It is in those two infallible moments that the two passions which define me today first came together in my life.

Second Inning

Moving to Israel and making Aliyah

"Life is not a spectator sport. If you're going to spend your whole life in the grandstand just watching what goes on, in my opinion you're wasting your life."
– Jackie Robinson

Through the 1980s and '90s, my life stabilized into "normalcy": I changed countries three times, got married to Ronit (only once) and we had three children together.

Those two decades can be divided into three periods:

- Moving to Israel and really getting settled, making aliyah, studying for my master's degree and getting married

- Moving to New York for one year, which stretched into five years; it's where my daughter Maya and son Amit were born

- Returning to Israel, re-establishing our home and welcoming a third child, Adi

When I arrived in Israel in 1979 at age 22 after 10 months of travel in Asia, I was an emaciated, long-haired nonconformist character who had just travelled halfway around the world, experiencing cultures and lives that most Westerners had no inkling of. Ronit and her family were quite shocked, to say the least, and definitely were not sure who or what they had on their hands.

I quickly realized that to fully integrate into Israeli life, I would need to learn Hebrew. The best option would be to live and work on a kibbutz, a collective farm, and study in an ulpan, an intensive language course combined with farm work: four hours a day in class and six hours in the fields. I went to live at Kibbutz Maabarot, near the coastal city of Netanya, for six months. The group I was assigned to was primarily Americans, with some Argentinians, Europeans and even Iranians who had escaped from the new Khomeini regime. We worked and studied hard, and played hard. The social fabric was an integral part of life there.

I was assigned to the citrus orchards to pick oranges, lemons and grapefruits beginning at 4:00 a.m. to avoid the late-morning heat. We used automatic forklift trucks and did our best not to damage the trees. (Forty-three years later, I would do much the same work during the first year of the Gaza war, when the foreign farm workers fled Israel and new labor was required to pick fruit so it wouldn't rot.) Exhausted, we would all have a siesta, then rush to our afternoon Hebrew instruction before socializing at night.

Barely a month in, I somehow came down with jaundice and was isolated in my room for two weeks. The kibbutz took good care of me, reassigning me for two months to non-laborious work with the elderly members, gluing cotton balls back onto the cotton stalks and creating decorative plants to sell in European markets. The pace was perfect for me to recuperate. I had no idea how I came down with jaundice. It was a good respite following the excitement of my travels in Asia.

Ronit would visit weekly, and I went to her home in Ramat Gan as often as I could. Our relationship solidified and I knew then that this was the woman I would spend my entire life with. We attended movies and concerts, went to the beach, had Shabbat meals and took trips around the country. It was wonderful period for both of us and our love blossomed. She gave me my first Hebrew book, *The Sixteenth Sheep*, by Yehonatan Geffen, consisting of poems and stories written from a child's perspective. I memorized all of the stories, which were later adapted into songs; many of the phrases became well-known among our generation. A comeback of sorts is happening today, with songwriters of that era performing throughout Israel and audiences reliving those childhood tales to sold-out theatres. This book actually helped to solidify our relationship and went a long way towards me feeling Israeli.

I decided to study for my master's degree at Tel Aviv University, but first wanted to return to New York for a few months to earn much-needed cash. The first day I got home, a letter waited for me: a job ofer from the U.S. Government Office of Management to work in its space-management department in downtown Manhattan. A few days later, I donned a jacket and necktie and began six months of government service, hating every bureaucratic minute of that job. The entire time, I had one goal: to return to Israel to be with Ronit, and with enough cash to pay for my studies at TAU.

I called Ronit each week from a pay phone, inserting coin after coin to speak with her. Our children have no idea of life before cellphones and would probably not understand how romantic this actually was. It wasn't the most convenient arrangement, but it was all we had and it helped the relationship expand and grow as we missed each other very much. After six months, on July 4, 1980, I returned to Ronit and the Holy Land.

I rented an apartment in Ramat Aviv, close to the university, together with an apartment mate, who later became a psychologist and was eventually accused of sexually abusing his patients, and lost his license (This was not only before cellphones, but also internet background checks). I always thought the guy was strange, but I never imagined these horrific acts, which only came to light years later.

Over the summer months I attended a more intensive university ulpan, and when the academic year began in October, I thought that I was prepared to attend the classes, which were given in Hebrew. Little did I know how ill-prepared I was, with every day being a struggle. The textbooks were in English and most professors allowed me to take the exams in English, but my first-year grade point average was in the high 60's, which at that time was not very encouraging. (Today in the United States, it would be considered reasonable). Ronit had her own challenges studying for her master's degree in psychology at Bar Ilan University, but she helped me — and I somehow muddled through that first year.

Here's an example of what life was like adjusting to my adopted country, with its different customs and a new language. I went to get my first mortgage, and a bank clerk presented me with sheet after sheet of paperwork to complete (that part is the same everywhere, I imagine). One form, he said, had to be signed by five "aravim". *Aravim* is Hebrew for Arabs, and I couldn't for the life of me understand why I needed five Arabs to sign this document, to say nothing of the fact that I didn't even know five Arabs! Turned out the word was "arevim", guarantors. Suddenly, the request made much more sense.

One professor I was especially fond of was Dov Eden, whose name in the United States had been Barry Fine. He prided himself on speaking proper Hebrew, so, strangely, he was the most difficult professor for me to understand. But I chose to do my thesis with Dov and, after three challenging years, I completed the requirements and received my master's degree in management science.

That summer I proposed to Ronit and, after months of preparation, we had a beautiful wedding on December 29, 1981, at the Plaza Hotel in Tel Aviv. Under the *chuppah* (Jewish wedding canopy), I waited for my beautiful bride a very long time, which I took as a sure sign of our future life together. (It turned out the elevator she came down on stopped on all the floors.) We settled in an apartment next to the Tel Aviv beach and began our lives as a married couple, still studying and working.

Once we both completed our master's degrees, we decided to move to New York for one year, so that Ronit could get a taste of life there and get to know my parents and friends better. We lived on the Upper West Side in a one-room apartment with a sleeping loft, and enjoyed the Manhattan lifestyle of the late '80s. The city was going through a period of gentrification, with the UWS leading the way, and every day new restaurants and cafes would open up. It was also a time of growing crime in the city. Subways became more dangerous and the homeless became more violent. Regardless, it was a grand time to live in the Big Apple as a young couple, and we took advantage of our time there, while also traveling throughout the country and Canada.

I landed a job with Solcoor, the marketing company for the Kibbutz Industries and Koor Industries, which was one of Israel's largest industrial conglomerates. I was dubbed "the American" who also spoke Hebrew, so all the factory CEOs from Israel naturally gravitated towards me. Ironically, my Hebrew improved tremendously during these years of working for an Israeli company in the United States. I found myself marketing an enormous range of products, including plastic faucets and brass plumbing parts, forklift tires, copper wire, Dead Sea cosmetics and ceramic tiles. Solcoor's head even called me into his office one day to show me a new hair-removal device that he tried on his hairy forearms. It was painful for him to use, and we ultimately decided not to take it on.

That device later became known as Epilady and sold millions of units. In hindsight, perhaps he should have asked for a lady's opinion.

Ronit found work with the New York City Board of Education's Brooklyn office and commuted to work on the subway, a commute she was none too thrilled by.

Of course, it helped enormously that the NY Mets were thriving at that time going through the greatest span of games in their history. From 1984 to 1989, they never had fewer than 90 wins, culminating in the championship season of 1986, when they went 108-54. I watched and attended many games, and those last two World Series games will always be etched in my memory.

I was home watching with friends, as the bottom of the 10th inning of Game 6 began at Shea Stadium. Boston was on the verge of its first championship since 1918. All their players were on the top steps of the dugout, just waiting on every pitch. It was a Saturday night, and I was pissed about the inevitable loss, and poised to go out and buy the Sunday NY Times (a Saturday night tradition), imagining the Mets needing to wait till next year, once again.

The end of this game has been documented ad-infinitum, but when the ball hit by Mookie Wilson passed between Bill Buckner's legs, it was as though a 100-ton weight had been lifted off my shoulders (Sadly, it was unfairly placed on Buckner's even though the game had been tied on a wild pitch). I celebrated with Michael and Andy, and it was a wonderful experience, even though it only tied the World Series at three games apiece and a crucial 7th game was awaiting the following night.

In spite of our incredible good fortune in that inning, game seven was rained out. Unfortunately, for me, I had to fly to Detroit for a business meeting the next day, and I'd have to watch the deciding Game 7 in a hotel lobby with a group of Red Sox fans, already down from the devastating loss in Game 6.

Although Boston scored first and held a three-to-nothing lead going into the bottom of the sixth, the Mets rallied to tie it and took the lead on a Ray Knight homer in the seventh. They tacked on enough insurance runs to stave off a Boston rally in the top of the 8th and secured their second ever, World Series championship. It was a bit disappointing to watch it with Red Sox fans rather than a Mets crowd, but it nonetheless was exhilarating to again, after 17 years, be the No. 1 baseball team.

As often happens, Ronit and my one declared year in New York stretched to five, during which Maya and Amit were born at the same hospital, Mt. Sinai, where I debuted. I clearly remember walking home after each birth, the first on the coldest day of the year in January and the second on the hottest day of the year in August, through Central Park to the Upper West Side, singing and smiling, and probably being stared at by passersby who attributed that to just another crazy New Yorker.

In spite of a Mets Championship and becoming parents of two healthy, beautiful children, we finally decided it was time to move back home to Israel. This decision would dictate the direction of the rest of my life, and it was not reached easily. But it was a decision made of a conviction, fervor and determination that after living in New York for most of my life, my adult home would be in Israel. My parents were distraught, to say the least, but Ronit and I felt that it was time to go back and embark on our lives as a family in Israel. It was a decision we have never regretted.

Starting this new adventure with two children in tow, I needed to find another job, outfit our home for double the occupants, find daycare, and become Israeli once again.

We had our apartment in Givatayim to return to. I had job offers from different Koor companies and went to work at Hamat, a manufacturer of faucets and sanitary ware, as the vice president of marketing and exports. This position involved travel abroad, so I attended plenty of baseball games across North America. I also was drafted for compulsory military service, which, at age 30, meant just four months. I specialized in firing artillery cannons, but in reserve duty was assigned to the home front command, where I served for 10 more years. Coming from an American liberal background of the 1960s peace movement, I found it strange to fire an M-16, but in Israel, everyone had to face the reality of life.

Returning to Israel was not easy for either of us, as we had to adjust to a different lifestyle and make friends. We were a full-fledged family, one that grew when Adi was born three years later, and our family was complete. The two oldest kids became Israeli very quickly, losing both their American innocence and accents. Were it not for summers in the United States with grandma and grandpa and American summer camps, they would have completely lost their American birth identities as youngsters. But Maya later enrolled in undergraduate studies in New

York for four years, and Amit and Adi both feel quite like native New Yorkers.

Raising two daughters and a son in Israel of the 1990's and 2000s was daunting. Israel's signing of the Oslo accords in 1993 was a time of optimism and hope for our country, and I had visions of my children being free of the mandatory military service both their parents had to do. But that optimism quickly evaporated with the assassination of Yitzhak Rabin in 1995 and the ascension of Benjamin Netanyahu to prime minister in 1996. Israel's excursions into Lebanon and Gaza were only precursors to the carnage of October 7th, but that will be discussed more in detail, later.

On September 11, 2001, I took Amit to a business meeting in Tel Aviv, because we'd then be going to a lecture on India in anticipation of a trip I'd be taking him on the following spring. In the lobby of the Hilton Hotel, the person I was meeting with received a frantic call from his wife in New York about a plane crashing into the World Trade Center. He immediately excused himself. Other people in the lobby also received calls. The lobby's atmosphere quickly changed. Amit and I rushed home to watch the events on TV, and en route I called my parents to ensure that they were safe. We got home in time to watch the collapse of the two enormous towers and the deaths of thousands of people. It was shocking and traumatic.

My friend Michael, who by then was a journalist with the *New York Times*, was off that morning and left his Brooklyn apartment immediately upon learning of the terrorist attack, not to be heard from for 48 hours as he wrote story after story. Cell phone coverage went out of service very quickly in lower Manhattan.

Ronit flew to the United States two weeks later to a previously scheduled seminar in Virginia and spent a few harrowing days in Manhattan. Debris was still swarming around lower Manhattan site of the towers, New Yorkers were in shock and disbelief, and she heard stories of horror, courage and panic. She saw pictures of the missing victims displayed everywhere. When I visited the city a few months later, I could feel the trauma. My Manhattan had changed after 9/11.

A few months later, Amit and I joined Michael and his son Nick in India to visit the country he and I had visited 23 years earlier, but this time with our teenage sons in tow. Seeing India through the eyes of your son makes quite a difference. India was rougher around the edges than I had remembered it, and it took Amit and me a few days to become inured to the prevalent poverty, hardship and deprivation we witnessed. By the same token, we found the Taj Mahal, the Red Fort and the Ganges River to be breathtaking, and we enjoyed experiencing the colorful Holi holiday in Rishikesh, as well as Passover at Chabad (along with 100 other Israeli backpackers).

My daughters were both quite successful in the fields of fashion design (Maya), as well as roller skating and graphic design (Adi), providing many instances of "naches" for their parents (naches is Yiddish and has no English definition– it's a term "that encapsulates the joy and pride experienced by parents when they see their children achieve something significant").

For me, it happened when Maya had her first fashion show, at Manhattan's Parsons School of Design. Meanwhile, Adi won the bronze medal at the European Artistic Roller-Skating Championship for her group performance and the silver medal at the Israeli Roller-Skating Championship for her solo performance. Today, they are both successful career women and I am very proud of what they have achieved. Amit has also provided us with *naches*, going from a high school kid who, in his own words, " barely attended class" to earning an M.B.A. and becoming a highly successful managing partner of a venture capital and private equity firm. All three of them have provided us with, in my father's own words, bags full of "nachos".

The only thing missing from my Israeli life of marriage and family was baseball. The internet having not yet been invented made it almost impossible to follow the Mets in any meaningful way, although it helped that they were a terrible team in the mid-90's Around 1998, Amit started getting interested in a Mets' team that was starting to look amazin' again. The great American pastime was about to become a major part of my life.

Third Inning

Serving as president of the Israel Association of Baseball

"In the European Championship tournament, we gave it everything we had, using the most important muscle —the heart. Though being a foreigner, I was and still am extremely proud to be part of the Israel Association of Baseball."
- Richard Kania

During my army reserve duty in 1998, I found myself in an Israeli desert, guarding terrorists held in a military prison. I had no contact with them, as I was doing perimeter patrols and watchtower guard duty, working four-hour shifts with eight hours off between shifts. That desolate location offered plenty of dead time. We had a barely functioning VCR and a TV with no reception. We only had one video tape: *Pretty Woman*, starring Julia Roberts and Richard Gere. I must have watched it 25 times and I can still quote it today. I served with a fellow American, who told me that his son was playing in an Israeli baseball league for kids. When I approached Amit with the idea, he shrugged his shoulders like any 9-year-old, and said very unenthusiastically, "sure dad, whatever you want...."

But it spurred a journey that would change our lives.

The following week we went to the Sportek in Tel Aviv, a sports complex in Tel Aviv. It included a very basic softball field, which is where we attended our first practice of the Israel Association of Baseball. Fewer than 300 children in the country played the game then, most of them the sons and daughters of American fathers who had moved to Israel. The IAB is a non-profit organization established in 1986 to develop and promote baseball in the country. It is recognized by the State of Israel as the sole governing body for baseball in Israel.

The IAB belongs to what today is called the World Baseball Softball Confederation. Israel plays in the WSBC's European division. Why in the Europe division, when Israel is in Asia? In one sense, it's a natural fit, since Israel competes in the Eurovision song contest and in the European basketball and soccer federations. It's true, too, that we in Israel consider ourselves a Western country that's very European. But the reason is far more onerous. We're part of Europe because of Arab countries' sports federations historical refusal to compete against Israel and their preventing us from joining Asian and Middle Eastern divisions.

Being in WSBC's Europe division offers Israel good competition, but not the top level. The Netherlands, whose national teams draw from the country's talent-rich Caribbean colonies, are perennial European champions, and Italy, the Czech Republic and Germany have powerful local programs; none are on the level of Asian powerhouses Japan, Taiwan and South Korea. National tournaments are held at different age levels, such as Under-12, Under-23 and adult. Each level is divided by talent/competitive designation, such as A pool, B pool and sometimes C pool. Each level will have eight to 16 teams.

Amit started playing on the Tel Aviv team in the juvenile level, where he quickly became one of the best players. Coaching the team was Leon Klarfeld, the "legendary Leon Klarfeld", who then was the president of the IAB. Leon is a great coach and greater human being who makes the game fun for all players, has an incredible knowledge of the game, served for years as the chief umpire of the IAB and loves telling very hackneyed jokes. We also became great friends who spent many evenings in European tournaments drinking whiskey, and to this day I value him as a mentor and guru.

Leon recruited me as his assistant coach, even though I had no coaching experience. He soon informed me that he was moving to Even Yehuda, near Netanya, and that I had to take over the Tel Aviv team. I was surprised. When I reminded him how green I was, especially compared to him, he replied, "You know a lot more about baseball than these 10-year-old kids, most of whom grew up here." He taught me a few drills, and with that bare minimum of training, I commenced my tenure as a coach with the IAB.

Later that year, Leon asked me to be the head coach of the juvenile level's national team (ages 10–12) for a tournament in Holland, one of the first teams we sent to play abroad. I protested, citing my lack of experience. He responded, "I only need a responsible adult who can take 15 kids to this tournament and bring back the same 15 kids." With that statement, the deal was finalized and I was taking a team to the Netherlands.

He did arrange for me to have an assistant coach who would be the real, on-the-field coach. The coach was Shlomo Lipetz, just 19 then and classified in the Israel Defense Forces as a *sportai*: a soldier who combines the required military service of three years with elite-level athletic training, in his case in softball. Today, 26 years later, at age 45, Shlomo still plays on Israel's national baseball teams, is a huge asset to the IAB, and is a warm and close friend. I would go through fire with Shlomo, and the experience in the Netherlands was only the beginning of our close relationship.

Amit came to that tournament, too, even though he was a bench player. He gained experience in the first of many national teams that he would be a part of. That roster – in 1999 – was stacked with players who still today, 26 years later, are involved in baseball in one way or another. Alon Leichman was only nine years old at the time, but he would play on numerous national teams, including our team at the Olympics in Tokyo in 2021, and is today the pitching coach of the Colorado Rockies — the highest position an Israeli native, a *sabra*, has reached in Major League Baseball. Another boy, Ophir Katz was on that team, and he is now coaching once again for the IAB. Itzik Levy, the son of legendary Raanana Regional Director Mel Levy, played first base. Jake Miller, brother of IAB coach Louie Miller, was our catcher.

We would face a future major leaguer on the Dutch team. Ours was a young squad and we lost all of our games, many by double digits. But in another sense, it was the best IAB team ever because of the prospective contributions from our players and staff, myself included. It was July 1999, my first IAB National team, and I felt like Charlie Brown.

Communication with the parents back in Israel was via fax, and I would write daily reports to them.

This was the final one:

> We lost all six games. Not the result we dreamed about,
> but Israel put up a fight in almost every game, and we
> were never out of them. ... The kids gave their all and
> the coaches ran them ragged. The talent on this team
> is much improved from what it was three weeks ago,
> and much of that credit has to go to Shlomo, who
> whipped them into the best shape possible under the
> circumstances. Many kids had to work on basic skills,
> things taken for granted in other national programs. ...
> Each kid who had this experience is a beacon to his own
> team back in Israel on how to train, how to practice,
> how to act and how to live and breathe baseball. If they
> got just a drop of this, it will be an achievement.

This was only the first of many Israel national teams at all age levels that I have accompanied to European tournaments, to the World Baseball Classic, to the Olympics and to friendly tournaments as a head coach, assistant coach, team manager, general manager, laundryman, cook, driver, and jack-of-all-trades. Quite impressive I think

The following season, Haim Katz, Ophir's father, and I jointly led the Tel Aviv region. We had both a cadet-level team (13–15-year-olds) and a juvenile team (10–12-year-olds); Amit and Ophir played for the latter. Friday afternoon practices each week were a great bonding time for Amit and me, as we became passionately involved with the game. The regular season, from March to June, would be full of road trips to games in nearby Raanana, Neve Elissa, Kfar Saba and Tzofit, as well as occasional weekend team retreats at Kibbutz Gezer. Baseball was always on my mind, and I totally enjoyed coaching those first teams with Haim.

For many of the new *olim* (immigrants to Israel) on the teams, baseball, the American game, ironically, provided a way to adapt to life in Israel. By bringing their kids to play on Friday afternoons, parents provided their children with a soft landing to the country, as they participated in an activity they loved in their country of origin, usually the United States or Canada.

One parent, Jordy Alter, would become deeply involved in the IAB. Of that period, as a parent, he said:

> Baseball was so important to our adaptation in Israel. Prior to coming to Israel, we heard there was a baseball league, and my kids were very excited about it. It was very important to them. So, we came and I coached, and the ability for my kids to integrate into Israeli society was incredibly enhanced by baseball. At baseball, they were the best, the best among the team, the best in the country. And they were good at something as they were struggling in every other area of their adaptation to Israel. They came with no Hebrew skills, so it was very hard for them. Baseball for them was special.

Mel Levy, at the time the regional director of Raanana, spoke about the transition of the baseball league in Israel from one played mostly by American *olim* (immigrants) to one played mostly by Israeli natives. "In the early years, most of our kids were American olim. We see a change now, as more Israeli kids are getting involved. In Tel Aviv and other places", he said, "it's mostly Israeli kids." He added: "For us to succeed in the future, we must have more Israeli kids involved."

In 2016 Hillel Kutler interviewed me for an article, and this is what I had to say about my first years in the IAB:

> There aren't a lot of other opportunities in team sports in Israel. The Israeli sports scene is very competitive: soccer, basketball and handball. If you're 10, 11 years old and you're not one of the top players, you can't play that as a team sport. Baseball is a great sport, because it can be played by any kid. You don't have to be tall, fast or strong, and you don't have to be the greatest athlete, although we encourage the great athletes to come out and play.

Amit's national team in 1999 was made up of non-religious kids from Tel Aviv and kibbutzim throughout Israel, along with religious kids from

Jerusalem, Beit Shemesh and Modiin. They all came together, practiced once a week at the Baptist Village (a top-notch field in Petah Tikva) and got to know each other. That still holds. Certainly, when they go overseas and live together for a week, they become a lot more friendly. You find non-religious kids eating kosher food together with the religious kids and learning more about Shabbat. For new immigrants, it's a fantastic thing. There are countless stories of families that have made aliyah (immigrated to Israel), whose kids are upset because they were in Little League in the United States and thought they'd have to forsake baseball in Israel — only to realize that baseball IS in Israel, and they can play the sport they love.

When I'm at overseas tournaments and see the Israeli flag with other flags and see our team on their field with their uniforms and *Israel* written across their chests and singing Hatikvah, the Israeli national anthem, it injects great pride, is an energy boost and gives me goosebumps. It's Zionism at its best. If on a Friday afternoon I'm at Tel Aviv's Sportek or other fields and see 50 kids playing baseball, I get a great feeling of achievement. I want to do more. I'm always thinking of how we can get more kids out there, how we can build more fields, recruit more coaches. It's never enough.

It's a chicken-and-the-egg dynamic. The cliché is true: If you build it, they will come. We've got to have more fields, and we need funding to do it. At the same time, we also have to have more kids playing baseball.

* * *

I was soon recruited by the IAB executive team Leon, David Shenkar, Sam Pelter and others to become a board member and in 2005 was elected secretary general along with the new president, Haim Katz. We served eight years together, years of growth for the IAB, a summer of professional baseball with the IBL (see next inning) and the start of the WBC.

The IAB is intent on using baseball to teach life skills. We became the first sports organization outside of North America to join the U.S.-based Positive Coaching Alliance. The first goal is to win, but the second, more important, goal is to use baseball to teach our youth important life lessons. I have felt very strongly about this mission. Soccer may be the most popular sport anywhere, while football has become the de facto national pastime in the United States. But baseball still has the richest history of cultural and historical change in the countries where it is played, and I can think of no better sport to teach life lessons.

The greatest period of internal growth and our expanded forays into international baseball occurred during my six-plus years as president, from June 2013 to November 2019. Jordy Alter joined me as vice president, Yaron Erel as treasurer and Margo Sugarman as secretary general. For most of that period, we worked well together and along with the IAB board, we brought baseball to more players, played in more areas and run with a higher level of professionalism than ever before. We had great support, particularly from board members Nathan Pomerantz, Lee Siegel, David Leichman and Dan Rothem, as well as the IAB secretary all those years, Miriam Fima, but the greatest impetus into making the IAB what it is today was done by the National Director that I brought on, Nate Fish. More on him later.

Throughout my tenure as president, I consistently worked on a 5-point program that I had personally developed. The goals were simple, easy to understand and implement, and could be measured readily. These points were:

- To increase the participation of players and coaches

- To raise the professional level of coaches and umpires throughout our program

- To make administrative and communications improvements throughout the organization, primarily decentralizing the IAB's national structure in favor of the local organizations, increasing transparency and becoming visible on social media

- To develop baseball fields and infrastructure

- To improve relations with the Israel Softball Federation and eventually combine forces.

This occurred as baseball and softball were expanding throughout Europe. The World Baseball Softball Confederation was established in 2013 to unite the international baseball and softball federations under one umbrella. WBSC founded a European division in 2018.

I'm proud to say that while our five goals advanced nicely, uniting with the softball federation proved challenging. Ami Baran and I worked tirelessly to remove the barriers blocking our two organizations from cooperating. In the fall and spring of 2015-2016, I worked with Ami to develop agendas, working proposals, organizational structures, and budgets to create the IBSA – Israel Baseball Softball Association. Basing ourselves on the European Baseball Softball Federation, WBSC, of which Ami was the Secretary General, we felt that by uniting forces and becoming the fifth largest sports federation in Israel, we could get more funding from the Israeli authorities, have a larger say in the allocation of those funds, have more policy influence in the Sports Ministry and Israel Olympic Committee and build on a larger base of players, coaches and fans. (Particularly in hindsight, seeing both baseball and softball return as Olympic sports in 2020, 2028, and hopefully 2032 as well)

Unfortunately, we were never able to overcome the inherent animosities and reservations in our two organizations towards one another, and our work and the concept of creating one united federation was soon sent to the document shredder, not to be renewed by my successors to this day. I do hope that in the future we can consolidate into one organization, to the benefit of both sports. A new discipline, Baseball 5, which is primarily geared towards schools and developmental work, was recently introduced in Israel on my initiative as the IAB CEO. In this endeavor we are cooperating with the ISA, each providing coaches and school time. I do hope the new administration will see the benefit of this cooperation and expand upon it, for the good of both organizations.

Much of my time was devoted to fundraising, primarily for the fields we wanted to develop, the national teams' travel expenses, the development programs we wanted to initiate, and for bringing American Jewish ballplayers on aliyah. All this costs money and there were times when I felt like a politician trying to win an election rather than build baseball in Israel. In February 2012, I signed an agreement with the Jewish National Fund (JNF), headed by Russell Robinson and Mitch Rosenzweig, and their team of professionals located in every major city in the United States. The JNF's Project Baseball held numerous fundraisers to benefit two fields we hoped to build, in Raanana and Bet Shemesh, and other IAB endeavors. I worked closely with the JNF fundraisers to identify potential donors who loved baseball, and to work on procuring their donations. I particularly want to highlight the help of Mark Rattner,

Lou Rosenberg, Sara Hefez, Roni Raab, Doug Liebman, Celine Leeds, and I just hope that I did not inadvertently leave anyone out.

We had great American partners over the years, such as Maccabi USA and Marshall Einhorn who enabled us to add a link directly on their website for financial contributions; the Pittsburgh Jewish Federation and other Jewish Federations; and countless other Jewish philanthropic organizations. In the early days we also had the help of close friends like Jeff Feinstein, who put on the first major IAB fundraiser that was held in Chicago, featuring a panel discussion with White Sox owner Jerry Reinsdorf; the team's broadcaster, Steve Stone; the Chicago Cubs' top executive at the time, Theo Epstein; and former major league outfielder Gabe Kapler. Jeff continues to help us to this day and is a Board member of the IBA. We also had a fundraiser that was held in Manhattan at the night spot City Winery, managed by our national team player Shlomo Lipetz and team, where David Broza performed (according to Shlomo, Broza is "Israel's Bruce Springsteen"). Ike Davis, our advertised keynote speaker, stood us up but has since more than made up for that disappointment. Over the years I have been at countless fundraisers organized by the JNF, as well as their annual conferences, involved in both fund-raising and friend-raising.

I targeted Jewish owners, presidents and general managers of MLB teams to meet with, and have reached approximately two-thirds of MLB teams to make my pitch. Jewish ownership is prevalent in MLB and I am always hoping to unearth the next Robert Kraft, the owner of the National Football League's New England Patriots, who has built two football facilities in Jerusalem and funds the Israel Football Association. I am still looking for the Baseball Bob Kraft.

I've also consulted philanthropists, and several have stepped up, like Jeff Rosen, Mark Rattner, Jeff Aeder, Josh Solomon, Jeff Royer, as well as any others I may have missed. Your help does not go unnoticed, and I thank you and appreciate your assistance. They and other contributors share my goal: to advance Israel baseball.

Field Development Projects

Regarding field development, Haim - and later Jordy Alter - worked with me for countless hours on planning, meetings, fundraising, and nudging these projects into existence. It has become part of the agenda for all IAB Presidents to declare the importance of new field development, and it remains a large part of the job. It is quite an undertaking, and I am glad that after 20 years I can show true progress on genuine baseball fields, in Bet Shemesh and in Raanana, as well as developments elsewhere.

When I first started coaching in the IAB, we had no legitimate baseball fields at the level of a decent high school field in the United States. Whenever I landed in New York, I would look through the plane window in awe and admiration at the countless baseball fields below. Israel had one, in Kibbutz Gezer, followed by a second, in Tel Aviv's Sportek complex in Yarkon Park, and another in the Baptist Village, in Petah Tikva. They were decent fields for the budding Israel baseball program at the time, and are still used today, but are far from the quality we needed and later developed in Raanana and Bet Shemesh as the program expanded.

When he immigrated from Queens, New York, in 1974, David Leichman was one of the founders of Kibbutz Gezer on land that had been a kibbutz established in 1945 and later abandoned. On Gezer, David romanticized about recreating the street corners in the Queens neighborhood where he and his friends hung out. He also imagined a field to play ball on. He didn't build the brick and concrete street corners on Gezer, but the dirt lot across from where he lives now eventually became a real field. He took matters into his own hands, asking the kibbutz's administrators for permission to build a baseball field. They acceded, partly because Leichman planned to do much of the work himself with tractors he used for landscaping. "I built the first baseball field in Israel, but really it was a softball field," David says. "It is a little smaller than a baseball field. We later made it into a baseball field."

Set in rolling farmland halfway between Jerusalem and Tel Aviv, the Gezer field is an expanse of manicured lawn and reddish soil. It is the favored site for games of the national softball league, and we have younger kids playing baseball there. Home runs bounce into fields that stretch toward the remains of ancient Gezer, a stronghold of King Solomon in biblical times.

"In Yankee Stadium you have a view of Bronx tenements, here you're looking out on 3,000 years of Jewish history," David would later tell the *New York Times*.

A less dramatic back story is attached to Sportek. Its softball field was a feature of the complex from as far back as I can remember. I played there in 1982 for a team known as 32 Flavors, named for a Tel Aviv ice cream parlor. When professional baseball came to Israel in 2007, the field was developed in its current location with outfield fencing that was removed after that season. Play has continued there over the years and in 2022, when the IAB was awarded the hosting of the 2025 European championship, we had detailed plans for expanding the field, adding lights and making it the showcase for the tournament. I wanted to turn the field into the premier location for baseball in Israel, but the October 7th war, shelved those plans and IAB's current administration is implementing only cosmetic upgrades to the field.

Then there's Baptist Village, which, while run-down today, remains the top baseball field in Israel. After turning off the main road and meandering towards the field, the green grass comes into sight, reminding one of first glimpses of the Shea Stadium field stepping off the subway in Queens decades ago. The Baptist Village field was built more than 20 years ago on land the government wanted to confiscate for housing but backed off on when the property's owners, American Baptists, agreed to change its designation to recreational land usage. On it, they built baseball and softball fields. It hosts the IAB's premier-level games, the professional Israel Baseball League played in 2007 and international tournaments. Many of our national players see it as their home away from home. I have spent countless hours on that field, and the ghosts of players past inhabit every corner of the BV.

In 2016, we reached an agreement with Moshe Abutbol, the then-mayor of Beit Shemesh, a town located east of Gezer. The agreement, negotiated by Jordy Alter, was to build a regulation size baseball field, two youth fields, batting cages, stands, a clubhouse and dugouts on land that would be donated by the city for a period of 10 years. The field would be built from funds raised by the IAB via the JNF. That field is due to be completed at the end of 2026 at a cost of $3 million. It will be the IAB's best field. The down side is that it's inconvenient to reach from the center of Israel and that could limit its use.

In July 2018, we reached an agreement with Eitan Ginsburg, the then-mayor of Raanana, a town about midway between Tel Aviv and Netanya. The agreement was similar to the one reached with Bet Shemesh, and that field was completed two years ago and is in constant use by the IAB. It is named the Ezra Schwartz Field in memory of an American youth killed by terrorists while studying in Israel. Donations came through the JNF, primarily from the Boston community where Ezra lived; Jeff Rosen also provided a substantial donation. The field has a storage facility and numerous batting cages, making it extremely versatile for practices, but is shorter than a standard baseball field and cannot be used by the premier league or for international tournaments.

The Beit Shemesh and Raanana fields represent over 20 years of faith and dedication and are highlights of my period as president of the IAB. I am very proud of these projects, which represent the growth of baseball in Israel. The voice in the film *Field of Dreams* wasn't just talking about Shoeless Joe Jackson when he whispered, "If you build it, they will come."

Baseball is best told through its people, and we at the IAB have had some good ones. Following are three of them.

Nate Fish - The King of Jewish Baseball

Nate Fish deserves his own chapter in this book (maybe even his own encyclopedia) to include all the roles he has played for Israel baseball: the King of Jewish Baseball; bullpen catcher in the WBC;   first National Director of the IAB; third base star of the Tel Aviv Lightning; CEO of the IBA. No individual has done more to advance the interests of Israeli baseball than Nate. If he were a character in a movie script, you wouldn't believe there could be anyone like him ... until you meet him.

Fish, as everyone calls him, had a very Jewish upbringing in Cleveland. He had a bar mitzvah, went to Hebrew school, and said the Shabbat blessings every Friday night. "By the time I was 16, I was collecting rabbi cards, " he says. "Thank God I found art." If not for baseball, in fact, he might have become a successful artist. But baseball captivated him and he played ball at the University of Cincinnati on the same team as future MLB star Kevin Youklis, and the two remain close friends to this day. Later, he played in Argentina and Germany and led the Los Angeles Dodgers' venture in developing baseball in Africa.

I first met Fish in 2007, when he played in the Israel Baseball League. We both attended the IBL's tryouts at the Duquette Sports Academy in Massachusetts: I as the IAB's secretary general and Fish as the IBL's burgeoning, floppy-haired heartthrob. We didn't have much contact that summer but stayed in touch over the years.

I invited him to be part of the 2012 WBC team; he was one of the few people we knew who was making a living in baseball. He was not good enough to be a player or well-known enough to be a coach, but as he told it, "there was a loophole" so he could be a 29th man on a 28-man roster: as a third catcher to catch only in the bullpen and be activated if someone got hurt.

But Fish was the one who ended up getting hurt in that WBC, and he had to be taped up prior to every game. He made it through the tournament and was one of the more colorful contributors to Team Israel.

On his blog, Fish, in his usual flamboyant manner, imagined what opening night of the WBC tournament would be like.

"Jews – nay, all mankind – will dance in the streets," he wrote. "Children will sing. Birds will fly high in the sky. And, if only for a moment, all human and plant and animal life on earth will exist in perfect harmony."

Vintage Fish for you.

I was impressed by his performance and proposed to Haim that we hire him as our new national director, making good use of our WBC winnings. I offered Fish the job.

This is how he remembered the discussion:

"Before we left, Peter Kurz, the GM of the team, said, "Fish, do you want to move to Israel and run the baseball program there?" And what did I say? Ye- Actually, I said no. I was still thinking about the loss , and I had never considered moving to Israel."

A month later, we met at Riverside Park in New York, where Fish was training some players. I again offered him the job, and this time he accepted. He lived and worked in Israel for three years as our first national director and was instrumental in establishing many of the programs still in existence in the IAB.

The job entailed the following:

- Developing and implementing a recruitment program for new players and coaches at the local level

- Overseeing national teams and developing an elite training program/academy

- Raising the level of professionalism of players, coaches and umpires

- Advancing field development projects

- Developing baseball-centered summer activities and summer camps

- Establishing a new and more efficient organizational structure

Fish and I saw eye to eye on what needed to be done and I, as the new IAB president, worked closely with him for the next three years in achieving most of these goals. Most important is that more players participated, we established a training academy and we decentralized and stabilized operations. Fish also created a Jewish-Arab coexistence program called Baseball Le'Kulum (Baseball for All) and started an important partnership with MASA, a program in which Diaspora Jews intern in their professions in Israel. Baseball for All received a rousing ovation in Washington, D.C., at the 2016 conference of the pro-Israel lobbying group AIPAC, where a video was shown and two participants, Niv Eytan and Fadi Abu Swees were introduced on stage. It was a unique opportunity to capitalize on a program that affected the hearts and minds of many participants.

The IAB was better after Fish's three years – unfortunately his time was cut short and there was no meaningful follow-up by the replacements we brought in for him

Sports Illustrated even wrote about Fish's challenges and first days on the job in August 2013.

"We have to change the identity of baseball in Israel a little bit," Fish said. "We have to make it cool, and we have to make it exciting and athletic." The article continued: "In his blog, part travelogue and part absurdist comedy, he styles himself "The King of all Jewish Baseball." He arrives at the practice in workout gear and runs around the field like a high school coach, yelling instructions and keeping the kids moving from drill to drill. He wants them active, engaged, and in the brutal summer heat, sweating. "The misconception is that baseball is slow and baseball is boring. Baseball is fast," Fish said. "For anyone who thinks baseball is boring, put them in the batter's box and zip a 95-mph fastball past them and see if they're still bo red."□

Fish is leading a grassroots push for "more baseball and better baseball." The association is focusing on improving coaching standards and building new baseball diamonds, of which there are currently only four in Israel. In many places, games are held on makeshift fields, plopped down in public parks or farmlands, with no backstops, base paths, dugouts or pitching mounds. □

Fish also spent much of the summer giving presentations to gym teachers and was granted the right to hold baseball clinics in Tel Aviv schools. Giving kids broad exposure to playing, he said, is key to pushing baseball out of its American box and into the Israeli mainstream.

As Fish described his tenure in Israel: "For three years I was the idiot and the expert. I coached, I umped, I delivered uniforms, and sometimes, I drove the bus – whatever needed to be done. I played for the Jerusalem

Lions in the Premier League, the shabby men's league that replaced the IBL, and played shortstop for the national team. A career I thought had been cut short was now being extended beyond any reasonable length. Youkilis had already made multiple All-Star teams, won a Gold Glove, and retired a legend after ten years in the major leagues, and I was still playing in front of two fans and hiding in the bomb shelter at Kibbutz Gezer when rockets came from Gaza."

On April 27, 2016, a few weeks prior to leaving the job and Israel, Fish wrote a summary of what his accomplishments were over his three years in his position. Following is some of what he wrote:

> I'm extremely proud of the things we have accomplished together in that short time (three years). I believe the organization is better off and healthier in every way than before. Two narratives have formed. One is that my tenure has gone well and we are making progress. The other is that the IAB has not grown enough and there are no financial resources to justify my salary. Both are true. After three years of being director, I do not see the current arrangement as sustainable for either side, for the IAB as employer, or myself as employee. I will suggest how the IAB should be restructured to continue to make progress. I hope to continue to be a useful tool in helping the IAB achieve our common goal of developing Israel Baseball.

Fish has indeed helped do this throughout his tenure outside the framework of the IAB, and now today as the chief executive officer of Israel Baseball Americas.

When Fish left the IAB and Israel in the fall of 2016, we were left floundering ahead of the WBC qualifiers in September 2016 and the main WBC tournament in March 2017. Justin Peedin took over for a short time, but he was not able to build on Fish's momentum. We couldn't really afford to pay a national director, but functionally we were in dire need of one. Only in early 2019 did we hire a new one. The choice was so tight between two strong candidates, Ophir Katz and Yaniv Rosenfeld, that we hired both: Ophir as the national team's coach and

Yaniv as operations manager. It was an unwieldy arrangement and we soon scrapped it.

In 2019, prior to resigning as president to oversee Israel's Olympic bid, I developed a five-year strategic plan for the IAB that the board approved. My vision was to develop baseball into one of the top five team sports in Israel in terms of player participation, fan involvement, and professional achievement. I wanted IAB leagues by 2024 to include 2,000 players on five baseball-specific adult fields and twenty youth fields. I hoped for Israeli teams to participate in European championships at all age levels, in the Olympic qualifiers and in the WBC. I also believed in fostering the support of Jewish communities of North America for Israeli baseball and re-establishing an Israeli professional league.

We reached some of those goals. Most important is that the document put in writing the milestones we sought to reach. It was a blueprint I also followed later on, as IAB's chief executive officer.

The Olympics diverted our attention from some of these goals, and the Covid crisis and the October 7 war significantly waylaid our plans. Since then, the IAB has tried to catch up.

Shlo-Mo

Like Fish, Shlomo Lipetz is a legend in the annals of Israeli baseball. He has played in international tournaments for more than three decades and there is not a person in European baseball who does not know him. When he comes to Israel, he always takes time out to work with our youth, and his workplace in New York, City Winery, is a mecca for Israeli baseball players. Shlomo never hesitates when I make any request of him for help and always comes through enthusiastically.

Before the European Championship qualifying tournament, held in Israel in July 2011, I said that Shlomo is our most important player. I wrote at the time: "He's a veteran, has a lot of experience and baseball IQ and this is important with the young team that we have. He's the best pitcher we have. He has a rubber arm. He can pitch a game, and after two days pitch again. He also has a very positive presence on the field and on the bench. He radiates a very positive energy. He told me that he's coming to Israel to win, and I hope this attitude will filter down to the other players as well.'

Shlomo started playing baseball in the Sportek in Tel Aviv and got turned on to the sport; at the age of ten he travelled with the national team to a tournament at the Ramstein U.S. Air base in Germany. That team, on which Dan Rothem also played, lost 54-0 to Saudi Arabia, a team made up of American kids. Two weeks after completing his IDF service, he travelled to the United States to attend junior college and try to play baseball. He was a walk-on at the tryouts, was selected and played college ball for four years, finishing as the team's closer and increasing his fast ball speed to 88 MPH. He was already considered too old to pla y affiliated baseball, and he soon became one of the founding members of City Winery and remains its music director to this day. But every summer, and whenever we need him, Shlomo answers my call and puts on the Israel jersey and rejoins the national team.

Fish describes Shlomo and his generation well: "By the time Shlomo stepped on the mound in Tokyo at the Olympics to throw a scoreless inning in relief against Team USA, a team comprised nearly entirely of Major League Baseball players, he was 42 years old. If you had told Shlomo or other players and coaches from that first Israeli national team that 30 years later Israel would win $1 million in prize money at the 2017 World Baseball Classic and, two years after that, become one of six teams to qualify for the 2020 Olympics, they would not understand what you were saying. It did not seem possible. But that is exactly what happened."

Richard Kania

Richard Kania is another gentleman who belongs in the Israel pantheon of coaches. Richard is Czech, not Jewish and a top international coach. He first came to Israel 18 years ago as an envoy from the European Baseball Federation (CEB). Aside from the Covid period, Richard has not missed a year joining us in a tournament, a summer camp, the WBC, for clinics, or just for a cup of coffee. Richard has been through wars — real wars — with us. He has lied flat on the side of roads as sirens went off and missiles flew overhead, he has joined us in bomb shelters, and he has travelled to every baseball venue in the country. The props he brings – a small garbage pail to flush down mistakes; ping pong balls with holes to try and hit with a stick; flat mitts to try and field ground balls —

are all legendary. Richard should have been the first to be awarded the Israel Prize for dedication and service to Israel now that the precedent was made to award it to a non-Israeli citizen (Donald Trump).

Back in October 2011, Richard explained to me how he decided to coach for us in 2007 as a CEB envoy:

I was a little worried: will I be safe there? What level is their baseball at? Well, to keep it short, I have been coming for four consecutive years, (and many years after that) and each year is better than the previous one. I wonder how far this can go, since this year we were one step from reaching baseball heaven. And safety: My son has been coming along to help for two consecutive years, and I am not afraid to let him go out with his local friends into the night life of Tel Aviv.□

All the fans, players and coaches enjoyed their baseball experience during the European championship qualifying tournament last summer. Yes, we fell one step short of reaching our goal: making it to the European championship (not to mention losing on an error). But we learned a lot. We learned (and showed Europe) that Israel is a strong baseball country that can compete with any team in Europe. We all knew that the chain is as strong as the weakest link, but we have learned that the weakest link becomes stronger if we pull together. And most importantly we made great friends on and off the field. Are we upset with the result? Yes, we are, but we gave it everything we had, using the most important muscle: the heart. This goes far beyond the disappointment. Though being a foreigner, I was and still am extremely proud that I was a part of the 2011 Israel senior national team. In fact, this has been my best baseball experience ever.

Following are some very successful accomplishments we had:

IAB Academy

Among the many activities that Fish and I worked on and I am most proud of was to organize the first IAB Baseball Academy in the fall of 2014. We selected the top 10 players, ages 14 to 19, from all over Israel to participate in a year-long weekly program at the Baptist Village, run at a very high level by Fish, David Schenker and Dan Rothem and recognized by Major League Baseball.

"This will open many doors that were previously closed to our players," Fish told *The Jerusalem Post* on October 30, 2014. "The goal is to develop our top players so that they are ready to compete at the highest levels, can train in the United States, and play college and even professional baseball."

The academy has been a rousing success, and today the IAB has academy programs at three different age levels that later in the year evolve into the national teams that travel to overseas tournaments. Approximately 15 IAB players and academy graduates have played college baseball in the United States and Canada and join Israel's national teams every summer at greatly improved skill levels. One academy player, Assaf Lowengart, became the first *sabra* (native Israeli) to play professional baseball in the United States, and we hope to soon see the first *sabra* play in the affiliated minor leagues and MLB. That has always been my goal and dream.

When New Jersey-born Tal Brody came to Israel as a 22-year-old to play on the United States' Maccabiah team in 1965, professional basketball in Israel was in its infancy and played on outdoor courts. It took 44 years for Omri Caspi to become the first *sabra* to play in the NBA, in 2009. Let's hope the first *sabra* plays in MLB prior to 2058.

European Championship

In late 2010, the WBSC (then called CEB) named the IAB as host of the 2011 adult European championships' qualifier round. This was the first high-level European baseball tournament to be played in Israel.

Over 38 European countries participate in the WBSC, and most compete either in the European championship (16 teams) every two years, or the B and C pool qualifiers, also every two years. Team Israel appeared in those qualifiers until 2019, when we rose to the A pool. We have not been demoted since.

The European championships at all age levels are national tournaments, meaning that you must be an Israeli national to participate on Israel's team. We have to present the players' Israeli passports prior to every tournament. A player in Israel with his parents as transient residents (journalists, embassy staff, etc.) is not allowed to play in a European championship, although he is allowed to play in the local leagues. By the same token, an Israeli citizen living overseas is allowed to play for the Israeli national team, and, indeed, we have recruited players who are the children of Israelis living overseas but holding Israeli passports.

We came to an agreement with the Baptist Village to host the tournament and arranged housing for the teams. In July 2011, players from Georgia, Lithuania and Great Britain arrived in Israel for the first international baseball tournament the country hosted.

I was the general manager of Israel's team, as I have been of most Israel national teams since. Our manager, Pat Doyle, was joined by assistant coaches Richard Kania and Nate Fish, who led intense practices during the month before the tournament. Pat is a coach from northern California, and one of his players came by to visit a practice session at the Sportek. The 15-year-old boy was Dean Kremer, whose Israeli parents moved to the United States before he was born. Dean went on to play well for Team Israel and reached the major leagues. He continues to be an important starting pitcher for the Baltimore Orioles, and holds the status of the first Israeli pitcher in MLB.

Israel and Great Britain were the two top teams, setting up a Friday morning showdown for a berth to advance to the 2012 European championship. Israel had already lost to Great Britain and needed to win this game to force a third, and decisive, meeting between the teams. Shlomo Lipetz returned to the mound on two days' rest and threw a shutout. Thus, the stage was set for a winner take all final between the two teams.

In the break between the games, as the team tried to cool off, a fatigued yet determined Lipetz came up to me and Doyle and said he could go another game. We were shocked and had already selected our starting pitcher. But looking Shlomo in the eye convinced us he could do it. The

Brits seemed shocked, and we started that day's second game with a huge advantage.

Israel struck first with a run and Shlomo continued to baffle GB until the 4th inning. Due to a miscommunication on the part of the third and first basemen, GB scored 2 runs on an error in the fourth inning and led 2-1. Shlomo ran out of steam after throwing more than 200 pitches that day. He was done for the day. We threatened in the ninth inning, loading the bases, but couldn't close the gap. With that, Great Britain won to advance to the A pool. Israel would not come so close to advancing for another eight years. Shlomo was awarded the most outstanding pitcher of the tournament. He'd earned two wins with complete games, an earned run average of just 0.44 and 18 strikeouts in 20 1/3 innings.

For the first time, a major newspaper, *Yisrael Hayom* (Israel Today), covered us, writing:

> The crowd, a few hundred family members, friends and baseball lovers, cheered the players on and left the game with a very positive feeling and full of optimism over what they witnessed today. Like proud parents who witness their babies take their first steps, here, on the banks of the Yarkon River, the baby that is called Israel baseball succeeded in crawling for the first time.   Next year there is a good chance the national team will participate in the World Baseball Classic (WBC), the baseball equivalent of the World Cup, and Jewish American professional base-ball players can represent us. That may be the only chance to see an Israeli national team in the World Cup.

This article was important in establishing baseball as legitimate among the Hebrew-speaking population of Israel and led to future coverage.

More than 3,000 fans had attended the four-day tournament, en-joying premier baseball competition. Hosting the tournament was the biggest project the IAB had undertaken, and we carried it out well. The IAB received accolades from the CEB officials who oversaw the tourna-ment, and our hosting it helped us tremendously when we applied in 2022 to host the 2025 European championship. Alas, the Gaza war led it to be relocated to the Netherlands.

The Maccabiah Games

The Maccabiah Games are dubbed the "Jewish Olympics." Every four years, thousands of athletes living in scores of countries gather in Israel to take part in different sports, at varying levels of international competition, with one thing in common: They are all Jewish. Beneath the radar, the event also is a prime venue for pairing Jewish singles, just as the Olympics are a hotbed for young athletic hormones.

At the end of the 19th century, Jewish athletes were not allowed to compete in many of their countries' official sports events, and few were allowed to belong to athletic clubs. The nonprofit Maccabi organization in each country provided an outlet for many of these athletes, primarily in Europe, and in 1932 the first Maccabiah Games were held, in Israel —what then was called Palestine. Only in 1961 did the International Olympic Committee recognize Maccabi competitions, and today the Maccabiah is the third largest sports event in the world, with more than 10,000 athletes from 50 countries attending the most recent one, in 2022.

I have been involved in six Maccabiah Games, including as general manager of the Israeli baseball team and commissioner of the baseball tournament. The 2025 Maccabiah was postponed to 2026 due to the Gaza war. In the 20 years that I have been involved with the Maccabiah, we have only been able to schedule youth (U–18) baseball tournaments, due to the inability of enough countries to assemble adult teams, and only in one Maccabiah, in 2009, were there more than the three core teams: Israel, USA and Canada. (Mexico added a fourth.)

Many great athletes who later made their names on the world stage competed in the Maccabiah, among them Mark Spitz, Yael Arad, Aly Raisman, Ernie Grunfeld, Danny Schayes and Alex Shatilov. Future MLB players who competed in the Maccabiah include Max Fried and Dean Kremer, who competed for the American team; with dual citizenship, Dean competed for Israel in all international tournaments after the Maccabiah.

The 2005 Maccabiah was the first to include baseball. A letter from Bud Selig, the MLB commissioner, was included in the tournament's brochure. In it, Selig wrote, "Being included in the Maccabiah Games is further proof that baseball continues to grow in stature across the world. Baseball may be known as 'America's Pastime,' but its reach extends to all corners of the globe."

At the 2005 tournament, I succeeded in recruiting two players with dual Canadian Israeli citizenship as future players for Israel: Oren Gal and Eitan Maoz; they would help our national team win many games. Also on that year's Israeli team was my son Amit, Ophir Katz and Alon Leichman, who continue to contribute to baseball in Israel. Matan Kaufmann was Team Israel's most valuable player in 2005 with a .444 batting average. Sagui Dekel-Chen, who attended every practice in the Baptist Village despite a four-hour, round-trip bus ride from his home in Kibbutz Nir Oz, played the outfield. 18 years later, on October 7, 2023, Sagui would be taken hostage by the Hamas terrorist organization and held in Gaza tunnels for 498 days until he was released in early 2025.

The 2009 tournament was played in the Tel Aviv Sportek. Jamie McCourt, the chief executive officer of the Los Angeles Dodgers, sponsored the baseball tournament and threw out the first pitch. The Dodgers provided plenty of giveaways — including pens, balls and pennants — and to this day, I still use their leftover notepads we were not able to give away. The assistant coaches on this team were Amit and Alon, and this was the tournament that the Mexican team also participated in and were almost thrown out of as they tried to use an over-age player.

The 2013 Maccabiah tournament marked the first time Israel defeated a U.S. team. The head coach of the American team that Israel beat 5–3 was Nate Fish, who right after the tournament became IAB's national director. It also was Dean Kremer's swan song as a member of the U.S. team, as he thereafter played for Team Israel.

The 2017 and 2022 Maccabiah baseball tournaments were both run by the IAB, and I acted as the impartial commissioner. Eric Holtz was the head coach of the 2017 U.S. team, and right after that tournament ended, he took over as head coach of the Israeli national team ahead of the European championships. That was the start of a long and close relationship with a man who became my friend Eric.

Also, at the 2022 Maccabiah, Ian Kinsler, a star second baseman in the MLB who played for our team at the 2021 Tokyo Olympics, attended and was honored as one of five torchbearers at the opening ceremony.

Field of Dreams Tournament

In January 2021 I contacted Roger Duthie, head of the Dubai Baseball Federation about our running a tournament together. In light of the Abraham Accords in 2020 that established diplomatic relations between Israel and the United Arab Emirates, we discussed holding a U–12 tournament later in 2021 in our countries, with additional Middle Eastern countries participating. He agreed.

The historical Abraham Accords "brought a promise for peace in our region," the brochure that we made for the tournament, stated in part. We printed t-shirts and drew up travel plans. Players in both countries were excited. But Covid travel restrictions forced us to cancel the tournament. The kids were disappointed and the organizers and parents were frustrated.

Unfortunately, the event, which we called the Field of Dreams Tournament, still hasn't yet come to fruition. One day, I'm sure, it will.

Fourth Inning

The short-lived Israel Baseball League in 2007

"We are on the map! And we are staying on the map — not only in sports, but in everything."
- Tal Brody

In November 2005, after only a few months as secretary general, a gentleman named Larry Baras approached Haim Katz with the idea of starting a professional baseball league in Israel. Though Haim originally scoffed at the idea, he asked me to follow up and when I visited the United States just before Thanksgiving, I met with Baras at a Starbucks on Manhattan's Upper West Side. I remember that meeting like it happened yesterday (and there are not many meetings that I do remember).

He told me that he sells frozen bagels with pre-spread cream cheese in a plastic bag to the U.S. Army. He explained what a Zionist he was and how much he wanted to help Israel. And he said he was a huge baseball fan who thought nothing could be better than starting the first Israeli professional league.

He regaled me with his vision of what he called "Holy Land Baseball." As my latte cooled, I realized that here was a man who was either deranged or a true visionary or both. I tried to dissuade him, playing devil's advocate to enlighten him to all the potholes that he would likely encounter. He would not be dissuaded, and I left that meeting thinking that if anyone could pull this off, it might just be Larry Baras.

19 months later, he had done what I tried to talk him out of.

I briefed Haim on the meeting and we forgot about it for a few months until Larry started making waves: holding press conferences, conducting player drafts and making announcements about coaches and staff sign-ings, all with the goal of opening a two-month league in summer 2007.

Larry is quoted as saying, "I'm fine during the day, but I have to admit that at 2 o'clock in the morning, when I wake up, I wonder if I'm nuts."

As Larry wrote to us in an e-mail in April 2006 that forming a baseball league also would play a role in his possibly making aliyah with his family.

"I really believe that the sport of baseball can benefit Israel substan-tially on many levels," his e-mail said. "Forming the business of baseball in Israel is a bottom-line goal not only for me personally, but for the fulfillment of baseball's development at the grassroots level as well."

Larry continued, "I know that all of you humored me as I mentioned my ultimate objective and made sure to let me know as accurately as possible what the facts on the ground actually are."

He told us of his efforts in the United States to establish a solid foundation for forming a league in Israel, his funding efforts, who were on board with him and what the next steps would be. He wanted to come public with all of this over the summer and initiate a prospectus to raise the required funds. He asked that the IAB agree to grant the league, which he called the Israel Baseball League, a license to run a professional operation in Israel and expected us to sign an agreement to this effect. After many months of negotiations, we did indeed sign such an agreement.

On February 26, 2007, the IBL held a press conference in New York and declared that the league would begin play that summer, with open-ing day planned for June 24. He arranged for three ex-MLB players, all Jewish, to serve as managers: Art Shamsky, Ron Blomberg and Ken Holtzman. Holtzman had earned the most wins in his career (174) of any Jewish pitcher, more even than the great Sandy Koufax. Blomberg, as a member of the New York Yankees, was the first designated hitter in MLB history. Shamsky was an important player for the 1969 World Series champions, known by me and everyone as the Miracle Mets. The commissioner would be Dan Kurtzer, an American diplomat who had been previously posted as ambassador to Israel. The league's baseball director would be Dan Duquette, who had been the general manager of the Montreal Expos and Boston Red Sox and was the only non-Jewish person in the group.

Kurtzer, the commissioner, had served as President George Bush's ambassador to Israel from 2001 to 2005 after four years as ambassador to Egypt. ESPN.com remarked that Kurtzer brought credibility as the new league's commissioner and quipped that when his sons learned of the appointment, "they congratulated him for finally doing something worthwhile with his life."

When Nate Fish read about the IBL in the *New York Times*, it "changed my life," he said. "For the first time, my two passions intersected." He flew to Duquette's academy in Massachusetts' Berkshire Mountains to attend the first tryout. He signed a contract to play for the Tel Aviv Lightning. "I was going to play professional baseball, sort of," he said.

The league had six teams. Baras imported 106 players from nine countries to go along with 14 Israelis. All 120 players were housed at Kfar Hayarok (Green Village) a 20-minute drive north of Tel Aviv.

Fish continues, "The league had the appearance of a professional baseball league. But once all the players arrived in Israel, the executives left. No one knew what was going on. One of the three fields hadn't been constructed. We quickly ran out of wood bats and game balls. And there was a player strike when the league ran out of money and they stopped paying us."

The teams were the Beit Shemesh Blue Sox and Modi'in Miracle, who shared the Kibbutz Gezer facility; the Petah Tikva Pioneers and Raanana Express, who split the Baptist Village field; and the Netanya Tigers and Tel Aviv Lightning, who played in the Sportek field in Tel Aviv. Games would be seven innings long, with ties to be broken by a home run derby.

Yediot Aharonot, Israel's largest-circulation newspaper, on June 18 published a full-page article about Baras and the league's upcoming opening. They wrote:

> One day, 11 years ago, Baras was sitting in his car trying to cut a bagel that he bought in Dunkin' Donuts, so that he could spread the cream cheese. The result was a cream cheese-stained suit and car upholstery, and unsatisfied hunger. But an idea came to his mind at that exact time: a

frozen bagel with the cream cheese already spread inside. This initiative became a hit in America and with the U.S. Army, and Baras felt that he could also do the impossible in Israel and successfully create an Israeli baseball league. "To love baseball, you need an environment that breathes baseball, and Americans lived that for 100 years already. When you have this historical perspective, the game that appears to be boring becomes magical," Barras said.

That sheds some light on Baras, revealing that only someone like him, with his initiative and determination, could seek to establish a baseball league in Israel.

On June 19, just before the IBL season, I had to go on a short business trip to Europe and planned to return after midnight in time for my 50th birthday on June 22 and for IBL's Opening Day on June 24. I had inklings that Ronit and the kids were planning a surprise for me.

Amit picked me up at the airport at 2:00 a.m., giving me my first birthday greeting and my best gift: a cap of the Netanya Tigers, the team for which he would be playing his first professional game. He signed the cap, writing, "Happy Birthday, from number 22" — the uniform number he chose to signify my birthday! It really moved me, and to this day, that is his number when he wears the uniform.

Returning from the airport, Amit informed me that I had to attend an important league meeting the next morning at 7:30. So, after a few hours of shut eye, we went to Kfar Hayarok, a boarding school on summer break. The accommodations were not quite what profession-al ballplayers were accustomed to. Then again, professional ballplayers never had stayed in Israel. As soon as we got there and saw so many of them lounging on the green lawn: Dominicans, Americans, Australians, Dutch, even a Japanese player. I knew we had found baseball heaven.

Kurtzer gave a short speech about ethics and being guests in Israel. Haim Katz, the IAB president, spoke about how baseball was the ulti-mate Jewish sporting experience because a batter starts at home, as our people did 2,000 years ago; runs the bases, or goes out into the Diaspora, as our people have been doing following the Romans' exile of most Jews from Israel; and in the end, comes back home, or to Israel, as our people did in 1948. I'm not sure how many players in that crowd understood or appreciated his words, as they were all itchy to get on the field, but it was a moving speech for me.

The players broke into teams to practice. I drove to the Baptist Village's field, where three teams were practicing. This is a field I am very familiar with, but so many players were there that every corner of the field seemed occupied by players throwing, playing fungo, fielding infield grounders or hitting in the batting cage, even talking baseball in several languages on the sidelines. The scene was a fantasy come true. I stood there in awe, in amazement, thinking of the last eight years and all of my struggles to field complete teams and recruit players to try this sport I love so much.

Amit later took the field, and although at 6'1" he is considered quite tall and well-built by Israeli standards, among those ballplayers he was not (Who ever said baseball players are not built?). I realized how much my son belonged on this field with them and this would be his opportunity to prove himself against international competition and see if he could pass muster. He did reasonably well as one of the 14 Israeli players and continued to a successful career on the national team. I was enormously proud to watch him play that season and attended as many games as I could.

I had planned to watch for an hour and go home to nap. The hour became four hours, and I enjoyed every second. I soaked up and savored the action, the small talk, the speculation, the memories. At home, my wife urged me to nap or I wouldn't have the strength to stay awake during the family dinner planned for my birthday. I fell into a deep sleep and woke up refreshed and exhilarated.

Haim told me that a press conference would be held late at Baptist Village that Friday afternoon with Shamsky, Blomberg, Holtzman and other IBL staff and that he could not attend. He asked me to go in his place. That made me a little suspicious because holding a press conference at 6:00 p.m. on a Friday in Israel is like holding a press conference in the United States at 8:00 a.m. on a Sunday.

I played along. When I approached the village, I saw Amit lobbing a softball to Haim. (softball, my god, how could he? That's sacrilegious!). A few friends were playing with them, as well as my co-workers at Hamat, my cousins and other friends. I realized that I was the guest of honor at a surprise party organized by Ronit and the kids. Next to the field there is a villa and lawn, where I saw balloons, tables and chairs.

Amit organized us all into a softball game. I had a nice hit actually, but if they tell you years from now that Haim grooved the ball in for me, I'll vehemently deny that. After an hour of play, we were called over to the lawn, where Ronit, Maya, Amit and Adi had prepared a huge spread of food, cold beer and wine. A band played live music - all tunes I love. Everyone chowed down and talked through the evening. I went from table to table, unable to eat much, but thoroughly enjoying myself with the very mixed crowd of native Israelis, American-Israeli's, IBL staff, cousins and in-laws. I had to change mentality, and language, as I went from table to table, thanking everyone for coming.

I gave a short speech, saying how I had in the last two months already received a lifetime worth of gifts, five in all:

- My eldest child, Maya, was going to study what she always wanted, fashion, at Parsons, the best university in her field in the world, and I awaited the day when she would have her own fashion show.

- I was seeing Amit as a professional baseball player, something he and I always will treasure, and knew that his future was bright and in his own hands.

- I took in Adi's huge smile, and two weeks later she earned a bronze medal in Israel's roller-skating championships, accomplished through determination and perseverance.

- Ronit was accepted to not one, but two Ph.D. programs, and had to make a choice of which she preferred.

- I was witnessing our field filled with professional ball players for the IBL's season and anticipating what surprises were in store.

"Those are my gifts and they have given me a tremendous feeling of pride and exhilaration and what keeps me going all the time," I told everyone.

After the party, after all the kisses and hugs and good wishes, after all the cleaning up, we came home and I had the pleasure of watching a video clip made by my two best friends in the United States, Andy and

Michael, as they spoke of our 50 years of memories, telling stories (well, maybe not all, but most....) and of the good times we enjoyed together.

It was a perfect ending to a perfect day and 24 hours after it began, I fell dead asleep, perhaps at the half-century mark in my life, but just beginning to really enjoy it.

Opening day was two days later, and the Baptist Village field felt electric with 3,112 people there to watch the Modiin Miracle defeat the Petah Tikva Pioneers 9-1. Although admission was charged throughout the IBL season, most spectators had free passes and came out of curiosity. The dugouts were open before, and during, the game and fans continuously came to greet the players in a carnival atmosphere. It was a great way to start a new league.

The Jerusalem Post being in English and with much of its staff and readership knowing baseball, had full league coverage on June 24.

"On a summer evening in late June, a dream was realized by bringing baseball to the State of Israel — and the league did rather well," its article began. "The access that the fans had to the players and managers was unbelievable. The fans were able to meet and greet anyone that their hearts desired."

In the paper's coverage on June 25, reality hit. The correspondent's report had this to say:

> On the way home from watching the first game of the IBL on TV on Sunday night, I popped into a grocery store in Talpiot, Jerusalem. *"Did you guys see the baseball game,"* I asked the two very Israeli-looking guys sitting behind the counter with their eyes glued to some soccer game on the television. *"Baseball?"* they replied with blank looks on their faces. *"There's no baseball here."* Clearly they and the majority of Israelis would have no idea what I was talking about if I began discussing the so-called first historic IBL game between Modiin and Petah Tikva. ... As much as the IBL management and staff constantly talk about bringing baseball to Israel, they seem to have forgotten one essential component — the Israelis themselves....there was not an attempt to Israelize the sport of baseball, but to bring New York to Petah Tikva.

The second game of the season drew just 20 spectators, and average attendance throughout the season was less than 100 fans a game over all three venues.

Haim and I spent hours talking to Larry and the management of the IBL about marketing directed at the Israeli public. We told them that America natives would come to watch the games — that was a no-brainer. But for the league to succeed, they had to convince other Israelis to come and to bring their families. Larry had to create a carnival atmosphere, such as activities for children, like at U.S. minor league ballparks, one that was different from the masculine-Israeli-dominated environment at soccer and basketball games. They had to do local outreach to fans in shopping malls, schools and community centers, to come to the fields to watch. They had to arrange with the players to "press the flesh," to greet the Israelis. But our advice fell on deaf ears, and Larry, the marketing guru of cream-cheesed bagels, invested little money in marketing baseball.

The Jerusalem Post put the IBL on the cover of its magazine on the first Friday edition after the season began. An article that day, June 29, dealt extensively with the league's promise.

> Everyone knew how momentous this was. Officially they came to see Petah Tikva play Modiin in the first game of the first season of the first professional league in Israel. Declaredly, they had come to support and celebrate the arrival of the sport they never forgot to the country they always loved. But really, deep down, they had all come for one simple pleasure: To feel like a kid again.

> The game ended in a 9-1 Modi'in victory — but that wasn't nearly as important as the fact that the game was played at all, and everyone knew it. ... On opening night, players from all six teams enjoyed the opportunity to mingle with each other at Yarkon Park — and to mingle with the fans, who greeted them all with equal zeal.

Another article in that day's *Post* said:

> While the Americans in Israel can't get enough baseball, it's taking Israelis a little longer to warm up to this all-American sport. ... The managers (Blomberg and Shamsky) recognize the importance of an Israeli fan base. "If we in the professional league can collectively talk to the youngsters and get them involved in the game, then the league can start developing Israeli players," suggested Shamsky. ... The key is to give the fans someone to root for. "It's very difficult when you have Israelis that have not played on this level," said Blomberg. "It's going to take time to bring the Israelis in. You've got to nurture them, and they have to go from one level to the next."

The Bet Shemesh Blue Sox, managed by Blomberg, but more so by Eric Holtz, won the league championship in dominant fashion. The Blue Sox had three of the best league players in Rafael Bergstrom, Juan Feliciano and Gregg Raymundo and led in the standings from day one. Bergstrom said after the final game, "I am very happy; this is a huge moment in my life." Blomberg couldn't stop smiling or cheering, as though this was the happiest he ever was in his life. "The truth is that all the credit goes to the players. They did an amazing job, as did our fans. Just look at the stands there — they deserve to celebrate."

The Israeli press was much more critical of the IBL, and much more pessimistic about baseball catching on in Israel. Two newspapers, *Maariv* and *Yediot Aharonot* (in its *7 Days* magazine) ran postseason recaps of the league at the end of August.

"The season opened with more than 2,000 emotional fans, but this week the first season of the professional league ended with a much weaker voice. The American national game is still very far from taking over the hearts of sabras, who still love their soccer," *Maariv*'s headlines and captions stated. The article had this to say:

> The first game reverberated, but the effect slowly died out. ... Shlomo Lipetz, the pitcher of the Netanya Tigers

and the first made-in-Israel local baseball star, said, "The most important thing was the existence of the league." Martin Berger, the league's president, said, "There were a lot of things that needed improving, and we are committed to doing that. You need to realize that this is a business in its first year. We all made mistakes, and successful businesses learn from them. If we learn from our mistakes, we will be in a much better position next year." Martin continued, "We survived the first year, and for me that is a huge success. We will be back next year. We are in the process of selling teams to private hands, and I hope we will be able to apply the business model we hoped for at the beginning. There are tens of people who expressed an interest. We need to be sure to choose the right people. We will be back next year and be a lot better. By the way, the memorabilia market for IBL items is flourishing. If you want to get a baseball cap or t-shirt of the league winners, Bet Shemesh Blue Sox, you can't find one. All the stock is gone."
The commissioner, Dan Kurtzer, summed things up: "I think in total it was an enriching experience for everyone. I think we started something here. Sort of a founding stone. As time goes by, we will be better. I have no doubt about that. You should know that there is lots of curiosity in America about this new venture. Everyone wants a souvenir from the IBL, and this will just grow and blossom "

If it's up to Baras, Berger and their friends, in the coming years the IBL will gather momentum and will soon occupy an honorable position among sports leagues in Israel.

Yediot's article, by Tzadok Yechezkeli, was more critical:

> The results, so far, signify well what happens in sports when money, good intentions, and dreams meet the Israeli reality of cynicism, pessimism, violence and indifference... At the end of the first chapter of this strange experiment, we can see the results clearly: 120 games were played in year one in front of mostly empty plastic seats, no ratings and weak press coverage. How shall we phrase it gently? The natives were not very excited about the package that came from America. They didn't even remove the wrapping.

"I will admit that it is offensive when they see us as a joke," says Larry Baras from Boston, who came up with the idea of baseball Zionism and takes too much to heart the indifference and disdain of the locals. "I have thin skin, I think. But I haven't given up. Far from that. Once, Israelis didn't want to eat a hamburger either and look at what is going on now. You can't stop wolfing them down." Everyone agrees that the hope for baseball in Israel depends on reaching Israelis. Kurtzer admits that he was disappointed by the difficult adaptation of locals to baseball. "We won't be able to exist only on the Americans in Israel. We must bring the game to Israelis. There is no doubt that we did not do enough to market the game. We will learn from our mistakes for next year."

Will there be another season? Not everyone is sure. The league lost at least $1 million in its first year, almost 50 percent of the funds invested. Lack of funds led to the cancellation of the weekly TV broadcasts, the vehicle that they hoped would help Israelis familiarize themselves with this strange and foreign game. But to be honest, it's a very difficult mission. On the first date, one doesn't fall in love with baseball. It takes time, lots of time.

Unfortunately, the IBL lasted only one season, but it did create a precedent that professional baseball can be played in this country. Slowly, greater recognition of baseball was forming both in the professional sports world as well as among the public.

IBL was the first big boost Israeli baseball received, a professional league funded entirely by Americans. Kids came to games and got excited about baseball. But it also nearly sank the ship, as Larry, the bagel man from Boston who founded the IBL, was detained in Israel at the end of the season because the league was bankrupt and he still owed so much money to the bus companies, caterers, the TV station and other vendors. The IAB was wise not to sign a document binding the financial fates of the two organizations, despite the pressures from Baras.

Following the IBL season, many of their vendors came knocking on our door to get their payments – the bus company, the caterers, and the TV station. The IAB had no legal liability at all, and Haim was very smart at making that very clear in the contract we signed with Barras. We sent all the vendors to Baras and Berger, who stonewalled. In the end, the IBL had to fold its operations and end any thoughts of an additional season. If we had acceded to him, both IAB and the IBL would have been bankrupted, and that would have been the end of organized baseball in Israel.

A year later, Elli Wohlgelernter wrote an article in *The Jerusalem Post*. It provided some perspective on what happened to the IBL.

> It's not that playing baseball in Israel is so important, when there are real bombs bursting in air and real rockets' red glare; it's just that the idea was so novel, the vision so grand, the imagination so captured and emotions so impassioned that few believed it could ever happen, he wrote. And then, amazingly, it did. And then, sadly, it died.

Wohlgelernter wrote that Baras had to sneak out of the final game of the season and leave Israel because of "serious financial issues" affecting everyone connected to the league.

> It started with the players claiming that checks they received had bounced. At least 23 vendors, companies and individuals were owed money at the end of the season. The list included the venue sites, the Kfar Hayarok dorms and Sports Channel. Baras promised numerous times to provide full financial disclosure, but his promises were empty.

The article stated:

> As the questions mounted and no answers were forthcoming, they [the IBL board members] grew impatient, sensing something was very wrong. The dream was falling apart. Two weeks after the season ended...details of the inside story were revealed of a problem-plagued season that included late paychecks; a players' near strike; a high-profile manager who trashed the league in the media and was subsequently fired; and substandard playing conditions and living quarters for athletes, including no laundry service, no weight room, no ice for sore muscles and poorly manufactured bats that kept breaking...While many were at first quick to excuse the IBL's troubles, attributing them to nothing more than the typical growing pains exhibited by any start-up company, the league's advisory board refused to accept that as an excuse. It wanted Baras to show financial transparency in his operation and insisted that he reveal how much money was raised and how much was spent. Baras never was forthcoming, and it was later revealed that close to half a million dollars was owed in Israel and $1.5 million overall.

In November, after Baras continued stonewalling and more stories came out about non-payments, Kurtzer and nine other board members resigned from the IBL board, while others requested that their names be removed.

Resigning board members Marv Goldklang and Andrew Zimbalist wrote: "It has become apparent that the business leadership of the league has ceased to perform in an effective, constructive or responsible manner, and has failed to manage its capital and other sources in a manner likely to produce successful results."

Additional attempts were made to renew professional baseball in Israel. When Baras' difficulties came to light, Jeff Rosen along with other investors and some ex-players, announced the creation of the Israel Professional Baseball League (IPBL), starting operations in 2008. A year earlier there was no professional baseball in Israel, and now two competing leagues might play. But the IPBL never got off the ground, and the IBL remained stranded as its debtors went unpaid. Baseball in the Holy Land went from two potential professional leagues to none.

The IAB was in the middle of all of this mess, and Haim and I struggled to get the IBL's bills to Israeli creditors paid while trying to maintain some semblance of a professional league. We had no financial liability – everyone realized that –but we felt a moral obligation to put this mess behind us and preserve the reputation of the sport as a viable commodity. We spent over a year cajoling, threatening, propositioning and negotiating with Baras, Berger and company, to little avail. Other investors were brought in, but they had no clout or money. The IPBL wanted to start a new league, but we were reluctant to sanction them if there was a chance that the IBL could still operate.

This situation went on for more than two years. Slowly, debts were paid off but some remain outstanding to this day. Baras has not been heard from in years. Berger has disappeared.

But the relationships started with people like Jeff Rosen, Jeff Royer, Marv Goldklang, Dan Duquette, Mark Rattner, Dan Kurtzer and other IBL investors, has continued over the years. They have helped the IAB financially and logistically and have been major supporters of the IAB's efforts in the WBC and Olympics and in developing baseball in Israel. As a result of the IBL, we were also introduced to Fish, Holtz, Shamsky, Dan Rootenberg, Ty Eriksen, Jason Bonder and the Rattner family, who have helped the IAB over the years, beginning with that glorious summer almost two decades ago.

A sustainable professional baseball league in Israel remains one of my unrealized goals. Upon our return from the Tokyo Olympics, I tried to renew interest in the IPBL and spoke with Rosen, Josh Solomon, Jeff Aeder and Jeff Royer, all long-time IAB supporters. It was the perfect time to do so, due to Israeli media coverage of the Olympic baseball games, which made the sport better known in Israel.

The IAB was also in the midst of building both the Raanana and Bet Shemesh facilities, both of which could be utilized for a professional baseball league. I started exploring how other professional leagues in Israel structure themselves, the challenges involved and how a professional baseball league can learn from past mistakes and do things differently. I sought legal advice, marketing help and community involvement, as well as the support of Israeli institutions, such as the sports ministry, the Israel Olympic Committee and of course the IAB. I wrote a detailed business plan with potential revenues and expenses, with a colorful presentation and prospectus for investors. The goal was for a professional league to start play in the summer of 2023. I was very gung-ho about this endeavor.

In addition to the Olympics, Israel had emerged from the Covid crisis. It all seemed as good a time as any to begin these explorations.

In hindsight, it was fortunate that no large investments were initiated, because the Gaza war of October 7, 2023, would have doomed the league. But I am still a big believer that professional baseball can succeed in Israel under these conditions: patience, long-term planning, investment and marketing to Israelis.

One day, this will be achievable and I will be at the forefront of it.

Top of the Fifth Inning

2012 WBC Qualifiers, Israel misses

"Long after I'm gone, this will get to be bigger and bigger and bigger."
-MLB Commissioner Bud Selig, on the future of the World Baseball Classic

In 2005, the International Olympic Committee voted baseball out of the Olympic Games for reasons I cannot possibly understand or defend. This is the same committee that often awards the Olympics to authoritarian regimes with deplorable records of human rights violations, so in fairness, cancelling baseball wasn't its worst decision ever. For global fans of baseball, however, it was a blow to the growing attempts at spreading the sport.

After the IOC's vote, MLB Commissioner Bud Selig responded with lightning speed, announcing the formation of the World Baseball Classic and having the tournament up and running as early as the next spring, 2006. Selig openly regretted not having acted sooner on the steroid crisis (although, given baseball's growth then, it is doubtful another commissioner would have done any differently), but he did not make that mistake here. Selig decided to put the strength of his office behind the WBC and the internationalization of baseball. He hoped that the teams from different countries would put on a good show and, thereby, grow the game he loves.

There were glitches and logistical problems, to be sure, but by the time Cuba defeated Japan in a championship game worthy of the word *Classic*, the event had caught the imagination of baseball-loving countries all over the world. With the exception of – believe it or not - the United States.

Japan won the second WBC in 2009 because ... well, the Japanese are awesome at baseball and their disciplined, fundamental, small-ball approach translates better to tournaments than the American and Latin styles. Since 2006, they have won gold medals in three WBCs, two Premier 12s and three Olympics. By contrast, no other country has won two. Their championship game with South Korea in Dodger Stadium in 2009 was the highest-rated program on Japanese television that year and remains one of the highest-rated events ever in that country. This just in: they really know how to play baseball in the land of the rising sun.

The tournament still hadn't quite caught on in the United States. In fact, the MLB Network's Jon Morosi reported widely circulated rumors in late 2016 that the 2017 iteration could be the last we'd see of the WBC.

In spite of the lack of interest in the United States, the biggest baseball market in the world, rumors had been swirling in 2011 of adding a qualifying round and that Team Israel would be invited to compete. Bud Selig; Michael Weiner, the executive director of the MLB Players Association; and many team owners who were Jewish were pushing for this to happen. We couldn't have been more excited.

The rumors were proven to be true when, on May 27, 2011, we received the formal invitation from Bud Selig, saying that he was pleased to inform us that our baseball federation "has been selected to receive an invitation to participate in the new qualifying round for the 2013 World Baseball Classic."

Michael Weiner wrote, "It's an honor to recognize Israel's standing among baseball-playing nations with this invitation to compete on a global stage."

In retrospect, this may have been the most important invitation the IAB ever received, considering what the WBC has meant for Israeli baseball ever since. Haim Katz, IAB's president then, called it "historic," and I agree. In accepting the invitation, he wrote, "It is a tribute to our efforts and progress in promoting the great game of baseball in Israel. We look at the mission as a partnership between the North American Jewish community and Israel and as a vehicle to strengthen the ties between us."

We were thrilled and ecstatic by all the possibilities this would bring. We had no idea how to move forward, how to recruit players, or even when and where the qualifiers would be played. Further complicating matters was that we had no idea under what eligibility rules they would allow players to play. It was all done by the seat of our pants.

The tournament uses what it calls a "heritage rule" to allow players who are eligible for citizenship in any country to play for that team. That enabled Team Israel to expand its roster beyond just Israeli citizens who were ballplayers and reach out to American-Jewish baseball players, who, on the basis of Israel's Law of Return, were eligible for citizenship and, thus, a place on our roster.

MLB recognized that Israel had the potential, under the heritage rule, of putting together a very competitive team. Several Jewish ballplayers played in the major leagues and dozens more in the high minor leagues. We were tasked with the job of assembling Team Israel, which would be the best Jewish baseball team ever established.

In an article in the *New York Times* in June 2011, sports reporter Ken Belson wrote, "Too bad Sandy Koufax is not pitching anymore." But Haim and I had no idea how to go about assembling the team.

Luckily, a few years prior, in the 2005 Maccabiah Games held in Israel, Team USA had been managed by Jerry Weinstein, a successful coach in American colleges and in international play, whom we had gotten to know very well. We contacted him while he was coaching a Class A team in the California League, and he said he would be thrilled to lead Team Israel. We thought we had our man, but Jerry contacted us a few weeks later and unfortunately had to bow out, as he had just received an offer from the Colorado Rockies to join their coaching staff, an opportunity no one could blame him for seizing. Disappointed, he did offer to help us find coaches and told us that three Jewish major leaguers had recently retired: Brad Ausmus, Shawn Green and Gabe Kapler. He was willing to join us at a meeting with them.

This was very exciting, as it was the first time we had the chance to meet genuine big leaguers, true Jewish legends of this high a caliber. The wheels were turning.

I realized that if I approached potential players as Peter Kurz, catcher for the esteemed Purchase College Burnouts intramural team, no one would listen. However, if it came from Green, Kapler and Ausmus, with their leading-men looks and impressive playing pedigrees, we would get a lot of ears all over America.

Ophir, Haim's son, was playing ball and studying at Cypress Junior College in southern California, where the legendary Scott Pickler was head coach. 'Pick' had led Cypress to five state championships and coached in the Cape Cod League, where 71 of his disciples made it to the majors. Weinstein knew Pick well, and since the players lived close by, he agreed to hold the meeting at the Cypress campus. On November 8, 2011, armed with a PowerPoint presentation and three Team Israel jerseys bearing the names Ausmus, Green and Kapler, I showed and told them what I knew about the upcoming qualifying tournament. This was a short presentation as I still did not know all that much.

Nonetheless, it was an exciting time for me to meet these Jewish legends and also a little humbling. They, especially Kapler, asked questions and at the end, when Jerry saw that I was too uncomfortable to ask the big question — Would you guys please join our coaching staff for the WBC? — he looked directly at them and said: "You guys need to step up. One of you needs to manage this team and the others to coach." They were surprised by his bluntness, but Ausmus suggested discussing it amongst themselves before making that kind of decision. I was sure that based on his inquisitiveness and his previous background as a minor league manager, Kapler would be the one to step up and take on the managerial position.

But how wrong I was...Ausmus, the former backstop, got back to me a few weeks later and on February 3, we received an e-mail about their discussions. They decided that Kapler would play and be the bench coach, and Green would play and be the hitting coach. Ausmus would not play (even though he looked fit), but he would be the manager. Through his relationship with Ausmus, former major leaguer Andrew Lorraine became our pitching coach. The die was set, and the ball started rolling.

The qualifiers were scheduled for November 2012 so that major leaguers could participate. This was a huge advantage for us, because several All-Stars were Jewish and had valuable playoff experience that could have a huge influence on our younger prospects. Ausmus, Kapler and I went over the names and what would be required for them to prove they were eligible to play for Team Israel. There were 10 known Jewish major leaguers and about 150 minor leaguers. Obviously, we started at the top with names like Ryan Braun, Kevin Youkilis, Ian Kinsler, Danny

Valencia, Ike Davis, Jason Marquis and Craig Breslow. Knowing that most would not want to suit up in November, their offseason, made this a tough sell. But none of them would be playing in the postseason that year, which may have made the decision to commit to us easier if they were hungry for the playoff-type action they had been denied.

That March it was announced that Team Israel would be in the bracket with France, Spain and South Africa and playing in Jupiter, Florida. It was a relatively easy group to try to get past and into the main tournament in 2013. We were told by a friend at MLB headquarters: "There is a desire [among the management] to see Israel advance to the finals. It is looked at as a potential economic plus for the tournament."

We saw the venue as an advantage due to the large Jewish population of southern Florida. However, we did not realize that Jupiter is a 90-minute car ride from Miami, an eternity for Floridians, and that the snowbirds would still be up north in November. We would learn this from all the empty seats in the stands.

Of the MLB's top four Jewish players (Braun, Kinsler, Youkilis and Davis), we felt that Youkilis was most likely to agree to play. As Katz wrote to Ausmus and me:

> His addition will have an impact on the future of baseball in Israel, the relationship between the US and Israel (both the Jewish and non-Jewish community) and the spread of the game of baseball around the world. Am I exaggerating? Maybe. We are being looked at very closely as a model for managing this tournament to develop baseball in our country. ... If Youkilis joins the team, it will be a statement heard not only in Israel and the U.S., but in every country where there is a core who wants to promote the game. I think of all the potential active players, Youkilis has the maturity to realize that this is not just a baseball tournament.

Katz was 100 percent right. I only fully realized the extent of Youkilis's reach and influence during his involvement with our 2023 team and, more recently, his total and complete support on social media for

Israel during this difficult war in Gaza. Youkilis had won World Series rings as a star first baseman with the Red Sox in 2004 and '07 and he'd played for Team U.S.A. in the 2009 event. He homered twice in that tourney and drew the bases-loaded walk that set up David Wright's walk-off hit against Puerto Rico, earning him the nickname "Captain America." That bases on balls ended up being Youk's last appearance in the tournament, as he was removed from the roster in the semifinals due to an injury. He was replaced by Evan Longoria, and the United States lost to the eventual champion, Japan.

The thought that Youkilis might choose Israel, rather than try to finish what he started with the American team, had me salivating. I wrote to Brad, "The ball is starting to roll and pick up speed." In March, Michael Schwimer, a pitcher with the Philadelphia Phillies, wrote to us to express interest in playing for the team, the first MLB player to actually reach out in this fashion. More would surely follow.

Then MLB shifted course in May, to our utter dismay. Our pool of the tournament, it decided, would instead be played in September, meaning that no MLB players on their teams' 40-man rosters could be used. That dashed our hopes of appealing to MLB players. This was particularly frustrating in that the other three countries in our pool lacked potential major league talent to draw from, which would have given us a greater advantage against them. Other teams in the qualifiers that would not be playing in September were able to recruit from both the MLB pool and available prospects. Padres shortstop Everth Cabrera, for example, suited up for Nicaragua, while Toronto Blue Jays catcher Yan Gomes, played for Brazil.

Our plans having been changed without our consent, we needed to make up a team with top minor league prospects and recently re-tired players. The first people we contacted were Mike Lieberthal, Josh Satin, Jake Lemmerman, Adam Stern, Jason Kipnis, Cody Decker, Nate Freiman. There was another player listed as on the cusp, Josh Zeid, then a 23-year-old pitcher in A ball.

In a 2011 article in the *Jewish Standard* by Ken Mandel, some of these minor leaguers spoke about being Jews in baseball. Zeid, an Astros prospect, said, "When you look across the major leagues, you see the Jewish players. I want to be one of those guys." Eric Berger, a minor leaguer for Cleveland, who also played the following year for Team Israel, said, "I love the fact of how few we are. ... The amount of professional [Jewish] athletes is so small. If kids can latch on to somebody, he can help inspire them."

For Zeid, furthering customs and a Jewish identity never stops. He sets an example by always wearing a Star of David and a chai. "If you become a successful athlete, you should let people know where you're from," he said. "Guys aren't afraid to say they're Jewish. The more you can tell people, the more everyone will understand who we are as a community."

A two-page spread in June 2011 in Israel's top newspaper, *Yediot Aharonot*, covered our invitation to the WBC, calling it the baseball version of soccer's World Cup. Understandably, it was met with skepticism, as the greatest sport in the world in my view — baseball, not soccer — barely existed in Israel.

"The rules allow American stars to wear the blue and white jersey because of their Jewish roots ... and the Jewish *kop* [ingenuity] continues to find new patents," the article said. "Here are the 10 players who will put Israel on the map!"

Unfortunately, none of the 10 players the article mentioned would don the blue and white jersey in 2012. Seven of them eventually did and we remain in close contact with the other three.

How were the players selected? The Law of Return states that anyone who has at least one Jewish grandparent, or is married to someone with one Jewish grandparent, can become an Israeli citizen by immigrating — known as making "aliyah." That differs from *halacha*, Jewish religious law, which states that only someone who has a Jewish mother is considered Jewish. The halachic definition of a Jew, in recent decades, has created divides between the Orthodox Jews, who are trying to maintain religious law, and secular Jews, who see Judaism as primarily defined bv heritage and history, and who want to open Israel up to more immigrants who have assimilated and intermarried. Did you follow all that? I almost got lost just typing it.

That was our "fair territory" that we could draw from.

We had to sell MLB on the aliyah standard to go by for purposes of our roster's construction. We also would have to make sure that all players were properly documented so that we could prove they were eligible to play for Team Israel. That task fell to Arthur Lenk, a veteran Israeli diplomat who was a volunteer on our staff and ex-Israeli Ambassador to Azerbaijan. That's not what qualified him for this task; rather, he is a huge baseball fan who took it on. Each player needed to send us proof of his affiliation to Judaism. We received a range of documentation, including bar-mitzvah and bris (the religious rite of circumcision) certificates, Hebrew school diplomas, pictures of grandparents' gravestones marked by a Jewish star and even a grandparent's U.S. Army dog tag that stated the religion. It wasn't enough to show that a grandparent was Jewish. We also had to show the parents' birth certificates, indicating the grandparents' names, and the players' birth certificates, indicating the parents' names.

It was quite an operation that Lenk undertook, and in later years I took that responsibility upon myself, made easier because those players who had been previously approved were now automatically approved, and anyone holding an Israeli passport was also automatically approved. That said, I needed to provide proof for more than half of the 2023 WBC team. My primary source for this information were the players' parents, who were thrilled to have their sons play for Team Israel and connect with their heritage and who searched frantically in dresser drawers for the documentation. In most cases, they found it.

Some teams, such as France, chose not to take advantage of the "heritage rule." Team France's general manager, Jean-Christophe Tine, said, "It's a choice made by each federation. I understand perfectly what the goal is. The goal is to take the team to the main tournament next year, which can bring sponsors, media coverage, and money to support a program. Take Israel. It will bring more baseball to Israel and help baseball to really develop there. I have no problem with that. It's just a different strategy. Our idea was to keep our own players, which we thought would get the full support of the French baseball clubs and the French people." This was France's strategy in 2012 but abandoned in later WBCs.

Larry Ruttman wrote a book in 2014, "Nine", and quoted me extensively:

> We said to Major League Baseball that to show your eligibility as Spanish or French or whatever, you just show a passport or birth certificate of a grandfather, and it's clear

that you're Spanish or French. We pointed out that you can't do that for being Jewish – there's no passport or birth certificate for being Jewish so how do you go about proving it? So, at first we said we would have an affidavit – every player would fill out a form and say how they were related to whomever, their parent or grandparents, and they would sign it. We did that and Major League Baseball said that's not enough, you have to have more than that. So, what do you do? You have to have some kind of objective proof ... and it took a lot of work to resolve.

Looking at the Spanish team's roster in 2012 or subsequent tournaments, you see that only a handful of players list their home country as Spain. Spain can draw from all Spanish people worldwide, France from all French people, South Africa from all South Africans. Sixty-five million people live in France alone, about fifty million in Spain and fifty million in South Africa. Many millions of citizens eligible to play for these countries live elsewhere in the world.

The Jewish people, in Israel and around the world, number only about 15 million. No one knows the exact number. That's it, the total pool that we can draw from. An IAB committee at the time discussed whether we should assemble a team of only native Israelis, sabras. If we'd have done that, we would have lost badly in every game. We decided unanimously that we'd field the best team assembled under the rules.

Once September was confirmed for the qualifiers, we needed to identify potential prospects. The ones we knew about for sure, who had Jewish-sounding names (Kaplan, Perlman, Cohen, Lemmerman, etc.) were easy. Players like Josh Satin, Cody Decker, Eric Berger, were known to be Jewish. But we had to find other sources to help us, and we did. *Jewish Baseball News* was a great source, and Scott Barancik, was instrumental. *Jewish Sports Review*, run by Shel Walman and Ephraim Moxson was also an important source. And just plain word of mouth got us quite a few ballplayers.

In September 2011, *Jewish Baseball News* listed the top Jewish minor leaguers of 2011: twelve players, including the best pitcher, best batter, best reliever and most valuable player. Nine of those twelve would play for Team Israel in the WBC.

Some players reached me by chance. Infielder Ty Kelly, who has an Irish father and Jewish mother, was signing autographs at a minor league ballpark for some kids wearing yarmulkes and he told them he was Jewish. They told their father and he e-mailed me.

Team Israel in 2012 was almost completely unknown to the baseball world (Although that guy in Menlo Park that I mentioned in the prologue was already a fan), so having Ausmus, Green and Kapler reach out to players was a huge help. By 2016, many of them had heard about us and Weinstein's job was made a little easier. By 2023, more prospects reached out to Ian Kinsler or me, having heard from him and other participants how amazing it was to play in the tournament.

The 2012 team would have a few guys who later reached the major leagues and enjoyed successful careers. One was Joc Pederson, a 20-year-old, single-A prospect with great potential that was soon realized. At one stage during our pre-tournament camp, Brad Ausmus told me we can't let Pederson into our courtesy suite, where alcohol was served, because he was under age. I told Pederson that I didn't care if someone else took a few beers out for him to enjoy in the privacy of his room, and he understood that. (He even played for us in 2023 as an MLB veteran and recent World Series champion.) Richard Bleier was also pitching in the minors but later played for us in 2023 and was on our designated-pitcher pool for 2017 but did not pitch. (The DPP was a pool of up to ten pitchers who are not on the roster but could be used as replacements as the team advanced in the tournament). Josh Satin made his MLB debut in 2011 and would play 116 games. Josh Zeid would play for the Houston Astros; he, Nick Rickles and Shlomo Lipetz played for Team Israel in 2012 and 2016–17 and also in the Olympics.

A document I drafted for the IAB, "The Roadmap for Team Israel in the WBC," set four goals:

- To win the qualifiers to reach the main tournament.

- To increase interest in baseball in Israel and enhance the strength of the IAB. Build a new field complex.

- To bring back a professional baseball league.

- To strengthen the ties between Israel and the North American Jewish community.

We organized committees to work toward those goals, and set a budget of $400,000. We established a steering committee, a baseball operations committee, a finance committee and a public relations committee. Many of the closest associates of the IAB assumed positions on these committees: Jeff Rosen, Marv Goldklang, Dan Kurtzer, Jerry Weinstein, Pat Doyle, Marty Appel, Andrew Wilson, staff from MLB and JNF. So did those already active in the IAB: Jordy Alter, David Leichman, Dan Rothem, Haim and me.

We brought Brad Ausmus and his wife, Liz, to Israel on May 20, 2012, for a red-carpet visit. They toured all over the country and came to Baptist Village for a press conference to introduce him as Team Israel's manager for the WBC. Ten reporters came, which was a nice turn-out for us. Ausmus answered their questions like the seasoned pro that he was.

The next day we went to see the country's president, Shimon Peres, together with Dan Shapiro, the U.S. ambassador. Ausmus wore his Team Israel jersey. Peres started regaling us about his baseball knowledge and said, "When I came to America years ago, there was one name on everyone's lips: Joe DiMaggio." Ausmus gave him a baseball and asked him to sign the "sweet spot," the narrow area nearest the seams. Peres returned the ball to Ausmus and said, "No, you need to sign here. You are the manager," Peres said while signing a different spot on the ball. He thanked Ausmus for a jersey and ball given as gifts and said, "The ball is easy to sign, but difficult to hit," summing up the very essence of the game. "There is nothing that helps connect between nations more than sports," Peres told us. "I wish the Israel national baseball team great success," and off we went.

Ausmus, an avid surfer, even glided upon the Mediterranean waves and still speaks today with great fondness about his visit to Israel as an eye-opening trip.

"I wanted to honor my grandfather and mother, who are my Jewish family side. They raised me to love baseball and it's a tradition I associate with my Jewish roots," he said. "Aside from that, when I was a player in the league, early in my career I started to see a lot of small kids who identified me as a hero because I was Jewish. That gives you a feeling of responsibility. I wanted to give something back to our community and to try and bring baseball to Israel."

His WBC role drew Ausmus closer to Judaism and Israel. In 2022, he readily accepted Ian Kinsler's invitation to be the bench coach for the team and has remained very helpful in fundraising and recruiting players throughout the years. In 2026 he will return as the WBC team manager.

In building the team rosters with Ausmus and then Jerry Weinstein, we struggled between the goal of winning the tournament and having more Israeli citizens on the roster. Some in the IAB leadership lobbied for a majority of sabras, to set an example for other players in Israel, while others (myself included) advocated that we field the best possible team and include a token presence of less qualified Israeli players. Winning was crucial, both for the resonance and for the financial considerations of the sizable prize money. Funds, after all, would enable us to pursue our goals to grow the sport in Israel.

Until the 2023 tournament, native Israeli players were significantly inferior to the non-Israelis. We always needed to strike a balance between providing the managers with enough quality players to be competitive, while including Israelis to gain experience and provide public relations and legitimacy to the organization. In 2012, three players held Israeli citizenship. In 2016–17, we had only two. But in 2023, 12 players held Israeli citizenship, primarily due to the requirements of the Olympics.

Barry Bearak of the *New York Times* wrote on September 19, 2012, about the internal conflict:

> Though Israel's national baseball team has many excellent pitchers, catchers, infielders and outfielders, the roster has a shortage of something that might be considered essential: Israelis.   Only three of the squad's 28 players hail from Israel....When Israel received an invitation to play in the qualifying round, a decision needed to be made: should it field an inferior team that would take its lumps or look to the United States, where the grass is greener with baseball-playing Jews. I asked our guys, "If people who have never been to our country get to wear Israel across their chests, is this going to bother you?" Kurz said. "Our guys all supported it. Oh, there were some who said we should be sure to have plenty of Israelis, and I said, "Listen, we want to win." "I'm happy to be playing for Israel, but it's kind of bizarre, too," Josh Satin said. "No one from my family has ever been there."

In the hotel lobby that night, Kurz watched his American ballplayers as they mingled. They looked like superb athletes, lean, muscled, and confident. "This is a dream come true," he said happily. "Look at them. They look like Jews, only bigger."

Stan Grossfeld wrote this for *The Boston Globe* on September 18:

Former major league All-Star Shawn Green calls Team Israel "the greatest collection of Jewish players ever assembled." "Oh my God, it's so humbling," says Team Israel pitcher Dan Rothem of Tel Aviv.
Team Israel manager and former All-Star catcher Brad Ausmus walks by Rothem, grins and says, "Nice job," and Rothem is thrilled. "I still feel nervous," he said. "I'm not a professional. This is so awesome." Like most children in Israel, Rothem grew up without much baseball. Soccer and basketball are the preferred sports in the country. But he fell in love with the game and played on a fledgling Little League team in 1989. They didn't have uniforms, just sweatpants and t-shirts. They had no batting gloves and had to borrow equipment.
"We were at the Little League regional qualifier in Ramstein Air Force Base in Germany in 1989," says Rothem. "We had to play Saudi Arabia. They were all American kids. They ended up beating us 51–0, and it was in all the Israeli newspapers. The next day the Saudi authorities denied the existence of the game, but I have pictures," he adds with a laugh.
Shlomo Lipetz says that when he hears the Israeli national anthem played in America, he will be ready. "It's not pressure, its pride, and the competitive juices will be flowing," he says. "The Hatikvah, it always gives you a little chill. I'm not a very religious person, but standing on the line, getting to give a high-five to Shawn Green, wow." Ausmus says he tried to pick as many Israeli players as possible. "It's a little strange that you're representing Is-

rael and the majority of the kids are American," he says. "But this is the framework of the WBC, and it applies across the board to all countries. The hope is that 25 years from now it's Israelis representing their country."

"My response was at first one of reluctance," says Ausmus. "I didn't really practice the Jewish religion. But once I started playing, the fans got real excited about having someone of Jewish heritage, and I'm glad to embrace that."

Shawn Green is glad to do his part. "It means a lot to Jewish Americans, because I think they have always had that stigma of being non-athletic," Green says. "To break the stigma, and to also have a team that Jews around the world can rally behind is great."

"Jews are going to be dancing in the streets when we win this thing," says bullpen catcher Nate Fish. "Every single one of them. I kid you not. This is happening. We're going to Muhammed Ali this freaking thing." A native of Cleveland, Fish blogs as "The King of Jewish Baseball."

We decided to bring to Jupiter the senior national team, known as the SNT, made up of passport-holding adults, most of whom lived in Israel. We thought this would be an opportunity for them to experience what being in a real MLB training facility and clubhouse would be like. They'd play exhibition games against local competition and be inspired by Brad Ausmus and others. We brought in two coaches just to work with them, Richard Kania and Steve Hertz - Steve had coached in the IBL back in 2007. It would also be a great opportunity to shmooze and be a part of Team Israel environment at the WBC.

On September 10, 18 members of our SNT team arrived at Roger Dean Stadium in Jupiter, Florida, shared every spring training by MLB's Florida Marlins and St. Louis Cardinals. Their jerseys were hanging in the clubhouse, their lockers prepared. It was also my first time in a major league clubhouse, and I was quite impressed by the amount of gear, or swag. Even today, I am impressed to be in major league clubhouses and to see Team Israel uniforms hanging in their lockers, the players' nameplates overhead with the IAB logo. Our players were in heaven, and from the swampy fields in Israel they entered a new world of manicured lawns in Jupiter. Like kids in a candy store, they examined the clubhouse, conditioning room, trainer's room, lunchroom, indoor and outdoor batting cages, six practice baseball fields, pitching mounds, and the main stadium itself.

The SNT guys practiced at the fields for three days with the coaching staff, and our WBC players arrived on September 13. Many came to the field to see the facility and eat lunch with our players The socialization between the teams was complete, although it was hard for our SNT players to give up on their exclusivity of the facilities and program. But they gladly cheered for the Team Israel players on the field. That evening we had an opening-night staff dinner organized by Adam Gladstone, our director of operations, an event that became a tradition at Team Israel events in the United States. It was great to have the full group together, some of whom I had barely met.

I spoke about what the IAB was, what our goals were for this tournament and how happy we were to have them on board. It was to be the beginning of a long relationship with everyone, which continues to this day, through two qualifying tournaments, three WBCs, one Olympics and who knows how many more events to go.

The teams had parallel workouts the following day on the Roger Dean backfields, then played exhibition games against college teams. They were good practices and allowed our coaching staff to become familiar with the players.

Sunday evening began the holiday of Rosh Hashanah and we held a traditional dinner. Prior to the dinner, Ausmus took me aside and told me that Kapler was hurt and would not be able to play, and that the coaching staff proposed adding Adam Greenberg to the roster. Adam was the only player in MLB history to have come to the plate yet not record an official at bat, as he was hit in the head on the first pitch he saw in the big leagues while a member of the Chicago Cubs in 2005. He suffered from vertigo for a long time afterwards, being stuck in the minor leagues until an online petition led to his being signed to a one-day contract with the Marlins. It was through them that he would have his first, and only, official at bat in the majors, in 2012, less than a month after playing with us. In that at-bat, he struck out on three pitches to the eventual Cy Young Award winner, R.A. Dickey, in the process earning a standing ovation. Ausmus and I called Greenberg over just before the dinner started and told him that he'd made the roster. His smile was a mile long, and I knew that the new year would be great for this guy.

Also from the Boston Globe article: "I was taken aback, "says Greenberg. "I was getting ready to sit down, and Brad said, 'Hey I need to talk to you for a second.' I was thinking he's going to tell me I'm going to be one of the coaches, thanks but there's no room. But he said, 'You're going to be part of this team.' I just couldn't stop smiling. Now it's real. I can contribute. I will be part of the greatest Jewish team ever assembled."

As the players came into the hall for dinner, all dressed in their fanciest clothes for the holiday and smelling of aftershave, I couldn't help feeling: Damn this is really something! These players, including past and future major leaguers, coming to play for the IAB was historic and emotional for me. Guys took it upon themselves to say different portions of the pre-meal blessings, and it was a pleasure to hear so many of them know and appreciate the prayers. Most players rarely get to celebrate Rosh Hashanah during their careers, being that it usually falls during their playing seasons, so they appreciated the opportunity and I received many compliments and thanks afterwards. The meal was the usual holiday meal of challah, gefilte fish, brisket and wine, paid for by a generous donor, and it was a grand evening and a great way to start the WBC tournament.

The team very quickly bonded together and guys who came from afar, but with similar backgrounds, quickly found common ground.

As Hal Habib of *The Palm Beach Post* wrote the following on September 23, 2012:

> Bond? What could they know about a bond after only a few days? Plenty, it turns out.
>
> "I've never played on a team where it's been solely Jewish players," Jake Lemmerman said. "When you go and play around the minor leagues, you run into one or two Jewish players and you're always excited to meet them. You share that bond with them. Everyone has that feeling now."
>
> "It's no secret that Jews are not a powerhouse in sports," said Lipetz, a pitcher. "And the fact that we could

kind of tap into that collective consciousness of the ultimate underdog and into that whole 'Jews can't be good in sports' — really, the response I've been getting from Jews in the United States has been overwhelming." For good reason, says Peter Kurz, the team's general manager. "One thing's for sure," Kurz said. "This is the greatest Jewish team ever assembled." Lipetz is what Kurz refers to as one of the "native Israelis," as opposed to the "new Israelis," many of whom have never stepped foot in the country but hope to visit in January. In the meantime, the Americans are picking up all sorts of clubhouse tips from their new *haverim* [friends]. "We've been trying to do our best to not only pump-up Israel and share as much of our experience and our passion for Israel, but also through teaching some key words," Lipetz said. "You know ... some appropriate, some inappropriate."

Designated hitter Shawn Green, a two-time All-Star and 15-year-major-league veteran, recalled a time in the mid-'90s when he was playing for Toronto and went to bat against Milwaukee during Rosh Hashanah. [Jesse Levis, who is Jewish] was catching. "We used to call each other 'Yid,'" Green says. "So, I go up to the plate, I say, 'Happy new year, Yid,' and he said, 'Hey, yeah, shana tova, Yid.' And Al Clark was the umpire. He goes, 'Happy new year, guys. Shana tova.'
"Al Clark? He goes, 'Yeah, I'm Jewish too,' and we're talking. Meanwhile, strike 1. I'm kind of focused on the conversation. But it was pretty cool to have that experience. Probably the only time in baseball when three Jews were at home plate at the same time.

One of the many characters on our staff was our team podiatrist, Dr. Glenn Copeland. He was added at the recommendation of Shawn Green, and although I did not quite understand why we would need a podiatrist, I quickly understood why we needed Glenn Copeland. The guy is your favorite Jewish uncle, a true mensch, who was probably the person most thrilled to be associated with this Jewish baseball team. "Doc," as he was called, gave a brief speech prior to our first game, probably the most moving and motivational speech I have ever heard. It was quoted in the *NY Times article* from September 24, 2012:

> In an impassioned speech before Israel's first game Wednesday, which has worked its way onto YouTube, the team doctor, Glenn Copeland told the players that although he has been in baseball 32 years as the Toronto Blue Jays' team physician, "it's as emotional as hell because there's never been a night in baseball that I've been associated with that I'm more excited and more proud to be a part of." He compared seeing an all-Jewish team in a world tournament to Jackie Robinson's breaking the color barrier. "You're the best and greatest Jewish baseball team that's ever played in the world," he said, "and every Jew is walking a lot prouder."

The *Times* that day mentioned a fan, Jay Dermer, who, while he "marveled at the community of Jews who flocked to this minor league park, talked about how comfortable it felt to be at a baseball game surrounded by skullcaps, mezuza and Stars of David. 'You can make a Jewish joke here and get a laugh because people get it,' he said. 'You can speak a little Yiddish and get a little Yiddish back. And kvetching, too,' he said, sighing. 'There'll be a lot of kvetching if we lose.' "

The next two days were light workouts, and the action began on September 19 in a 7:08 p.m. game start against South Africa. Israel was ready.

So was Nate Freiman, who homered in the top of the first inning off Dylan Unsworth, who many predicted would be the first South African born player to reach The Show. (Shortstop Gift Ngoepe, his teammate in both the 2012 and 2016 qualifiers, would have that distinction.) Unsworth pitched five more innings without allowing a run. Seven years later, we would run into him again in perhaps the most historic game Israel has ever played. But, that story is for later.

We thought we broke the game open with a five-run eighth inning and sealed it when Freiman homered again in the ninth. With a large Jewish contingency in the crowd, Israel looked as though it would cruise to its first ever victory in international competition and needing only one try to do it. Ausmus called on Israeli born Shlomo Lipetz to close it out, and he promptly let the South Africans back into the ballgame, allowing three runs and three walks. Mets prospect Jeff Kaplan, who never made it to the Bigs, came in to close out the game and cleaned up the mess before we almost snatched defeat from the jaws of victory, and won 7-3.

We next faced Spain, which relied heavily on Caribbean ballplayers who had played long enough in a WBSC-sanctioned league in Spain to qualify to represent Spain. Its team in the 2022 qualifier a decade later included only one Spanish player — this despite Spain's having played baseball for over a century and winning a European championship in 1955.

Conversely, Israel hosted only one unsuccessful season of professional baseball, matching, at least until 2000, the number of fields we had. We had no choice but to begin our WBC experience with mostly American Jews. In 2019, while Spain continued to neglect the development of local and youth talent, the Israeli U–18 team made it out of the B pool to compete in the main tournament with a roster of players born entirely in Israel. So, while we were heading toward a future of true Israeli teams in international competition, Spain was going in the opposite direction.

In this game, Freiman belted two more homers, looking like a lock for tournament MVP, and we came out on top, 4-2.

Freiman was, and still is, one of the most interesting players in our team's history. He's 6'8" and was Duke University's career home run leader. Later, with the Oakland A's, he was the American League Rookie of the Month, shortly after they snatched him from the Astros in the Rule 5 draft. In the movie Bull Durham, Max Patkin *(played by himself)* tells Annie Savoy *(Susan Sarandon)* that 'Crash' Davis *(Kevin Costner)* is different than most other minor leaguers, explaining that he had actually seen Crash read a book once that didn't have any pictures. That line makes me think of Nate, a very quiet person, but highly articulate when he did speak, and a guy who was always curled up, all 6'8" of him, reading a book somewhere in our hotel. And much like Costner's classic character, he was not without sly wit. In 2017, when asked if Team Israel wasn't basically just Team USA's junior varsity team, he replied that we weren't, adding that most of our guys couldn't have made that team.

Spain then played South Africa to determine which team would face Israel for the pool championship and a trip to the 2013 WBC. Unsworth had gone over the pitch limit against us, so was ineligible for the game and Spain trounced the South Africans, 13-3. Our rematch with Spain was set for the night of September 21. We were the home team this time but expected a similar outcome. Fish said before the game, "We're gonna go out like savages if we win today," visualizing a seedy club in South Florida with reveling Jews.

This was a back-and-forth affair that went into extra innings. Our pitching was mostly dominant in the first two games, but now we had trouble getting outs. After clubbing four homers, Freiman's bat went silent as Spain's pitchers refused to give him anything to hit.

We led 6–4 in the fifth inning. Shawn Green, who'd socked 327 big league homers, came to the plate with a runner on third base and only one out. Shawn, who had looked really uncomfortable in his last at bat, popped out to first base and promptly took himself out of the game. It turned out that he had just gotten new contact lenses and in the twilight hours, couldn't see the ball at all and spoke to Ausmus about coming out. Spain quickly retook the lead before we tied it in the bottom of the eighth inning on a wild pitch.

We had the potential winning run on third base with two outs in the bottom of the ninth. Joc Pederson, a man who would become no stranger to post season heroics, stepped into the left-handed batter's box with a chance to send Israel to the third World Baseball Classic. Showing a glimpse of what was to become commonplace for him, Pederson put a charge into the ball, lacing a scorching line drive that everyone but the right fielder knew was a walk-off hit. As the ball took off over the infield, we all rose up in unison, certain the game was now won by Israel. If I close my eyes, I can still see it was a base hit, the vision marred only by the leather glove that caught it before it hit the grass.

Then came extras and, to paraphrase President Franklin Delano Roosevelt, the 10th inning would live in infamy. Josh Zeid was on the mound. After pitching flawlessly against South Africa in Game One, he found himself with runners on second and third with two outs and Spain's hottest hitter, Yunesky Sanchez, who'd gotten three hits, in the batter's box. Josh is the last guy in the world to make excuses, but I think his composure was rattled when our catcher, Charlie Cutler, was ejected a few moments earlier for arguing a ball four call that he thought was strike three.

In fairness to the home plate umpire, the pitch looked clearly inside to those watching on TV. In fairness to Charlie, umpires can't have a short fuse in tournament play and throw out a catcher in extra innings of the final game for arguing balls and strikes. Ausmus was livid and came out to protest the ejection, but to no avail.

The delay, the new backstop setting up an unfamiliar target behind the plate and the jam he got himself into proved to be too much. Josh yielded a two-run single up the middle. After coming so close to walking it off in the bottom of the ninth, we were now fighting for our WBC lives.

We brought the tying run to the plate in the bottom of the inning, but went down without a run. Team Israel, the oddsmaker's favorite, the Jupiter crowd's favorite, the wouldn't-it-be-a-good-story favorite, lost 9–7 and watched Spain celebrate on the infield grass.

We were devastated, and Josh was particularly heartbroken. His shoulders slumped so low that he could almost scratch his knees without bending. It's one thing to carry a loss into to the next game or the next season. But to carry it for four years, not even knowing if you'll be playing when the next opportunity comes, is a killer. The only solace was that as hard as he took it, his character was that of a man who could bear it. Yes, baseball is just a game, but anyone who remembers the name Bill Buckner knows that sometimes passion for the game comes at price. In retrospect, it may have been a blessing that he was the one asked to live with it. More on that later.

We got back to the hotel in deathly silence. It was as though someone had punched me in the stomach, and all the air in me was gone. I was exhausted from the emotional pain. We had the better team, the much better team, but that was on paper and baseball is not played on paper. Our catcher was thrown out at a critical time, our outfielder almost won the game in the bottom of the ninth, but then our closer lost it in the top of the tenth. He wasn't to blame; the cosmic stars just were not aligned that night. We may have found ourselves in the darkest hole we could possibly be in, but in hindsight, this was all groundwork for what would happen four years later.

Prior to that final game, Gladstone told me that it is customary for the two teams in the finals to split the cost for the champagne and keep it on ice for whichever team wins. I said to him, "You aren't serious, are you? We are going to win." Then I instructed him to buy bottles and put them on ice in our locker room. My career as a soothsayer notwithstanding, the guys gathered after the game in our hotel courtesy suite to say their goodbyes, in defeat and not in victory. A few did drink some champagne, but when we all left the suite at about 2:00 a.m., there were quite a few bottles left. So much for my giving the team good luck.

Three months later, Ophir Katz was in South Africa playing baseball and when some local players heard he was from Team Israel, they laughed and related the story of South African players after that 2012 game reaching the Team Israel courtesy suite at the hotel at about 3:00 a.m., finding the leftover champagne and enjoying it. For Team Israel, that became known as champagnegate, and I have certainly learned my lesson.

On the bright side, Adam Greenberg summed up his experience this way: "Talking to the guys from Israel, and hearing their passion and desire to play but also getting to know that there's only one real baseball field in the country, gives you a greater appreciation of how great it is that these games [were] televised on a couple of stations in Israel. It's making the newspapers over there too. That will raise awareness and educate kids there about baseball and get them to say they want to play."

Haim Katz wrote a blog during the WBC, albeit containing just three entries. It was brilliant commentary at the time. Allow me to quote him extensively:

> In my eight years as president of the IAB, there have been many ups and downs, starting with the rise and fall of the IBL to our successful European qualifying tournament last summer. For most of these activities, I was very active in the organization and execution of the events, often trying to put out fires and never able to take the time to soak in the moment until the event has passed.

On the eve of the most important event in the history of the IAB, I find myself a complete spectator. I am not complaining. Much work, thought and planning has been done in the last year and a half to allow me to walk around as president without having to do anything. Most of the credit belongs to Peter, who is still working very hard here as the point man for the Israeli federation. Much of the credit goes to our staff we have assembled to put this thing off, primary Adam Gladstone and his three interns, who have all the technical aspects running as clockwork.

In fact, everything we have been planning for the last year and a half to date has been executed as planned. We were able to bring over 15 Israelis for a training camp in the best facilities any Israeli team has ever played on. We assembled a coaching staff that is the envy of all 16 teams in the qualifiers. And we have put together the greatest Jewish team ever assembled.

More importantly, we have created the chemistry we had hoped for between the native Israeli players and the Israeli players who have yet to make aliyah. Everyone, from the ex-major leaguers to Adam Greenberg (who is one of the big stories of this tournament) to every A, AA and AAA player on the roster, is 100 percent identified with Israel and what it means to play on this team. Before their base-ball practice yesterday, they had singing practice. Singing Hatikvah. I have heard better renditions, but none more moving to my soul than the one in that clubhouse.

The impact of this team on the Jewish community here is even beyond my fertile imagination. This is not a just team of Jewish All Stars. This is a team of the Jewish people, and each and every one of them is proud to be representing Israel. Not only do they come to me and thank me for this opportunity, but their parents also come to me and tell me that their kids have not had this much fun playing baseball since Little League. On their teams, they are Jewish but are reserved about it. On this team, they can celebrate it together with their peers both from Israel and from the U.S. We are all one family.

I enjoy watching our Israeli players having fun with the Israeli players who have yet to make aliyah, and to have our players address Shawn Green as "Greenie." The warmth we receive from the entire Jewish community is overwhelming. The game scores are linked to almost every Jewish newspaper's web site. Last night, Yaron Erel was stopped by a cop. He showed him his Israeli license and the cop said, "You're from the Israeli team, so go ahead."

It is four days and two victories since my last post, eight hours until the first pitch of Israel baseball's definitive hour. Two exciting baseball games. Two huge steps for Israel baseball. My barometer for our success is the Israeli Hebrew press. They, with few exceptions, have ignored Israel's participation in the WBC and certainly do not "get" what this is all about. After the victory over South Africa, we made it to the bottom of the sports pages' headlines. The victory over Spain has moved us to the bottom of the *front*-page headlines. We have had interviews with IDF Radio and Mabat [television station], so we are getting there. (I make no future projections in this blog).

It is important for me to write these words now, before our final game, without knowing the outcome. I am proud of Team Israel. I am proud of everyone. I am proud of our manager, Brad Ausmus, who I believe is the best active manager in baseball today. He has conducted himself with total integrity and with the two goals of winning the tournament and developing baseball in Israel. I am proud of his coaching staff, his players and the players who came and did not make the team. I am proud of our support staff, and I am proud of our eight-year-old minors' team in Modiin who have to throw down bases every Friday in the middle of a traffic island to play baseball. All of us are Team Israel.

Over the last year and a half, this entry has been written many times. I had visualized what I needed to say after the great victory, the historic advance to the World Baseball Classic, just as many players visualize the ball hitting the bat and soaring over the fence, just as every Israeli in the stands in Jupiter on Sunday visualized Joc Pederson's shot to right field falling for a single and winning the game. Even in the last two days, during the euphoria hanging around after the last victory, imaginations ran wild. As I teach my eight-year-olds, however, one cannot always win. The game is played on the field, and you need to focus on the effort, worry about the things you can control and not on factors out of your control. For the most part, that is what we did. We focused on our coaching staff. We wanted people who were not just professionals but would lend legitimacy to the team. We wanted to project both to potential players and donors alike that this team is viable. We wanted someone who would identify with our goals of utilizing this opportunity to promote Israeli baseball both in Israel and abroad. We succeeded with our recruiting of Brad Ausmus as manager and Shawn Green and Gabe Kapler to our coaching staff. I cannot visualize anyone doing a better job than Brad did, both in preparing for this tournament and in his game management, all in keeping with the goals and objectives we have established. But baseball, as life, is humbling. Even when you make your best effort, it's not always enough. In sport, as in life, sometimes the competition wins. On Sunday, Spain executed better than we did. If you concentrate on the process, the results more often than not will come. After all, it was only a baseball game. As I tell my eight-year-olds, some you win and some you lose, and what is important is how you play. If you play well, you will win games. I cannot blame this game on lack of effort of the players. If anything, there was too much effort. (If Joc's ball was hit a little less hard, then this post would be considerably different!)

Our biggest fear was to assemble a "Jewish" all-star team which had no affiliation or connection to Israel. This did not happen. We had 28 proud Jewish players. To a man, they all came to me and apologized for not wining. Twenty-eight players and five coaches all came to me and Peter and thanked **us** for this opportunity to play for Team Israel. Peter had mentioned several times that he didn't want to change this team if we made it to the main tournament. They were really a great bunch of kids, all mensch's.
In the end, we lost a baseball game. But some baseball games are not just baseball games. I can feel a little what it's like for an owner to just miss the playoffs. He loses a lot of money and opportunity. Israel Baseball hasn't lost any money, but we have lost future opportunity. Objectively, we are still much better off than we were before the tournament. More people are aware of Israeli baseball not only in the United States but Israel as well. We have made many more friends, all of whom have contacted either myself or Peter telling us that while we may need to regroup, the mission must continue. Support to build the Raanana field is still strong, and MLB is still committed to helping us design and plan the field. Had we won, we would have had many, many challenges to transform the publicity to

success on the field. Maybe it's more important to build baseball in Israel the hard way: one kid, one coach, one field at a time.

If anything, what we have done by this tournament is prove that there is no greater bridge between the North American Jewish community and Israel than baseball. I know I have a penchant for exaggeration, but had we won, pride in Israel would have swollen to levels just below the victory in '67 and the Entebbe rescue. In this world, where people are tired of hearing about the Middle East conflict and the Jewish identity of the North American community is weakening, baseball has now proven that it can play an important role in turning this trend.

Bottom of the Fifth Inning

2016 WBC Qualifiers, Israel thrives

September 2016, Brooklyn, New York

Fast forward four years to Brooklyn in 2016, where once again, the feeling was that we were the home team. After all, so many flags displayed the Star of David and blue-hued team yarmulkes and other Israel swag dotted the stands. This time, we weren't the favorites, and while we had confidence and determination, the memory of Jupiter in 2012 kept us from being cocky. With many of the players from that previous team returning, we were looking for both redemption, and to finish what we had started.

We'd built the team over the previous two years. Jerry Weinstein was now available to manage for us, and we felt that he, with his vast experience in college and playing in short tournaments, would be preferable to an MLB managing style that accounts for a 162-game schedule. Jerry understood what it meant to play one game at a time and that today's game was the most important one on the calendar.

Not that Ausmus didn't understand that, but there's a difference between knowing the principle and living it. I met with Jerry in Arizona during the 2015 season, and he was ready and willing to take the team on. This time, we knew far in advance that the qualifiers would be in September again and that we again could not draw players from MLB teams' 40-man rosters. Instead, we drew up a long list of possible players, and Jerry started talking to them with my help.

I spoke with Alex Bregman, a very successful AAA infielder who we felt could be our shortstop. We chatted in early July 2016, and he was quite interested in playing for us. We had him penciled in — with a very thick marker. Unfortunately for us and fortunately for him, the Astros called him up on July 25. He would go 0-for-4 in his first game and 1-for-32 to start his career, so while I pulled for his success, I knew he could be sent back down to AAA. Then I thought, "Maybe he isn't good enough for us." Obviously, I was as wrong about that as the studio that rejected *Star Wars* thinking that nobody would want to see a space Western.

I did speak to Bregman again about playing for Team Israel in the main tournament, which would be played during MLB's spring training, were we to advance from the qualifiers. He said he would do that if he didn't get a call from Team USA. He did get that call and played for the American squad, but with only a handful of at-bats. Bregman later said that in retrospect he probably should've played for Team Israel because he got just those four at-bats as a backup for Team USA. In 2017, he won both the gold medal for the U.S. team in the WBC and a World Series ring as a member of the Houston Astros. In 2023, Bregman was recovering from a broken finger and could not play for us. He announced that he will be playing for the U.S. team in the 2026 WBC, which was a huge disappointment for us, after speaking out for Israel in the wake of the October 7th attack.

Ike Davis, who reached the majors with the Mets, was another player I had been pursuing for many months in 2015. He hadn't shown up to our Manhattan fundraiser in 2012 at Lipetz's City Winery, and by the summer of 2016 was no longer playing in MLB, having been released by the Yankees in early August.

But it presented a perfect opportunity for him to play in our qualifying round in Brooklyn in September, only Ike was not returning my or Weinstein's calls. Jerry Narron, ex-MLB player and manager who can best be described as a true Christian Zionist, was in Israel just then, one of the rare summers when he wasn't playing or coaching. Narron has visited Israel more than 15 times, because his daughter Callie lives in Jerusalem. (In fact, now, in 2026, she runs IAB's Jerusalem program.) Jerry's grandson, in fact, plays in the IAB youth leagues. Callie first contacted me in the winter of 2013 and said her dad would be visiting, and she wanted to see if we were interested in having him help us out on the field. Naturally, I jumped at the opportunity and, ever since then, we make sure to arrange for Jerry to address the young players in Jerusalem during each of his visits. They look up to him and savor his words of wisdom. After all, he has played, managed, and coached baseball at the highest levels of the sport, and he is a true *mensch*. In an interview with American sports reporter Hillel Kuttler in 2015, Jerry opened his heart thus: "I love the game, I love the Jewish people and I love Israel."

In that summer of 2016, we sat together and I mentioned to Jerry the difficulties we had in getting Ike Davis to play for our team at the WBC or even talk to us. Narron immediately picked up his phone and dialed Ron Davis, Ike's dad and former major league pitcher. Jerry and Ron were teammates on the Yankees in 1979 and remain close friends. Narron, with his heavy southern drawl, and Ron Davis, from Texas, spoke about my interest in recruiting Ike to play for Team Israel. The next day, Ike called me.

I came to really like and appreciate Ike. He would play for us in 2016 and 2017, came to Israel in January 2017 and has become a close friend and a proud Team Israel player. Millie, his mother, is Jewish, so after he and I first spoke, she searched for several days for documentation of her being Jewish. She eventually found her confirmation records, thus putting the kosher stamp of approval on Ike.

My lifelong friend, Michael Powell, in his "Sports of the Times" column in the *New York Times*, wrote in late September about my activities. In the column, headlined "Good Bat? Great. Jewish? Terrific.", Michael wrote:

> Every few weeks during the baseball season, I receive an irrationally optimistic email from my buddy Peter Kurz, who is a lifelong and thoroughly demented Mets fan. "Demented" is the adjective that attaches like a lesion to those of us who belong to the Mets' tribe. In August, however, I received a worried-sounding message from Kurz. He framed the dilemma this way: Should he root for Ty Kelly, a minor league infielder, to be called up by the Mets in their mad, not to mention highly improbable, dash for playoffs? Or should he hope that Kelly remains in Class AAA, in which case he would be available to play shortstop for Team Israel? Some explanation is needed here. Kelly's mother is Jew-

ish, which means he is eligible for Israeli citizenship and therefore can play for the Israel national baseball team in this week's World Baseball Classic qualifiers at the Brooklyn Cyclones' stadium in Coney Island. Four nations — Israel, Brazil, Britain and Pakistan — are competing.

Kurz is president of the Israel Association of Baseball, and he is charged with assembling the best possible collection of baseball players for Team Israel. He is also an Israeli by way of 86th Street on the Upper West Side of Manhattan. Growing up, we were next-door-neighbors, schoolmates and batterymates. My imaginary Tom Seaver would toss strikes to his imaginary Jerry Grote.

Baseball, it is fair to say, is not a dominant sport in the Holy Land. ... Major League Baseball permits national teams to act as yogis and take an elastic definition of nationality. Anyone who can qualify for a passport or citizenship can play. So, the Italians recruited Mets catcher Mike Piazza. ... The Israeli team features many Jewish former major leaguers and minor leaguers, from catcher Ryan Lavarnway to the former Mets Ike Davis and Josh Satin to the former All-Star Jason Marquis. The team features a few Israelis. How many Israelis? Two.

To stay competitive, my friend Kurz and his baseball codependents pursue Jewish ballplayers with the determination of Ahab after that whale. Kurz has bona fide baseball scouts and bona fide experts of the Jewish diaspora, baseball division. The informal team includes Scott Barancik in Florida with the *Jewish Baseball News* and Ephraim Moxson and Shel Wallman of the *Jewish Sports Review*. They are detectives of the Jewish and the athletic.   They study rosters and photos — oy, is that possible Jewish minor league second baseman wearing a cross? — and call parents and friends and cousins. Rule No. 1: No assumptions. "You quickly learn: Not every Cohen and Schwartz is Jewish," Moxson, a retired parole officer, said.

Israel baseball hews to the Israeli definition of citizenship, which is available to those with at least one Jewish grandparent or parent. From time to time this causes tsuris for the Orthodox, who prefer religious law, which is that Judaism is traced only through the mothers' side.

Team Israel appeared short of middle infielders this summer. Kurz confided to me that he had an interesting prospect in Panama, a young shortstop who said his grandparents were Jews. The who-is-a-Jewish-athlete investigative apparatus swung into gear. It turns out that the shortstop's grandfather had emigrated from Portugal to Panama to work on the canal. Kurz's sleuths found a list of Jewish-sounding names, and the shortstop's family name was in there. Yet there was no paperwork to prove the lineage. Reluctantly, not to mention longingly, my friend turned elsewhere.

New York being New York, which is to say a cacophonous Tower of Babel, the Cyclones' stadium should be bubbling over Thursday and through the weekend, and by no means just with Jewish fans. The Little Pakistan neighborhood sits 20 blocks to the north, and Brazilians and Britons are easy enough to find.
Alas, Ty Kelly will not be among the assembled Israeli

baseball athletes. He will be found in Queens, sitting on the bench for the Mets' improbable late-season playoff run. I'm guessing that my friend is enough of a lunatic fan to find that acceptable.

Team Israel had a three-day minicamp at the Boulders facility in Pomona, New York. After the first practice day, Weinstein gathered the players together in the dugout to introduce themselves. Josh Zeid was one of the last to speak, and I still wish I had a recording of it, all these years later. He quietly said how he lost the final game for Team Israel in 2012, how he thought of retiring from baseball at that time, how he was just kicking around the minors the last two years waiting for this opportunity to pitch again for Israel, and how much he welcomed the chance now to redeem himself. Everyone there hung on his every word, and it was truly motivational. His heartfelt words made them all want to give Zeid that one last chance.

When it came to be Cody Decker's turn, he said how he also was with the team four years ago, what a difficult loss that was and that he was back for revenge. Decker was another player who was a very colorful character. He held the home run record for minor leaguers, but his major league career lasted only 11 at bats with no hits (He did hit a sacrifice fly for a run batted in as a pinch hitting for the San Diego Padres at Dodger Stadium.) He has had a lasting effect on Team Israel, playing for our 2012 and 2016–2017 teams. His most renowned contribution extends to introducing the team in 2016 to the Mensch on the Bench, a plush doll of a religious jew sitting on a bench traditionally given on Hannukah to children.

Cody described the mensch thus: "He's a mascot, he's a friend, he's a teammate, he's a borderline deity to our team. ... He brings a lot to the table. ... Every team needs their . He was ours. He had his own locker, and we even gave him offerings....and....He is everywhere and nowhere all at once. His actual location is irrelevant because he exists in higher metaphysical planes. But he's always near." Although the mensch may have been the most talked-about feature of Team Israel during that period, to me he represented the Diaspora image of a Jew that the creation of the State of Israel in 1948 was trying to dispel. I was more in favor of Team Israel being represented by a warrior, a fighting *sabra* and not an East European *hasid*. But Cody got the headlines for it. He even brought a five-foot version of the mensch to South Korea for our tournament appearance. In that country, mascots are highly valued, and the mensch was sought out the most for selfies, practically a leading man in the documentary that was soon to be made about the team.

In Brooklyn in September 2016, Brazil was the favorite and as the top seed in the pool drew bottom-ranked Pakistan in the first game. Brazil won 10–0, with the game ending early due to the WBC's mercy rule. Pakistan often looked like Little Leaguers in the contest, misjudging fly balls, getting picked off at first base by Brazil's catcher while forgetting how many outs there were and never getting a baserunner past second base. One might have wondered how they received an invitation to the tournament, but in hindsight, I'm glad they did.

Pakistan was managed, and still is, by Syed Fahker Ali Shah, whose late father was important in baseball being played in that nation. Syed, who loved the game while learning it, also served as president of the Pakistan Baseball Federation. Though his country is 80 percent Muslim, and Pakistan does not recognize Israel diplomatically, Syed willingly posed with me for media photos before the tournament, and I found him to be a delightful gentleman. I was a little concerned about what would happen to him if he had to play Team Israel, but that matchup did not happen. We became Facebook friends, and he has been more than generous on social media by complimenting Israel's baseball program and me. In just the last year, Pakistan has risen 11 slots in the international rankings, and I couldn't be happier for Syed, because he deserves it. I remember fondly my visit to Pakistan in 1979 during my great Asian adventure.

We never got to play head-to-head because Pakistan's loss to Brazil put his team in the loser's bracket, where it was again mercy-ruled this time by Great Britain, and eliminated from pool play. Though I'm certain we would have had an easier time against Syed's 2016 team than facing Great Britain, I have a different reason for pondering the possibility of what might have happened if our two nations had matched up. Certainly, there would be no joy in beating Syed, as he is a colleague and friend. Yet, I can't help but wonder about the image of Jewish ballplayers shaking hands with Muslim ballplayers on a baseball diamond in Brooklyn, with the New York skyline beyond the stadium's walls. For all I know, that might have been MLB's motivation in putting our teams in the same bracket.

When Middle East analyst and die-hard St. Louis Cardinals fan David Makovsky spoke to players whom we brought to Israel prior to the 2017 WBC in South Korea, he alluded to American politicians always trying to hit the "home run" in trying to solve the Middle East conflict. He mentioned President Bill Clinton's summit in 2000 and those of two secretaries of state: Condoleezza Rice in 2008 and John Kerry in 2014. It would be unfair to say they struck out, David said, but they didn't hit home runs. David told our players that what we needed were a few singles and doubles to get the rally started and that this team would make one of those hits. I'm not suggesting that the image of our players shaking hands with Muslim players on a Brooklyn ballfield would have been the home run that prevented what is happening right now in Gaza, but who knows? It may have been an infield single, just as what became known as ping-pong diplomacy led to President Richard Nixon's historic visit to Beijing in 1972 and opened the gates to American relations with China.

Back in Brooklyn, Great Britain played us tough in our opening game of the tournament, thanks to its strong pitching and defense, as its offensive skills were developing more slowly. Its pitching was no doubt buoyed by retired relief star Trevor Hoffman, a future Hall of Fame inductee, running clinics in England, and its speed came from the surplus of Bahamian athletes. The team was fast and agile and made some of the most impressive plays in the tournament, especially in the outfield.

Great Britain scored in the second inning off Jason Marquis, who was otherwise stellar, pitching five innings and keeping his pitch count low enough to return if needed in another game. We tied the game in the bottom half, and it was a pitcher's duel for the next five innings. Josh Zeid struck out the side in the sixth.

The Brits took the lead with a run in the top of the seventh. It didn't rattle our squad, which remained calm, sensing that their bats would come alive, while the pitching would bend without breaking.

We responded with four runs in the bottom of the seventh, the big hits being RBI singles by Zach Borenstein and crowd favorite Ike Davis. Great Britain brought the tying run to the plate in the ninth with two outs and runners on second and third, but Brad Goldberg struck out the opponents' last hope with a fastball in on the hands, and we were in the winner's bracket, 5–2. All in all, it was the perfect start to the tournament, with Marquis giving us five innings, the bullpen building confidence in a few pressure situations and the bats responding every time we were scored against.

Marquis was definitely the team leader at that tournament as the most decorated player who had suited up for Team Israel by far. He held court in the dugout and bullpen, regaling players with his accomplishments and the finer points of the game. Marquis did not stay with the team at the hotel, preferring to remain at home on Staten Island, but he was an integral part of our squad. After one practice session, he had 20 pizzas delivered for all the players. He certainly performed for us at the level of the All-Star he was.

All four teams stayed at the same hotel in Brooklyn, just across the bridge from Manhattan's famous skyline. The hour-plus bus rides through New York traffic were gruesome, but it was better than staying at a hotel near Coney Island or in the boondocks. The stadium was wonderful, home to the Mets' Class A team, the Brooklyn Cyclones. It was called at the time MCU Park, after New York's largest credit union, but it was later renamed Maimonides Park, honoring the renowned 12th-century Jewish sage, a more fitting moniker for Team Israel's games. The park's opening in 2001 marked the return of professional baseball to Brooklyn (albeit on a minor league level) since the Dodgers left in 1957. Its location next to the Coney Island amusement park, with the Cyclone roller coaster perched just past the outfield, made the ballpark iconic. During the pre-tournament practice sessions, I snuck away to the legendary Nathan's Famous to get a true New York hot dog with sauerkraut and onions. Turned out that the New York reporter for the Israeli newspaper *Haaretz*, Haim Handwerker, who wrote quite a few articles on Team Israel, is the grandson of Nathan's founder, Nathan Handwerker.

Our second game was against Brazil. Corey Baker blanked Barry Larkin's team for five innings, giving up only one hit and finishing the fifth by striking out the side. His only trouble occurred in the fourth, when, with runners on second and third and two out, Bo Bichette, son of a former major leaguer, Dante Bichette, and a future major leaguer and New York Met himself, grounded out weakly to third to end the threat.

Brazil put a few guys on base after Baker's exit, but our bullpen kept stranding them. If you're thinking this game sounds like an easy victory for us, guess again. We scored only once in the entire ballgame, on a sacrifice fly by Cody Decker in the fourth, scoring Nate Freiman from third. I wonder if the Brazilian catcher felt the ground shaking as the huge Nate ran home.

We couldn't get an insurance run, and it was up to Goldberg to seal the deal in the ninth inning again. I don't remember exactly where I was when he came out of the bullpen, as I have trouble sitting still in the stands during games. I need to watch alone during tense moments. I often wander around and visit fans and people I know, making sure the conversation remains on us. Because it was such a tight battle and we did not want to go into the loser's bracket and play a fourth game (although Marquis and Baker had made that possibility seem a little more palatable), this was the most concerned I'd been since the late innings against Spain in 2012.

Brad had an easy inning and when, with two outs, Luis Camargo rolled out meekly to second, we won 1–0 and were back where we were four years ago with a record of 2–0. We waited to find out who would face us in a championship game for the right to participate in the main field of the World Baseball Classic.

I did not particularly care who our opponent would be, as both teams had given us a pretty good fight and we had come out on top. Our chances seemed better against Great Britain than Brazil, the latter having entered as pool favorites, but the Brits had held a lead twice against us, while Larkin's lineup couldn't scratch out even a single run. Marquis would be back out there no matter whom we played, so we were confident, especially with a bullpen that had allowed only one run in eight innings. Weinstein seemed to be pulling the right strings with every decision, and I was grateful that we had his calm demeanor to lead the team. It definitely felt different from 2012, and when we watched those two potential opponents square off for the right to face us, we were more scouting them than rooting for who might be easier to defeat.

Great Britain prevailed in come-from-behind fashion. Both of Dante Bichette's sons playing for Brazil, Bo and Dante Jr., had left key runners in scoring position that could have sealed the game, and the game ended, 4–3, when Juan Carlos Muniz, already in scoring position, inexplicably tried to steal third. He was caught easily, and with that blunder, Manager Liam Carroll's British squad was heading for a championship game showdown with Israel.

If I could build the drama, I would, but the game never really gave me an opportunity. Great Britain was not as built to play a short tournament as we were, and while it put up a valiant effort for four innings, it was never a matter of if our bats would break out, but when. That happened in the fifth when Blake Gailen, whose biceps looked like Popeye's triceps, launched a two-run homer into the right field bleachers. Blasts by Ryan Lavarnway and Cody Decker made it a laugher, and the only real drama was whether we could achieve a combined no-hitter. The British bats couldn't stir tea, and except for a vicious line drive that almost took Zeid's head off — he caught it falling backward and quickly got up like nothing happened — they barely sniffed at a base hit for the first seven innings. Eventually, they would muster an unearned run in the eighth, following a bloop hit that spoiled the no-no.

The game ended 9–1, Israel, and even though it was a breeze, our guys stormed out of the dugout like they had won a playoff series in the major leagues. The Brits had played their hearts out, but they were already a shattered team by the time they got to us. (They qualified again in 2022 under manager Drew Spencer, just two days after the death of Queen Elizabeth II.) Though I had been having constant flashbacks to that loss against Spain four years earlier, I was more relieved postgame than elated. I had learned my lesson from Champagnegate and did not buy any bubbly, but Ike Davis had sent someone to get six-packs of beers for the guys in the clubhouse when they got back.

And who got the win for us in the clinching game? Josh Zeid, the losing pitcher against Spain four years before. He got his just rewards. We hugged and chugged and I told them all we would meet at the bar next door to the hotel.

The clubhouse celebration was glorious, and I was basking in the festivities. After we all got back and showered, we met at the dive bar next door to the hotel, and the booze was flowing freely. We were up until at least 3:00 a.m., all hugging and saying our goodbyes. Amit was with me. It was a scene, one that I'll never forget. The tab came to a few thousand dollars, money the IAB didn't have then, but I didn't care that night. The guys deserved to party, and we would make it up with the higher fundraising profile as the 16th and final team to qualify for the WBC's main draw.

Three hours later, I flew with my wife, son, and daughter to Aruba for four days of much-needed rest, although in the middle of our stay a hurricane sideswiped the island and we had to evacuate our rooms on the ground floor to higher ground. The baseball gods apparently targeted my vacation instead of the last game. But all those four days I was just fantasizing with Amit about having a WBC roster of strong MLB players: Ryan Braun, Sam Fuld and Kevin Pillar in the outfield, Ian Kinsler at second base, Youkilis at third base and Alex Bregman at shortstop.

We were really going to the main WBC tournament in Seoul! It was five months away, but there was so much to do — first and foremost, to recruit all 12 active major leaguers who are Jewish. I thought that most would jump at the chance, but little did I speculate that few of them gave Israel any chance to advance and one of the biggest could end up playing against us.

But first we had that memorable visit to Israel and the beginnings of "Heading Home" ....

Sixth Inning

2017 WBC, Israel rocks Seoul and Tokyo

"**You may not think you're going to make it. You may want to quit. But if you keep your eye on the ball, you can accomplish anything.**"
—**Hank Aaron**

I returned home from Aruba euphoric but didn't have a second to celebrate, since we had a new team to build.!!! It was clear to me that our first goal would be to convince the Jewish major leaguers to join our squad in South Korea, which, if successful, would mean telling some of those who got us there that they would no longer be playing for Israel. I did not relish doing that. For one guy in particular, Mitch Glasser, that was hard, although he would play for us often again and deliver one of the biggest hits in our team's history. Like so many other alumnus, Mitch continues to be a key part of our team.

Together with Jerry Weinstein and Adam Gladstone, we talked about our priorities and mapped out how we would approach each player we wanted to recruit and who was the best person to do the recruiting. The main WBC draw encompasses three rounds, starting with 16 teams competing in four divisions. We started in Seoul, together with South Korea, Taiwan and the Netherlands. The top two winners would go on to play the top two winners in the Tokyo division: Japan, Cuba, Australia
top two winners in Asia would go on to Los Angeles to
the of eight teams that started play in North America.
ssues would be the long schlepp to South Korea in the
training and whether Team Israel would make it out
l. I spoke to Brad Ausmus about recruiting Ian Kinsler,

who'd played for him with the Tigers, but he told Brad that he was committed to his manager with Team USA, Jim Leyland.

I spoke with veteran infielder Danny Valencia about playing, and those were not the easiest of conversations. Valencia wanted to bring his wife to Seoul, and I told him that would be fine, that MLB was paying for either one business class ticket, or two economy tickets. He insisted on two business class tickets, but the IAB could not afford that for all the MLB players; in the end, Valencia elected not to play for Team Israel at the WBC. Valencia later made Aliyah, played for us in both the 2019 European championship and the Olympic qualifiers, joined our Olympics squad and played for Israel in the 2023 WBC in his backyard of Florida. Once you get to know him and appreciate him, Danny is a true friend, and we've had many soul-searching conversations. As with many of our players, he will be part of the Team Israel family for many years after his official retirement from playing.

But first, the trip!!! For years, we had been toying with the idea of bringing a group of MLB players to Israel, and Jonathan Mayo of MLB.com even got them all on a video expressing their interest. Now was the time to put that plan into motion, and I approached Ron Dermer, who was then the Israeli ambassador to Washington. I had met Dermer the year before, when I was in Washington for the AIPAC conference, when he told me about the huge baseball card collection that his mother eventually threw away. That conversation reminded me of my own comics collection that my mom got rid of. Dermer was very close with Sheldon Adelson, the Jewish casino owner and philanthropist, on anything having to do with the image of Israel in the world. Adelson also supported right-wing political causes in Israel and the United States. I don't let politics interfere with my business, especially regarding Israeli baseball. Just a year before, Dermer and Adelson had sponsored a successful trip to the Holy Land for a group of football Hall of Fame players which was very successful.

Dermer approached Adelson about allowing us to use one of his planes for the trip, and before I knew it, together with our good friend Jeff Aeder, a major supporter through the years and the man behind the Chicago-based Jewish Baseball Museum, the plan proceeded. Aeder met with the Adelsons, arranged for one of their jets and provide funding for the rest of the trip, All we needed was for the players to come along for the ride. The trip was set for January 3–10, 2017.

At the same time we were recruiting players for the WBC tournament, we were planning the pilgrimage to Israel. I tried to get the top major leaguers, but just as they rejected our offer to play for the team, they also found excuses not to come on this trip. I then offered to bring our core players from the qualifiers — Lavarnway, Zeid, Kelly, Davis, Decker and Baker (Marquis couldn't make it) — as well as new players who would play for us in the tournament in Seoul, like Jeremy Bleich and Sam Fuld. I also decided to bring Jon Moscot, who I knew wouldn't be able to play for us in March because he had just had Tommy John surgery. I knew that he would be an investment for the future when he returned to health, and Jon indeed paid dividends, helping us in the 2019 European championship and qualifiers and as an integral part of the Olympic team.

We told each person he could bring either a significant other, (Lavarnway, Zeid and Decker did), or the Jewish parent (Kelly brought his mom and Fuld brought his dad) or a good friend, as Davis did. Gabe Kapler, the head of player development for the Dodgers and a future MLB manager, also joined the group and brought his two teenage sons.

We had been planning such a visit even before the 2012 WBC, but now, with team going to the main event, seemed like the most appropriate time to do so. Although asking for money is never easy, this may have been one of the easiest periods to raise funds, with Team Israel always in the news and constantly on the minds of our admirers, competitors and fans.

With the Adelsons' plane, we could now offer the players a luxurious way to fly. In addition, Jonathan Mayo, Jeremy Newberger, Seth Kramer and Daniel Miller expressed an interest in making a documentary about Team Israel's run in the WBC and the trip to Israel, which eventually became the award-winning film *Heading Home: The Tale of Team Israel.* Their production company, Ironbound Films, produces top documentary movies, and had gotten an Emmy nomination. Little did they know at the time what a Cinderella run this would turn out to be, and what a different film emerged from the one they had planned.

I went to the airport in Israel on January 4 and entered the VIP waiting area. Passengers on private planes do not need to go through the same customs and passport checks of ordinary passengers; they get their own private areas and are personally cared for. I was excited to meet them all again and overjoyed that we could finally host them in Israel, show them the beauty of the country they had printed across their uniform chests and introduce them to our constituents.   It was there that I first met everyone, as well as the tour guide hired by Aeder, to spend six glorious days together.

It was a whirlwind tour, as documented in the film. The schedule was carefully prepared to include historical and cultural heritage sites, some fun and of course baseball activities with our players throughout the country. We took them on a graffiti tour of Tel Aviv, where they drew Sandy Koufax near the Jaffa flea market; on a bicycle trip along the Tel Aviv waterfront; and into cockpits of fighter jets at an air force base. We made a somber visit to Yad Vashem, took a mud bath in the Dead Sea and, of course, walked in the Old City of Jerusalem, including to the Western Wall, and celebrated Shabbat together. They enjoyed top restaurants and Tel Aviv nightlife. On the baseball side, they gave a clinic for three hours at the Baptist Village field, punctuated by a home run derby with Ike Davis, Cody Decker and Ryan Lavarnway pounding more balls over the fence than have ever been hit there before. Hundreds of kids were there, mobbing the players as they came off the bus and lining up for selfies and autographs. The players loved the attention. I bemoaned the number of lost baseballs, but it was for a worthy cause.

It was sobering for them to hear about Ezra Schwartz, an American teen who visited Israel on a study program the year before and was killed by terrorists. In his name we dedicated the future Raanana field. There was also a dedication ceremony at the yet-to-be-built Beit Shemesh field site, as the mayor and the players planted a baseball in the ground that symbolically would grow into a field. (we are good at dedicating yet-to-be-built fields, although these two did eventually get built) And, unfortunately, a terrorist attack occurred in Israel during the players' visit, a reminder of what we need to deal with in this country.

The players were all smitten with the Holy Land and there is no doubt that this visit laid the foundation for the kinds of relationships we went on to forge with each other. It went exactly as I had hoped, providing them with enough of a taste of Israel that they could connect with their personal roots and pass this message on to other players and fans. The kids and parents in Israel were also thrilled to be part of this experience and could point to the visit years later as a highlight of their IAB days. I was delighted over what this visit accomplished.

Ty Kelly would later be quoted in an article as saying: "I was a little skeptical how I should take it because I didn't have a huge background growing up. But everyone who is Jewish feels connected to Israel, and it was really emotional for a lot of guys seeing all the religious and historical sites, especially the Western Wall."

Ike Davis said: "The cool thing about Israel is that Jewish people have a home here no matter where we live. We might stay here if you want us to. When you get here, it feels a little like home."

Lavarnway was smitten: "I personally feel a part of this, of Israel — the Jewish state of Israel. I feel a big part of this."

The trip was a huge success..........

Kelly, Lavarnway, Zeid, Moscot, Bleich, and others would eventually become Israeli citizens. But first we had to play some games in South Korea.

* * *

I decided not to attend the minicamp we held in Arizona to acclimate the players before the team flew to Seoul but instead arrived early in South Korea to visit the country with Ronit. We spent time on Jeju Island, with its volcanoes and ancient stone statues and sisterhood of deep-sea divers. It was all quite interesting, but I was antsy to start the baseball part of our visit. We met the players at our hotel just after their arrival from the United States, and it was great to see many of them once again after a five-month hiatus. Amit joined us a few days later as part of the official IAB delegation, so the team was complete.

The squad we built had a lot of potential, but few major leaguers. Ty Kelly was the only player on a current 40-man MLB roster, although Jason Marquis, who played 16 major league seasons and went to the playoffs in 10 of them, was certainly an illustrious name. The rest of our squad with MLB experience were towards the end of their careers, and none of our prospects and minor leaguers were on any "can't miss" lists. You can't blame the press for reporting the truth that while our nation's baseball program was building fields and developing youth talent, our current roster was primarily American-born. We didn't mind the honesty, as it fueled our belief that we were better than we looked on paper, and we weren't playing for the media, anyway. We were playing for our team, and that team included the entire population of Israel, even the ones who didn't know what the WBC was, let alone that we were competing in it.

The coaching staff remained the same from the qualifiers, with only Pat Doyle added as a bench coach at the last minute in place of Jerry Narron, who became manager of the Diamondbacks' AAA team and needed to be with them. Weinstein was our manager, Lorraine the pitching coach, Tom Gamboa and Fish were third- and first-base coaches, respectively, and Leichman was the bullpen coach. It was an experienced staff, led with a strong hand by Weinstein, and you don't change a winning horse in mid-race.

Our operations and training staff has remained fairly consistent for the past 10-plus years, including the WBC tournaments and Olympics. They have been Jewish for the most part, not just because of the natural affinity, but also because it seems like Jews hold many of these positions in baseball. We were quite happy to have these professionals, and they were all glad to help Team Israel. As with the players, there was a feeling of solidarity and commonality. And all did so as volunteers.

Adam Gladstone is our operations manager and has the system down pat. He has the experience in establishing a mini-camp operation, housing the team in a hotel, providing transportation, even taking care of the more esoteric things without breaking a sweat. (Try placating a major league player at 3:00 a.m.) Adam is a true pro and has been particularly helpful putting together our staff of interns, many of whom have continued with us in other capacities, such as Alex Jacobs, Ali Recht and Ethan Gold. Alex has continued working with us in many capacities: scout, coach, video replay — you name it, he does it. Adam introduced us to Eric Blum, clubhouse manager par excellence, who can wash a clubhouse full of uniforms, dry them, and hang them within 30 minutes (I exaggerate not...).

The Team Israel training staff has been anchored throughout the years by Dan Rootenberg. I first got to know "Root" when he played in the IBL and spent the entire summer as the centerfielder of the Netanya Tigers, together with my son Amit. I spent a lot of time with his wife Shelby and newborn son, Jack, who came to all the games that summer. Root later established Spear Physical Therapy, with 43 physical-therapy locations throughout New York and New Jersey, including about 20 in

Manhattan, where he lives. Root spends his time running and managing the operation. Every few years, I pluck him out of his office, and he joyfully comes to help us in the clubhouse and on the field, giving the players rubdowns, stretching their taut muscles or running warm-up drills. Here he is completely in his element.

Root has been with us on all the WBC teams, at the Tokyo Olympics and at far-flung locations of European championships. Root's dad was born in Israel and immigrated to the United States as a young man, and Root was born in New York. Root's father passed away many years ago, before I could meet him, but I am thankful that he raised such a *mensch* who will always be an integral part of Team Israel.

Another physical therapist, who leaves his well-established operation in Baltimore and enthusiastically joins us on every occasion, is Yoni Rosenblatt. Yoni brings his non-traditional methods to our players: cupping therapy, acupuncture and probably many other treatments that I am not aware of. As an Orthodox Jew, together with Jordy and others, he provides us with the touch of religion so crucial to Team Israel.

One of the most colorful people on our staff has to be our head trainer, Barry Weinberg, who held that position for close to 30 years with the Oakland A's and St. Louis Cardinals. Barry has vast experience and knowledge and regales us with his stories, many of which cannot be requoted here. The walls of his home in Jupiter are filled with pictures of him alongside the biggest names in baseball, including George Bush, Bud Selig, Mark McGwire and Sandy Koufax, and his two World Series rings are impressive pieces of jewelry. Barry as a trainer has been privy to some of the best kept secrets in baseball.

We had many terrific fans following along with our successes and failures, none greater than Zack Rabb, who has been to all of our tournaments, save for the Olympics in Tokyo, where no fans were allowed due to the pandemic restrictions. Zack is often captured by TV cameras cheering us on and likely losing his voice. He came to meet the players when they visited Israel and can be seen talking to Cody Decker in *Heading Home*. He's now friends with most of the players on the team and continues being a big part of Israel baseball. He has worked the last few years in minor league baseball and is perfect for the job. We have other great fans throughout the world — in northern California, New

York City, Detroit, even in South Korea and Japan — and I do my best to keep them involved with the team.

* * *

ESPN, as I alluded to earlier, did dub us 'The Jamaican Bobsled Team,' but most of the guys either shrugged it off or used it as motivational, locker room, bulletin board material. Though the network would do recaps of the games on Baseball Tonight and Sportscenter, the Seoul games' broadcasting rights were with the MLB Network, and our three games there would be called by Paul Severino and Joe Magrane, who was briefly a teammate of Andrew Lorraine on the 1994 Angels. Being in Seoul, I obviously didn't watch the games on TV, but I heard from others that Severino several times stated that our goal was to grow the game in Israel and have future rosters contain more Israeli players. Magrane was impressed by our defense and said that our pitching staff was better than the Netherlands', widely considered the favorite of our bracket.

I met quite a few South Korean fans who were worried about facing us, and our opponents had been around the game long enough to know that baseball is the one team sport most likely to see a David slay a Goliath. Since David was a Jew and South Korea ranked number three in the world and would be facing us on its home field, the host certainly qualified as Goliath.

We played two exhibition games, against the Seoul police and fire department teams. We had our usual pre-tournament staff dinner at a Korean barbeque restaurant, which was my first exposure to that cuisine. I went with Ronit, Amit and some players to a restaurant in the fish market, which was quite an experience. I had never seen such a variety of fish as in that market, although some of the offerings were not very appetizing. Zeid and Lavarnway conducted a culinary tour and made a video about it on YouTube, but I was way too busy to enjoy the gastronomic wonders of Seoul.

The team was also invited to the home of the Israeli ambassador to Korea for a reception, although he was in Jerusalem at the time and his top assistant hosted us. Many embassy people attended our games. I spent my days and nights dealing with the WBC, with the team's staff needs and desires, with players' requests, with IAB matters and with the Israeli, American, South Korean and Japanese media. I was running on adrenaline during my 18–20 hour days.

Sam Fuld was to be our centerfielder and leadoff hitter, and we were confident with him at the top of the lineup but concerned about his damaged throwing arm. He wore a brace off the field, and we had practices with our infielders going out much farther than normal to take relays. Weinstein was hoping to hide Fuld's injury by having him casually underhand the ball to infielders or flip it to his fellow outfielders after routine fly balls. Other teams quickly learned of his condition and took advantage of it. Fuld still had well above average range and speed, was probably the smartest baserunner on the team and had a good eye at the plate.

He would be followed in the batting order by switch-hitting Ty Kelly, whose versatility on defense would give us flexibility in the late innings. We had some big-league power with Nate Freiman and Ryan Lavarnway and with Ike Davis coming off the bench. Cody Decker and Blake Gaillen could also run into one, and both did just that in the game that brought us here. Switch hitter Tyler Krieger and Scotty Burcham, who had a great glove and was a good bunter, gave us good speed at the bottom of the lineup.

Veteran Jason Marquis, of course, was our starting pitcher in the first game. Unlike in Brooklyn, his control was inconsistent, and he battled through three innings, not allowing a run while staying just under the pitch limit. Things looked to be off to a strong start offensively, however, as we scored first in the top of the second inning on a two-out, bases loaded walk by Krieger. But that was the only run pushed across in regulation, even though we would load the bags three times in nine innings.

Our bullpen came up huge, even without Brad Goldberg, who was not available in Seoul but would be joining us in Tokyo if we got there. Our relievers allowed a run in the fifth inning, but gave the home team's hitters fits at the plate. Our defense converted the few hard-hit balls into outs.

Josh Zeid was the last of five relievers to follow Marquis, and he started the eighth by walking the leadoff hitter on four pitches. That prompted a visit to the mound from Lorraine. Whatever advice he gave worked as Zeid struck out the next hitter, Dae Ho Lee, on three pitches. The following batter blooped a soft single to center. Sam Fuld's arm came into play, just as we had feared. Though Fuld got to the ball quickly and even attempted to deke pinch runner Jae-won Oh into thinking he was going to run it down, Oh read it perfectly and knew the injured centerfielder could not throw him out at third. So, after battling back from a four-pitch walk with a strikeout, South Korea now had runners on the corners with only one out. Unfazed, Zeid induced a one-hop grounder to Ty Kelly at third that was too slow to turn a double play. He alertly threw out the lead runner at home. The next batter hit a weak pop-up to end the inning.

Fuld led off the ninth inning with his second single of the game, but we couldn't get him any further, as the big hit continued to elude our offense. Luckily, South Korea was faring no better and Zeid got the first two outs in the bottom of the inning before walking Yongkyu Lee. Lee tried to steal second, but Lavarnway gunned him down with a bullet to Burcham for the third out.

Though we were happy to make it to the tenth, the last thing we wanted was to go into extra innings after already using six different pitchers and with Zeid needing to quickly retire the side to stay under the pitch limit.

Of course, we needed to worry about scoring first, and it looked like we were in a great position to do so after Ike Davis walked with one out and Lavarnway moved him to third with a clutch single. Krieger was asked to bunt, which was a smart play given how anemic our offense had been and with Scotty Burcham, having struck out twice already with the bags full, in the on-deck circle. Not having time ahead of the short tournament to work on our bunting drills, Krieger was rusty and popped up to the catcher, leaving it up to Burcham to try to push a run across.

I suppose now would be as good a time as any to tell you just how Burcham made our team. One of our staff members, Alex Jacobs, felt that Burcham's name sounded Jewish. Alex was a scout for the Pirates, and his instincts were always on target. He looked up Burcham's mom and dad on Facebook and concluded that his mom "looked Jewish" and was from a Jewish area of New York. Her maiden name, he said, sounded Jewish as well. *(I swear to God, I'm not making this up!)* Jacobs mentioned that to Weinstein, who asked Scotty what had to be the oddest first question in the history of baseball recruiting; "Are you Jewish.?"

The answer was yes, and that his mother had the appropriate documentation. We had our shortstop. While Team USA was choosing

Brandon Crawford as its shortstop based off of his three Gold Gloves and two World Series rings, ours made the team because Jacobs thought Burcham's mom looked Jewish. Truth be told, Burcham, who had played high school ball in Lehigh Valley, California, was rated Southland's top player at his position by the *Los Angeles Times* before the start of his senior year.

He had already made a few terrific plays in this game and was a big reason we were still alive in extras. After falling behind in the count, 1–2, he hung in on a well-placed fastball on the outside corner and hit a hard grounder up the middle. The second baseman made a great play to backhand it on the outfield grass, but Ryan Lavarnway had gotten a great jump at first, taking away any chance at a force play. Burcham was too fast to be thrown out at first from the outfield and, finally, after seven consecutive innings of not scoring when we were given plenty of opportunities, we had a lead and our best reliever was still on the mound.

Korea almost put the leadoff hitter on base to start the bottom of the tenth, but Burcham ranged far into the hole and made a brilliant diving catch of a sinking line drive. Unlike in Jupiter, Josh Zeid was so relaxed that he forgot how many strikes there were on the next hitter and started circling the mound on a swing and miss for strike two. When he saw that the ball wasn't being thrown around the infield, he looked back at his catcher, was informed that the count was only 2–2 and simply replied, "My bad" before striking out the batter for real.

At 44 pitches on the night, he had only five more tosses before reaching the limit and being disqualified for the rest of Seoul. Dae Hoe Lee, Korea's biggest power threat, whom he had struck out on three pitches in the eighth, came to the plate. Two fastballs later, we were one strike away from possibly the biggest WBC upset since the 2009 Netherlands team beat the Dominican Republic twice to knock them out of the tournament.

With two pitches to spare, Zeid only added to the drama by throwing a couple of sliders out of the zone. We were one pitch from either an historic victory or losing our best arm for at least the rest of Pool A. All the Jewish fans in the crowd were on their feet while our players were on the top step of the dugout. Baseball fans in Israel were watching on their laptops, former Team Israel manager Brad Ausmus was watching on a TV in a spring training clubhouse and one diehard, gentile fan was watching on a computer screen at a Menlo Park, California, hotel.

They all saw what I saw: Zeid blew a fastball by Dae Hoe Lee, and baseball's equivalent of the Jamaican bobsled team, ranked 41st in the world, had just beaten third-ranked South Korea, 2–1, on its home turf. The noisy crowd suddenly went silent, forced to listen to the cheers of Jewish fans they outnumbered 20 to one. I made my way to the dugout to congratulate Jerry and the coaches first, while the players hugged and high-fived on the field. The first game of the 2017 WBC had concluded, and the ladies and gentlemen of the press would be reporting that Team Israel was the victor. I was overwhelmed but knew we would have a short turn-around before our next game *(we had an 8am bus)*, so I did my best to herd the happy players onto the bus and back to the hotel. I was up until 4:00 a.m. talking to media and friends in Israel and the United States.

Ken Belson of the *New York Times* wrote this on March 7, 2017, after that victory: "Miracle of miracles, Israel won its tournament debut on Monday by beating South Korea, 2–1." The game was "an emotional lift for a team tied together not only by its underdog status, but also by its heritage."

"But what Israel lacks in baseball firepower, it makes up for in pluck and humor" Belson continued,"… the team has a David-versus-Goliath feel to it……'We have free agents, we have guys who have been kicked around a bit in their careers,' said Decker. 'Under the radar is where we live.'"

Belson also had this to say:

> Laughter has been a key ingredient in building team spirit, and nothing has unified the team as much as the Mensch on a Bench, a Jewish version of the Elf on the Shelf, a doll that is supposed to remind children to be nice so Santa Claus will bring them a lot of gifts. The team adopted the pint-size mensch, which means an honorable person, as its mascot during the qualifying round. The players put the mensch in the dugout during games and gave it a locker of its own. The manufacturer sent Decker a five-foot version of the mensch to take to Korea. … Whether the mensch

will provide enough luck to propel Israel to the second round is unclear.

Our next match up against Taiwan was scheduled for noon, so barely half a day later, we were starting our second game of the WBC before any team other than Korea had played its first. In spite of the quick turnaround, Team Israel looked well rested. Sam Fuld singled leading off the top of the first, followed by a scorching double by Ty Kelly that one-hopped the right field wall. On the next pitch, Ike Davis singled them both home and before Taiwan could catch its breath, it was down 2–0 and facing our clean-up hitter with a runner on first and nobody out.

We loaded the bases for the fourth time in 11 innings and after entering the game one for nine with runners on base, we were now two for our last three. Tyler Krieger quickly fell behind 0–2, but the young switch hitter, batting lefty, ground a sharp single up the middle for a commanding 4–0 lead. The boys couldn't have looked more relaxed.

Ryan Lavarnway, swinging the hottest bat on the team, hit a two-run bomb to center in the third, and after five scoreless innings by our staff (10 straight over the last two games), we looked to be in complete control. Taiwan put a man on first with one out in the sixth when pitcher R.C. Orlan induced an easy comebacker. But, just as our bunting wasn't fine-tuned due to the short training schedule, our pitchers' fielding practices also had been limited. Orlan threw wide of second base, the ball glancing off Krieger's glove and rolling into centerfield. After not allowing a hit until the fourth inning, one of our pitchers had turned a would-be inning-ending double play into a rally, and our opponents jumped on the opportunity. They loaded the bases and scored two runs on a C.S. Lim double that bounced high off the blue left field padding, almost becoming a grand-slam homer. Taiwan added a sacrifice fly. The momentum definitely had shifted to the opposing dugout, and we needed to get it back before the game got away from us.

Ike Davis was our first man up in the top of the seventh inning and he tripled high off the centerfield wall for his third hit since pinch hitting in the eighth inning of Game One. Nate Freiman singled him home two pitches later. The momentum swung back in our favor, and the game was about to be out of reach.

After we loaded the bases again, Kreiger hit another solid single up the middle. Jerry Weinstein made the brilliant move of calling on Scotty Burcham to bunt, even with a force at home. Taiwan never saw it coming. and not only did Scotty lay it down perfectly, but the pitcher who fielded it was caught so off guard that he threw the ball to first base, where no one was covering. The ball rolled deep into foul territory and on a bunt that traveled less than 30 feet from home plate, we scored three runs and were now up by seven. Freiman added a three-run blast in the ninth to secure a 15–7 win and give us a 2–0 record.

That seemed even bigger when considering that the other teams had yet to play a single game, except the two that lost to us. In the blink of an eye, we were in position to advance to the second round in Japan and could do so without playing another game. Advancing also would give us an automatic slot in the 2021 WBC. Yes, Team Israel: ranked 41st in the world, dubbed the "Jamaican bobsled team" and with Las Vegas odds against us, was now 2-0 and awaiting the Kingdom of the Netherlands.

The Dutch team, managed by the San Francisco Giants' hitting coach, Hensley Meulens, was scheduled to play later that evening against South Korea and the following night against Taiwan. The Netherlands had no trouble recruiting big-league talent, and even had Japan's reigning single-season home-run champion, Vladimir Ballentin, batting cleanup.

They handled South Korea. with even more authority than we had and while our guys were enjoying the next day off, the Dutch and Taiwan teams were going head-to-head in a contest that had huge implications on our future. Meulens and company opened up an early lead, but the pesky Taiwanese hitters battled back to take a lead into the bottom of the eighth. Didi Gregorious tied the game with a two-out double and the Dutch won on a walk-off free pass. Both Taiwan and South Korea had now been eliminated, and we would go to Japan for Round Two and be assured of playing in the next World Baseball Classic. I was overwhelmed and spent hours on-line, being interviewed by the media back in Israel.

Our match-up with the Netherlands would be for seeding only, but it was an important game for reasons even our players weren't yet aware of. The pool champion would get to take an earlier flight to Japan and receive an additional $200,000 in prize money. No underdog in its right mind would want to face Japan in the first game of a pool, so beating the Netherlands meant we wouldn't have to face Japan until at least the second game. We were growing so confident that we thought we could beat anybody, but it wouldn't have hurt to see Japan later rather than sooner.

Though Jason Marquis was available to start the Netherlands game, having stayed under the pitch limit against South Korea, it was more of a tune-up for him than anything else. This would end up being a game of bullpen by committee for both teams, with ours on a roll, while the Dutch relied heavily on its offense to maintain the status as favorites. It was a powerful team with impressive MLB and Nippon League players on its squad, but we would have the advantage in a close game in the late innings. In spite of the Netherlands' great line-up, its domestic-born pitching staff was its weakest link.

For the third straight contest, we scored first, putting up a three-spot in the bottom of the first, and our pitchers responded yet again with a shutdown inning. Credit our defense for backing them up. Scotty Burcham threw out Jurickson Profar in the third as he sought to stretch a leadoff double into a triple, with a laser from shallow right center. Then, with a runner at first and nobody out in the seventh, Burcham made what probably would have been the best play of the entire tournament had Adam Jones not robbed Manny Machado of a homer in Petco Park — the greatest defensive play of all five WBCs. What happened was this: Dylan Axelrod induced a comebacker from Dashenko Ricardo but made an awful throw that seemed headed to right-centerfield. Burcham, running across the bag as you're taught on double plays, somehow kept his foot on the bag while bending over and scooping the one-hop throw. In one motion, he maneuvered around the charging base runner and gunned Ricardo out at first to complete the twin killing. The greatest writer in the world couldn't possibly capture how spectacular the play was, so I highly recommend looking it up on YouTube.

With runners at first and second and one out in the eighth, Weinstein called again on Josh Zeid, who was still available after finishing the South Korean game one pitch under the limit. Once again, he walked the first batter he faced, bringing Andrew Lorraine out of the dugout to talk to him. Lorraine's visit again did the trick, and Zeid induced a double play ball out of Jonathan Schoop. Unfortunately, Krieger made an errant toss to second that not even Burcham could field and the bases remained loaded with the score now 4–2. With ice water in his veins, Zeid induced another grounder on the very next pitch to Didi Gregorius, the Netherlands' hottest hitter. Krieger had no trouble this time in turning our sixth double play of the tournament.

The bottom of the eighth inning saw a true oddity when the Netherlands brought in 7'1" (216cm) pitcher Loek Van Mill, who would face our 6'8" (203cm) Nate Freiman. Elias Sports Bureau was not available to tell us if this was the combined tallest matchup between a pitcher and batter in baseball history, but it was a sight to see. Heck, you couldn't miss it if you tried, those guys were so big! Sadly, Van Mill passed away in 2019 after trying to come back from a head injury suffered in a fall while hiking. What made his death all the more untimely was that he announced his retirement from the game the day before he passed. Freiman drew a walk.

Once again, there was no 9th inning traffic on the base paths as Zeid closed the door in the ninth, completing our sweep of Pool A and guaranteeing that we would face Cuba instead of host Japan in the opening game in Tokyo. Ryan Lavarnway would be awarded MVP of Seoul, which he richly deserved, although it also could have gone to Zeid or Burcham.

Unfortunately, the Israeli press was much less enthusiastic about our victories, continuously reporting that the team members had no connection whatsoever to Israel. I had many long nights of arguments with them about the importance of these games, emphasizing players with very strong connections to Israel, like Shlomo Lipetz, Tal Erel and Dean Kremer, and coaches Alon Leichman and Nate Fish, as well as the long-term development of the sport in Israel. They refused to see it.

When the wins continued, Oren Aharoni from *Yediot Aharonot* was the first to report about the connection of the players to our Jewish heritage and tradition. He was contradicted by Ben Mitelman, reporting for Channel 2, the country's primary TV news channel, who said we were not representative of Israel and insinuated that the players were not at all connected to their Jewish heritage and roots. I had long discussions with him about that afterwards. He was ultimately convinced that our path was the correct one to take and would apologize for the story. His son later took up the game in Tel Aviv and Mitelman became an enthusiastic baseball parent.

Now, the U.S. press, and especially the *New York Times*, started to see us as a feel-good story, while our upcoming opponents saw us as a serious threat instead of an underdog. If we didn't win another game, we'd still walk away as one of the biggest headlines of the 2017 tournament. One look in the eyes of any one of our players and it was obvious that they intended to give the media more to write about.

Tokyo

The next day we flew in class on our own charter plane to Tokyo. Even the Mensch on the Bench got his own row. The media presence in Seoul had been modest, but we were mobbed in Tokyo by a press corps who wanted to know what sauce Team Israel was drinking. When we got to our hotel, scores of fans waited out front begging for autographs on their baseball cards of our players — or the few who actually had baseball cards. Our guys were in heaven.

It needn't surprise anyone that Jason Marquis was our starter against Cuba, our fourth consecutive challenger ranked in the top 10. Actually, the WBSC rankings didn't mean much, as proven by our three wins in Seoul. For one thing, rankings are based on points allocated to all national teams at all levels of the federation, meaning that the more teams federations send and the more tournaments they play well in, the more points they get. Japan, while deserving of all the kudos they received, earns points that other countries don't by playing in sanctioned tournaments that feature only Asian teams. Our 41st-place ranking is directly related to our lack of national teams at the youth level, something that has been corrected in the last few years.

Another under-discussed element of tournament play is the lack of preparation time most teams have before the games start. Some of the best countries in the world don't have the infrastructure to assemble a squad and get ready for the regular season, save for Japan, whose 2023 WBC players already were scrimmaging the previous December. This lack of training time together serves as something of an equalizer and is a big reason why the WBC, Premier 12 and the Olympics and their qualifiers usually feature close games and rarely produce blowouts.

Cuba had been a dominant force in international baseball for decades, but in recent years, that had changed dramatically. In 2017, Cuba had a dearth of talent. Its roster had a lot a veterans well past their prime and youngsters (like Yoelqui Cespedes, Yoenis's brother) who hadn't fully developed. Cuba did have power-hitting Alfredo Despagne, whose eighth-inning grand slam against Australia in Round One got it here. And they were still Cuba, traditionally a baseball powerhouse, and to be on the same field with them was overwhelming.

The game was played on the Jewish holiday of Purim, when the scroll, called a *megillah*, is read. It tells the story of Purim, how Queen Esther overcame the plan of the king's evil advisor, Haman, to murder all the Jews in ancient Persia. Jordy Alter read the *megillah* aloud in the dugout as the players were warming up for the game. Some wandered over occasionally. Eric Blum, our club house manager, was very attentive and at one stage was quite overcome with emotion, as it was the *yahrzeit* (anniversary of the death date) of his father, who'd passed away one year before. We were all emotional when he told us that, and we said the Kaddish prayer in his honor.

Marquis breezed through the first inning, but in the second, Despagne tagged him for a monster homer to left. For the first time in our brief WBC history, we trailed. The next batter walked and, after a rare miscue by Scotty Burcham, Cuba had runners at first and second with nobody out, prompting a mound visit from you-know-who. In a regular-season game, a veteran like Marquis would probably have received a visit from his catcher in this situation, but this was tournament ball and, experience aside, he hadn't pitched in a major league game in two years.

Lorraine worked his magic yet again and Marquis retired the next three batters to escape with one run allowed. Lavarnway, still swinging a hot bat, doubled home Ike Davis with two outs in the fourth, and Marquis would pitch 5 2/3 solid innings before giving way to Zach Thornton. We now had Brad Goldberg with the team, and he would relieve Thornton, who was flawless for 1 1/3 innings. We got a pair of runs in the bottom of the sixth, thanks to two-out hits by Zach Borenstein and Blake Gailen. It was great to see more of our guys in the lineup contributing.

Without getting hit hard at all, Goldberg got himself into an eighth-inning jam, with runners at first and second and two outs. Weinstein already had Josh Zeid warming up in the bullpen and called on him to clean up the mess. Zeid came in, immediately walked Despagne on four pitches and do I really need to tell you what happened next? Well, for the sake of completeness; Lorraine came to the mound, Zeid [ba]tter to ground out weakly to third and the threat was over. [I cou]ld have just cut and pasted that last part.

[... a]n insurance run in the bottom of the inning on a beauti[ful b]unt by Gailen, and it was on to the ninth, three outs away from our fourth win in four tries. Zeid came within one pitch of striking out the side, but the last hitter for Cuba grounded to short on a 2–2 pitch to end the ballgame for a 4–1 Israeli win.

It was our most complete victory thus far, with the offensive contributions more evenly spread throughout the lineup, our longest outing by a starting pitcher and nearly flawless relief. In spite of this becoming common place for Zeid, he was more animated after securing the last out than after the first two games he finished. It was great to see him showing such emotion after being so quiet in defeat five years earlier. We were now 4–0 in the WBC, and visions of flying to Los Angeles for the semifinal and final were on my mind. In defeating Cuba, ranked fifth in the world, Israel beat a country with three Olympic gold medals and two silver medals to its credit, not to mention a silver medal in the 2006 WBC.

During the press conference after the game, a Cuban sportswriter, through an interpreter, asked Jerry Weinstein "Israel has not properly recruited a team of its country, but in fact, experts are calling it United State 2 or United States 3. What is your opinion on a team that should represent Israel, but actually represents the United States?" Weinstein politely responded, "Well, I don't agree with that. All our guys qualified with the heritage rules. The attitude in our clubhouse is we are *not* the JV for Team USA. We're Team Israel. Make no mistake about that."

There's one misconception about the WBC that seems to elude a lot of people, especially fans. While I'm grateful to those fans for caring enough about the WBC and international competition to have passionate opinions, I wish they had a better understanding of what it means to play for your country as opposed to rooting for it.

If the trip to Israel proved anything to the 10 players we brought over to visit in January, it is that you don't just play for your country of birth, you play for your heritage. When Ike Davis's mother was putting together a family tree, he noticed that his father's side could be traced back six generations while his mother's only had a handful of names. Confused, he asked her about that, and she had to tell him those names represented the only members who made it out of the Holocaust. Not only did the Nazis almost eradicate an entire religion and its people, but so many of the records of their existence. Over one-third of the Jewish people worldwide were murdered during World War II, and our players were representing them as well as Israel.

Ken Belson, in his coverage in the *New York Times*, wrote this on March 13, 2017:

> A week into the tournament, Kurz and Team Israel are more than halfway to Los Angeles. The team, which has just one Israeli-born player, swept its three first-round games in Seoul — against the Netherlands, South Korea and Taiwan.
> Then it was on to Tokyo, where, on Sunday, the minor miracle continued as Israel downed Cuba, 4-1, in the opening game of the second round..............
> Its string of victories has turned Israel into the darling of the tournament and left baseball fans asking, as Paul Newman put it to Robert Redford in *Butch Cassidy and the Sundance Kid*: "Who are those guys?"
> Despite its unlikely pedigree, Team Israel has blended in an organic, if slightly peculiar, way. No member is currently on a 40-man major league roster. What resulted has been a team a lot better than people expected, although the players themselves say they are not surprised by the victories they have now strung together.
> "Once we won the first game against Korea, I knew we'd be O.K.," said Kelly. Decker laughed when he saw the team's insulting world ranking. "There's no way I didn't think we were going to L.A." he said.
> Kelly, whose mother is Jewish, but who went to a Roman Catholic high school, saluted the Jewish holiday of Purim, which arrived this weekend, and can now say a few words in Hebrew. Decker, who was not religious growing up, has embraced Jewish humor more than anything. Like Team Israel, the Mensch has become a curiosity among Japanese and Korean reporters, who snap photos of the doll when it is in Israel's dugout. ...
> And Team Israel is starting to be celebrated in Israel itself, where soccer and basketball normally dominate. Prime Minister Benjamin Netanyahu congratulated the team on

Twitter, and at least some Israelis are staying up late to watch the games.

Oren Aharoni reported the following in the Hebrew Language top-selling *Yediot Aharonot* on March 14:

> Meanwhile, back in Israel, whoever wanted the stamp of approval that there are indeed fans of baseball in Israel just had to come yesterday to Mikes Place, a pub in Jerusalem, where more than 200 fans of the national team and a number of players gathered to watch the game against Holland. During the happening, shirts and hats of the national team were given out in a raffle, a video clip of national team players thanking their fans was screened and beer flowed like water.
> Proof of international interest in the Israeli team could be seen by the media representatives who went to the Jerusalem pub, among them a Japanese TV station, a team from CNN, and reporters of international news organizations.

While we were in our bubble in Tokyo, savoring the feeling of having four victories in our first four game with no losses, including the huge win over Cuba, the rest of the baseball-loving world was rubbing its eyes and not believing that Israel could achieve this. I was up every night until the wee hours talking with the Israel press and then unable to sleep after because of the excitement.

Oren Aharoni wrote this in a double spread in *Yediot Aharonot* on March 13:

> Kurz knows now that his team is the hottest thing in Israeli sports. The team is the Cinderella of the tournament, with a perfect record at this stage in the competition, having defeated baseball powerhouses. It's true that these are players who understand that this is a very special opportunity for them to participate in an event like this —

but there is more to it than that, and they all have a special connection together. A connection of heritage that is important to them, of a country they have succeeded in captivating, of a roster that has no superstars, and is totally focused on one goal. This is the Israel National Team, no doubt about it.

We would again play the Netherlands, this time after its tough loss in extra innings the night before to Japan, which, like Israel and Puerto Rico, were the only undefeated countries remaining in the tournament. Japan and Puerto Rico would carry that unbeaten record into the semi-finals in Los Angeles, and we were hoping to join them.

Before my trip to South Korea, I had packed my Israeli and American passports, because the latter one would mitigate the need for my having to get a visa to enter my birth country. We were one win away from that practical decision being a prophetic one and, since I don't believe in jinxes, I wasn't worried about angering the baseball gods with my whimsy. I was overwhelmed by the prospect of traveling to the United States to play, both from the personal and fundraising-promotional perspectives. We would finally get the platform we were seeking, I figured.

The baseball gods didn't beat us that night, The Netherlands' offense did. Corey Baker, who was brilliant against Brazil in the qualifiers, was no match for the Dutch and its lineup loaded with major leaguers. He gave up four runs in the second inning and we trailed 10–0 in the fourth inning, the death blow a three-run bomb off the bat of Didi Gregorious, who went 6–11 in South Korea and stayed hot in Japan. Jair Jurrjens, a former starter for the Atlanta Braves, looked like a current MLB starter, giving up only a solo homer to Nate Freiman in six innings. He was suspended for 80 games three months later for drug use, so you have to wonder how much of his success against us was due to being juiced. The Netherlands' bullpen, their weakest link, gave up only one run in the last three innings. We lost for the first time in the tournament, 12–2.

It was only the second loss in our WBC history, including in both qualifiers, but not nearly as crushing as the first one, against Spain in 2012, that knocked us out of the main event. Though we didn't come to this tournament expecting to go undefeated, it was a blow to our confidence to lose so badly after winning four straight games, especially to a team we had already defeated. Had we beaten them again, we would have advanced to the semi-final in Los Angeles and played another tune-up game against Japan. Instead, we were now playing to stave off elimination. Even if we upset the host country, we would need another upset — by Cuba over the Netherlands — to force a one-game playoff.

We had our backs against the wall and did not fully control our own destiny. Too many managers fighting for their lives had left their best relievers in the bullpen during pressure situations in the seventh and eighth innings, preferring to save them for a save opportunity that never came. With that in mind, Jerry Weinstein decided not to leave Josh Zeid in the bullpen and let Japan potentially do to us what the Netherlands did the day before: open up an insurmountable, early lead. Zeid started the game and was brilliant again, rewarding his manager's confidence with three more spotless innings. He'd become Israel's lone representative on the 2017 All-Tournament Team.

We hung tough for five and half innings, blanking their offense but being unable to generate any of our own. Every time we did get good wood on the ball, it was hit right at someone, or they made a great defensive play. Second baseman Ryosuke Kikuchi, whose defensive gem in extras against the Netherlands saved the game for Japan, victimized us as well with his glove and his bat. With a diving stop, he denied Sam Fuld of a sixth inning hit while the game was still tied. He then was in the middle of a rally in the bottom half that pushed our dreams away from us. It wasn't easy watching all these plays from the stands. My stomach was as twisted as the ballpark pretzels that I could smell all over the park.

Yoshitomo Tsutsugoh, the Japanese league's home run and RBI leader in 2016, led off that half for Japan with his third homer of the tourney. After a mental error by Nate Freiman cost us a crucial second out, Kikichi singled home two runs, and we were suddenly down 4–0 and looking like the team many expected us to be.

It was 8–0 in the top of the ninth when we did something special, proving that Israel still was the competitors that had swept Pool A and beaten perennial powerhouse Cuba. While other teams might have packed it in and emptied their benches with pinch hitters who hadn't gotten into a game, Jerry Weinstein still had his best players on the field and Israel did not surrender. Ike Davis singled home a run with a blistering single and Ryan Lavarnway capped his amazing performance in the WBC with a two-run double. We put runners at second and third with two outs and somehow had the tying run two batters away. Alas, the Cinderella story ultimately came to end when Tyler Krieger struck out, but the inning was still a reminder of how far we had come as a team.

Our dream of WBC glory was over.

Not only was I proud of our boys while watching this, I also admired our fans, led by the eternally faithful Zack Raab, who were cheering that last rally as if the score were much closer than 8–3. Just like our players, they showed the world what being Jewish is all about: never give up and always fight for each other. That feeling was rampant among the team, and the guys were hugging each other, not quite ready to leave the field, but feeling they'd accomplished a lot. We headed back to the hotel and then on to our respective countries with our heads held high.

Unlike Cinderella, the glass slipper had been just too far out of reach and that U.S. passport never made it out of my suitcase.

Seventh Inning

The Olympic dream and miracle

"If you're not practicing, somebody else is, somewhere, and he'll be ready to take your job."
—Brooks Robinson

When I returned to Israel from Tokyo after the WBC tournament, I was sure that baseball in Israel was on the right foot. I expected us to receive continued press coverage and for hundreds more kids to come out to play baseball that spring. Unfortunately, that was not the case and there were no celebrations, no parades, not even press coverage. The people of Israel, or at least those who knew about the WBC, had moved on. We did have a slight bump in registration of players, but it was far from what I had hoped. Something else had to be done.

In August 2016, that "something" had started to happen. The International Olympic Committee's executive board decided to bring back baseball and softball at the 2020 Tokyo Olympics. "Baseball and softball are global sports that belong in the Olympics," MLB Commissioner Rob Manfred said in a news release. "We are grateful to the IOC executive board, the Tokyo 2020 Organizing Committee and the World Baseball Softball Confederation for their collective efforts, which will allow fans throughout the world to again enjoy baseball and softball on the Olympic stage."

I had forgotten that back in 2014, we sent Nate Fish, then the national director, to the WBSC conference in Tokyo that voted to work on reinstating baseball back in the Olympics. As Fish put it, "I had flown to Tokyo to cast the vote on behalf of Israel. At the time, I slipped that small piece of paper with my favorite word into the ballot box: yes, Israel votes in favor of reinstating baseball back into the Olympics. It never occurred to me that we might actually be one of the teams in the tournament."

My vision for the future of Israel baseball was set: We were going to the Olympics.!! I dared not tell anyone else, though, or they would have put me in a straitjacket and thrown me into a padded room. How could a country of only seven million people, with almost no baseball history whatsoever, go up against the sport's powerhouses, like the United-ed States, Japan, South Korea, the Dominican Republic, Venezuela, or countries with strong baseball programs, like Italy, the Netherlands and Mexico? We had been playing in the boondocks of the European B pool, our highest level as a national team, and the WBC's heritage rules didn't apply to the Olympics, which required players to be bona fide citizens of the countries they represented. We looked years away from being competitive in that regard, but my Jewish *kop* started working.

It was right around this time that I received a Facebook message from a man who had just seen *Heading Home* at a film festival in Santa Cruz, California. He had been following Team Israel since 2012 and was, like the rest of us, heartbroken when we lost that qualifier in extra innings to Spain. His name was Michael Ignagni, and though he was not Jewish, he was one of our biggest fans and wanted to congratulate me after seeing the documentary. I was appreciative of the kind message and curious as to why he was following us so closely. He told me that he was an avid WBC fan — an understatement, as he knew more about international baseball and Team Israel than a lot of our players — and wanted to see baseball being played throughout the Middle East, hopeful that it might unite the troubled region. Realizing that the road to such a destination had to go through Israel first, he became a die-hard supporter of my guys.

The conversation continued after I told him of my desire to reach the Olympics. Michael pledged his support and would make numerous small donations, purchase lots of our merchandise and defend Israel (the country and the team) on social media. He became known as perhaps, our biggest gentile fan. We remain friends to this day, and seldom does a week go by when we don't discuss the past, present and future of Israeli baseball. I wish I could name all the people who made donations and supported us in ways large and small. Every one of them is important and, like Zack Raab, I know Michael Ignagni will always be a true friend of Israel.

So, in July 2017, we planned to go to Belgrade, Serbia, to play in the European championship's "B" pool. We had rejoined the "B" pool in the 2015 championship in Vienna, finishing a very respectable third. The first player with Israeli roots to be taken in the MLB draft, Dean Kremer, led the way. But we had to do better than third and this qualifying round would be a test to see how good we were. The first order of business was to find the right man to lead us to the Promised Land.

I first met Eric Holtz during the 2007 IBL season, when he played third base and led Beit Shemesh to the league's only championship. He was the de facto team manager for most of that summer. In 2013, Holtz joined Nate Fish on the staff of the U–18 U.S. Maccabiah baseball team and spent two weeks in Israel. It was like he never left. Holtz had his bar mitzvah at the Western Wall, and his pride in and bond to Judaism was unmistakable. After the WBC, I asked him to become our manager, and Holtz accepted immediately. He said at the time, "Being asked to coach the SNT team was somewhat breathtaking. I was overwhelmed with emotion, as it's not like any other position of employment or any other position in baseball," he said.

"You're being recognized for doing something well, and it made me incredibly proud. I now have another opportunity to be part of Israel and I get to represent the motherland. I cannot explain the pride I feel."

Holtz was indeed overwhelmed, and I was happy that we found someone so connected and proud of his Judaism.

But there was one other tournament in the way of his managing the team. He had previously agreed to be manager of the U.S. Maccabiah team in that same summer of 2017. That's what he did, and as soon as the Maccabiah tournament was over, he would change uniforms and become the manager of our SNT team.

"It will be fine and a smooth transition, as I will be strictly business on the field until the Maccabiah is over, and then my royal blue hat will go forth," he said. "I think that my passion, knowledge and experience of playing as well as coaching will help Team Israel."

Holtz and I put together the team for the 2017 tournament with Israeli passport holders, and we reached the finals against Austria. In the final game, Shlomo Lipetz pitched against Christian Tomsich. The two knew each other well, having pitched often against each other in New York's Central Park baseball leagues. Tomsich outpitched Lipetz this time and Austria won that tournament, 12–2 and moved on. We'd have to stay in the B pool for the 2019 tournament. Team Israel was improving, slowly but surely.

In March 2018, the WBSC announced the qualification system for the Olympics. Six teams would be competing at the Olympics, with Japan, as the host, automatically qualifying. There would be four qualifying tournaments, allowing all WBSC-affiliated national federations the opportunity to compete for the five remaining spots in the Olympics through one of the qualifying tournaments. Two teams would come from the Premier 12 tournament and one each from the Africa-Europe, Americas, and intercontinental qualifiers.

I paid careful attention to how to qualify for the Africa-Europe tournament, along with 35 other national federations.

I met with the Israeli Olympic Committee's secretary general, Gili Lustig, and the chairman of the Elite Sports Department, Danny Oren, on March 27, 2018, to update them on the path for Israel to qualify for the Tokyo Olympics. Lustig and Oren are the two key people regarding Israel's participation in the Olympics and the make-up and administration of the Olympic delegations. They wished me luck but did not commit to providing any financial support at this stage. They did say that if we qualified, their door would be open, and it has been ever since. Both are true professionals, attentive to the needs of the athletes and always willing to consider supporting initiatives. I walked out of th e office with the feeling that they thought they would never see me again. They looked at me, nodding their heads, seeming to say, "Yeah, sure. You're a dreamer." Little did they know that I was intent on attaining this dream.

In May 2018, I met Holtz for breakfast at a Holiday Inn Express in Manhattan for breakfast. I'll never forget that meeting if I live to be 100. Anyone familiar with a Holiday Inn Express breakfast knows what they are like- eggs that taste like sandpaper, muffins that are hard as rocks and coffee that tastes like water. But it's free and there was a table available so we could sit and talk. There were also napkins and I proceeded to map out on napkins what our qualifying path looked like:

1. We had to win the European B pool's championship in July 2019 at a still-undecided site.

2. The next month, we'd have to win a three-game playoff with the winner of the other B-pool .

3. We'd then have to finish in the top five in the European championship's A pool the month after that in Bonn, Germany.

4. After all of that, we'd have to finish first at the Africa-Europe Olympic qualifiers sometime in 2020.

I said to Holtz, "We can do it!!!" He looked at me, stunned, and said, "You're crazy, but I'm with you on this." The conversation cemented my vision and our relationship to the end of the Tokyo Olympics and beyond.

I put together a detailed business plan, which we followed very strictly. This plan would be used to convince players, potential donors and investors that we were serious and presented logical reasoning in our vision.

My plan had four phases:

- To win the B pool, we'd have to scout players and bring them on aliyah so they'd be Israeli citizens. We'd have to improve the local Israeli league and arrange exhibition games prior to the tournament. The budget: $163,000.

- To finish in the top five in the A pool. The budget: $125,000.

- To win the European qualifier. The budget: $22,000.

- To win an Olympic medal. The budget: $90,000.

Total to be raised: $400,000.

I was ready for the battle.

There was lots of work to do, and I had to get Jewish American players from our WBC team to buy into this as well and to persuade them to make aliyah. There was a "ghost" requirement, never made official or written anywhere, that they needed to be citizens for at least one year prior to the Olympics, so it was incumbent on me to bring them in as quickly as possible and not have to deal with that question at all. I spoke with some of them and they were all gung-ho to do it, after the extremely positive experience with the WBC team. Their eagerness to help Israeli baseball, the deepening of their Judaism and heritage and their desire to play for Team Israel in the Olympics were real. They bought in.

A few words on making *aliyah*, which in Hebrew means "going up" and usually refers to immigrating to Israel because doing so is thought to be to ascend spiritually. Moving to Israel is not a simple process. It involves a great deal of paperwork, submitted to the Israeli interior ministry, to prove that one is eligible to make aliyah under the Law of Return. This law, passed by Israel's legislature in July 1950, states that anyone who has at least one Jewish grandparent or is married to someone with one Jewish grandparent can become an Israeli citizen. Proving one's being Jewish involves submitting such items as a *bris* (circumcision) certificate, a bar-mitzvah certificate or a picture of a parent's or grandparent's tombstone with a Jewish star on it. One also has to submit relevant marriage, birth and death certificates, have a criminal background check and provide a letter from a synagogue or rabbi attesting to the applicant's being Jewish. The documents must be notarized and apostilled.

Aliyah is a cumbersome process requiring constant monitoring. Depending on the political party running the interior ministry for a given government, citizenship could be more, or less, difficult to obtain. It was also important to me to bring players who identified with their Jewish roots and would be willing to help advance baseball in Israel in later years.

It was clear to players going through the *aliyah* process, to those assisting them from the IAB side, and even to government officials working with us, that few of these players would actually live in Israel and were only gaining citizenship to be eligible to play on the Olympic team. The formal explanation was that these players were all in the midst of their professional baseball careers, which consisted of a short time period, but that they might later choose to move to Israel. Those were the realities of the *aliyah* process.

To be competitive and have any chance of advancing to the Olympics, it was clear to me that, as the team advanced through the qualifying stages of the Olympics, we'd have to incorporate more top-level Jewish-American players eligible for *aliyah*. Utilizing only our *sabra* players would mean certain elimination in an early round. I also needed to be very selective about which players I approached, both from a Jewish-heritage perspective, to bring players who were dedicated to the cause and could contribute in later years as well and also based on the positions they played. I'd have to determine where we were lacking the necessary team skills and bring on players accordingly.

From April through August 2018, I was heavily involved in both recruiting players to make *aliyah* and fundraising. I was in constant touch with a number of players who were going through the *aliyah* process with an organization called Nefesh B'Nefesh that prepares English-speaking potential immigrants for life in Israel. A woman assigned as the organization's *shlicha* (emissary) for our team, Aleeza Kessler, possessed the perseverance, dedication and determination that allowed us to bring the first 10 players on *aliyah*. Kessler was a fanatical Mets fan, and a baseball fan generally, which certainly helped us as she felt an extra bit of incentive from that. She and I exchanged hundreds of e-mails during those months, and my phone bill was keeping Verizon in the black.

The first two players to complete the process were Joey Wagman and Corey Baker, who would be instrumental in the 2019 tournaments and beyond. I was also in touch with Jon Moscot, who was a professional gamble, as he was still recovering from Tommy John surgery, but a personal "guaranteed bet" being the mensch that he is. Through him, I made a connection with Zack Weiss and brought him along as well. Nate Freiman connected me to Jonathan deMarte, a player who happened to have a Jewish mother. Blake Gailen came on board in July and Jeremy Wolf in August. Benny Wanger had to delay his *aliyah* because he was subject to being drafted by the Israel Defense Forces: only those coming on *aliyah* after the age of 22 could receive military-service exemption. Two other American players, Josh Wolf and Jacob Steinmetz, contacted me; they would play for Team Israel five years later. By the end of August, we had 10 players who would make aliyah in October.

We would need pitching, and lots of it, so that was my primary focus. On October 15, 2018, the 10 immigrants-to-be arrived in Israel, eight of them pitchers. Five of the 10 had played for us in the WBC (Corey Baker, Gabe Cramer, Blake Gailen, Joey Wagman and Alex Katz) and one, Moscot, was an ex-major league pitcher whom we'd brought to Israel in

January 2017. The others included Zach Weiss (a future major leaguer), Jonathan deMarte, Eric Brodkowitz, and Jeremy Wolf. We put them all up in one apartment in the heart of Tel Aviv and they had a great time travelling around the country, conducting baseball clinics, meeting our Israeli players, visiting tourist sites and enjoying the night life. They had a very intense, Birthright-type experience, going to Jerusalem and the Western Wall, Yad Vashem, and an air force base and the Golan Heights. It was a grand tour. They were all mesmerized by Israel.

We took them to the interior ministry to receive their Israeli passports, and that afternoon we had 10 new players for the SNT team!!! It was an incredible accomplishment. All 10 helped us the following summer to reach the Olympics, and six played for Team Israel at the Olympics. Some of them are still playing for us five years later and will continue for as long as they can. I told the Israeli news web site Ynet that the players "showed great enthusiasm for working in Israel to reach the Olympics in particular and to develop the game in Israel in general." Those who'd played in the WBC, I said, "were exposed to Israel and saw how they can help the country become a force to be reckoned with in international baseball. The players will ensure that the professional level of baseball in Israel continues to grow."

It was an exciting visit, and I was riding high, knowing that these guys really improved our chances to advance.

Two weeks after making *aliyah*, Moscot, who has relatives in Israel, said this to the Israeli newspaper *Haaretz* on November 1,

> When I was in college, the first WBC was held in which Israel played in the qualifiers. I saw the games and said to myself, "I'd love to play for Team Israel. That would be super-cool. That would be a dream come true," says Moscot, a Jewish pitcher who in 2015/16 wore the MLB uniform of the Cincinnati Reds but was later injured and underwent Tommy John surgery. "The second WBC arrived, and I was supposed to play for the team, but I got hurt just before and was unable to play. When I heard the plan to play for the Olympic team, I jumped at the opportunity. First, because I didn't get the chance to play two years ago; and second, because we are talking about

something much bigger: the Olympics! This is an incredible opportunity for Israel and for Israeli baseball.

But I wasn't finished yet. I realized we needed some position players to catch the balls put in play, and in April 2019, I brought four additional players on *aliyah*, and Eric Holtz came for a visit as well. Mitch Glasser and Zach Penprase were middle infielders, while Rob Paller and Matt Soren are still playing for us and were on the 2023 squad. They held clinics all over Israel, toured the country and went to the interior ministry to get their passports.

I was still not done. I was in touch with some of our bigger Jewish stars at that stage: Danny Valencia, Jeremy Bleich, Ty Kelly and Nick Rickles. Although I didn't bring them on aliyah for the B pool, I knew we'd need their help once we reached the A pool in Germany, so I expedited the process. Valencia, Kelly and Rickles came to Israel in August and Bleich came in September, and all went directly to Germany. They were of enormous help in the Olympic qualifiers and really came through for us.

The European championship B pool, Blagoevgrad, Bulgaria

But I'm getting ahead of myself. We first needed to win the European championship B pool in Blagoevgrad, Bulgaria.

I barely knew where Bulgaria was on the map, let alone Blagoevgrad. We needed to fly to Sofia and then drive for about an hour to southeast Bulgaria at the foot of the Rila mountain range. Blagoevgrad has two universities and a lovely downtown pedestrian mall with many restaurants and cafes where we spent a lot of time. We stayed in a newly opened hotel, set within those mountains, a 10-minute drive to the baseball field. We were practically the only guests in the hotel and had the run of the place. We ate traditional Bulgarian *shopska* salad and drank the refreshing local beer.

Sydni Holtz, Eric's daughter, who works as a pediatric oncology nurse in Manhattan, made the trip and helped out as an extra trainer. It was the second time we had a woman in our dugout, the first being Justine Siegel, our mental skills coach at the 2016 qualifiers. Team USA had a female trainer for its WBC title run, and we are seeing many more women in baseball as broadcasters, coaches and executives. Team Israel is proud to be a part of this progress.

The field itself was also in the Bulgarian mountains, with beautiful views all around. Goats grazed on the field when we arrived for our first practice there. The head of the Bulgarian baseball association told me that goats are cheaper than a lawn mower. The Bulgarian team also served as the grounds crew, and they did a better job maintaining the field than playing competitive games. It was a wonderful atmosphere, being in the middle of nowhere and beginning our quest for an Olympic medal.

The story of the B pool might as well have been called *A Tale of Two Countries*, as Russia and Israel utterly demolished every opponent en route to two head-to-head match ups. Russia beat its first three opponents by a combined 48–4. We were similarly dominant, winning our first three contests, 33–8.   All the teams in this pool knew this would eventually lead to the Olympic qualifiers, and they were gunning for that, with Greece, Ireland and Serbia padding their rosters with American players who also carried those countries' passports. Russia had on its team Cuba-born players with dubious Russian credentials. (At the time, only national identity cards were required as proof of citizenship, and no one could figure out how these Cuban players obtained theirs.)

The event wasn't streamed, so Haim Katz filmed and announced our games with his phone and posted it live on Facebook. The Internet signal was weak and kept cutting out. Haim was no Vin Scully, and his color commentary repeatedly was interrupted. With audio and video transmission not working, our relatives and friends could follow us only on a European sports Website that apparently had someone at the field typing in the results, batter by batter.

Mitch Glasser, Blake Gailen and Noam Calisar were the hitting heroes in our opening game against Greece. Each homered, and they drove in eight of our 14 runs. Eric Brodkowitz struck out seven batters but struggled through 4 1/3 innings, giving up four runs and leaving the game with the bases loaded. Shlomo Lipetz came in and calmed things down, limiting the damage and giving up an earned run and recording a strikeout in 2 1/3 innings before Corey Baker closed out the 14–7 victory. We were very concerned about the opposing team because it had quite a few Greek Americans who played in college, so this victory was important to us. It's always good to get that first victory under your belt.

In our second game, we limited Serbia to a single run after it had scored 17 against Ireland the day before. Gabe Cramer was flawless for five innings, while Joey Wagman allowed only an unearned run in three innings. The contest ended in an 11–1 mercy-rule victory. Our pitchers combined for 11 strikeouts and only one walk. Our catcher, Tal Erel, had an easy enough time behind the dish, but took a beating in the batters box, getting plunked twice to go along with a walk and a single. There are actually a lot of hit batsmen at this level, and it's a wonder we didn't lose anyone to injury because of an errant pitch. Glasser homered again and drove in five runs, for seven combined in the two games.

The next day, Matt Soren, Dean Pelman and Dan Rothem threw a combined two-hitter against the winless host country, Bulgaria, for an 8–0 win. Jake Rosenberg led the way on offense with a grand slam, while Gailen added three more hits and an RBI. Back-up first baseman Ari Fabian had a hit and a run scored as he filled in for Simon Rosenbaum. Our pitching again was superb: nine strikeouts and only two walks.

After three days, Israel and Russia were undefeated and about to play what was supposed to be a meaningless game, with both teams having secured a slot against each other in the championship game. But neither squad played as if this first encounter didn't matter. It was also the Fourth of July, and although we were Team Israel and our Independence Day is celebrated in May, it was a special day for our American players on the roster, and some felt that playing Russia on that day was meaningful. When I first saw the schedule that spring, I knew this would be *the* game of the pool, and the significance of it was not lost on the players or our manager.

The starters were Victor Cole for Russia and Alon Leichman for us. Each gave up seven runs and couldn't make it past the fifth inning. Cole was born in Russia to an American father who was at the game and in the stands with us, and I got to know them both. Twenty-five runs were tallied by the two teams, although there were only three homers, including one by our Zach Penprase.

Jonathan deMarte gave up four runs in the 10th. Only two were earned; he had started the inning with men on first and second, as per tournament rules for extra innings. It looked like Russia would remain undefeated and secure the home-field advantage in the championship game. Our guys, however were not ready to quit, and scored three runs and loaded the bases before making an out. And who was coming to the plate with a chance to complete the comeback victory? None other than our hottest hitter, Blake Gailen, stepped up to bat. He was 9 for 16 in the tournament with six RBIs. Blake ripped a single up the middle to win the game, 13–12, and secure the top record in the pool and the home field advantage for the rematch. It was a huge psychological boost for our team and a blow to the Russians.

We had a tune-up game against Ireland, which ended after seven innings due to darkness, but Holtz managed to get 15 players into the game, including Haim's son Ophir. He went 1–3 with an RBI, a walk and two stolen bases in the 10–3 victory. As expected, Russia won its game against Serbia.

After scoring 128 combined runs in our 10 B-pool games, this winner-take-all matchup turned out to be a low-scoring affair. The stalwart Joey Wagman tossed three innings of one-run ball before taking a vicious line drive right between the shoulder blades. He was hurting, but he wanted badly to stay in the game. He threw a few pitches to prove he could, but was in such great pain that Holtz had to take him out. As he was being worked on in the dugout, the area where he was struck was swelling, and it did not look good.

We wanted him to be x-rayed. I did not want the trainer to leave the team, so I rode with him to the local hospital along with his girlfriend and her friend. We got directions and off we went. The hospital looked like it was out of the 1950s, and the x-ray machine may have been from before World War I. I somehow was able to tune in to the play-by-play results while Wags was being tightly wrapped up. The staff said nothing was broken and sent us back to the field with a supply of painkillers. He was one happy guy. We made it back just moments after the game concluded, having missed a lot of excitement.

We were up 2–1 when we left, courtesy of a Simon Rosenbaum homer. Gabe Cramer followed Wagman with an inning of scoreless relief. When Dean Pelman gave up a two-run homer to Russia's Cuban shortstop in the sixth inning, we were down a run with 12 outs to go and made the first six of those outs without pushing a run across. Amit was preparing our protest to the tournament organizers, as players and staff of other teams were getting us proof that the Cuban players on the team were not Russian citizens and therefore ineligible. It would cost us 100 Euros to file, but doing so seemed appropriate, especially if we would lose on a homer by an illegitimate player. The protest and fee were submitted to the tournament's technical director in the seventh inning, while I was at the hospital. All of this was communicated to me while I was at the hospital.

Jonathan deMarte entered in relief and came up huge, blanking their offense for the last three innings. Our bats would have to come alive if we were to win the pool; otherwise, we'd fall just short of our Olympic dreams. Simon Rosenbaum led off the eighth with a clutch solo home. That lifted our entire team. The Russians imploded, loading the bases and allowing two more runs to score on wild pitches. deMarte made the lead hold up for a 5–3 win, sending us to the championship round with an undefeated record.

The other pool winner would be Lithuania, who would be the host country. Amit's protest letter was ultimately irrelevant, and the 100-Euro fee was not refunded. We received the trophy, still the biggest and best one I have, and even drank beer from it. As soon as we returned to the hotel, many of the players jumped in the pool, led by the documented splash of Matt Soren. We felt exhilaration, completing the first step of the Olympic plan. A lot of work remained to be done to get the team up to the A-pool level and the Olympic qualifiers. But for the next 12 hours, we partied and drank beer in a very quiet, breathtaking corner of Bulgaria that will never be forgotten.

We had a month to go until the playoff tournament was due to start. We had a lot to consider.

Lithuania lacked proper baseball fields, as far as I knew, so we told the European federation we would be willing to host the games in Israel. Four months prior, a lottery was held as to which pool winner would host the playoffs, and the other pool won. They told us the Lithuanians were considering major improvements to an existing field in the four weeks we had, something I was very skeptical about. I felt pressure because I needed to buy plane tickets for 24 players and had no idea where to fly them to. At least two weeks passed before a final decision was made. The games would be held in Lithuania, whose baseball federation claimed the field would be ready. We now had to raise funds to get our team to Lithuania.

We realized we needed to improve the team. I wasn't overly concerned with winning the playoffs, but I wanted to upgrade our squad prior to the European championship's subsequent A-pool tournament in Germany in September. To make the Olympic qualifiers, I knew that we needed a few big bats and focused my attention on Danny Valencia and Nick Rickles. I had to make sure they could prepare all the paperwork and send it to the Jewish Agency for approval, then fly them to Israel in time to get their passports. It was a race against the clock. The clock lost.

We also needed new uniforms. For the B-pool games, we used existing jerseys we had in Israel, but I wanted to outfit the players better going forward. Margo Sugarman took on this project. She contacted a South African manufacturer, but the team wasn't happy with what we ordered, so I had to improve upon that for the A pool.

B Pool playoff, Utena, Lithuania

Upon arrival at Vilnius airport, we were greeted by the head of Lithuanian baseball, Virmidas Neverauskas, a good friend. His son, Dovydas, would become the first Lithuanian major leaguer as a pitcher with the Pittsburgh Pirates. Virmidas came with a broken-down school bus that looked almost as old as that x-ray machine in Bulgaria. He drove us to Utena, in northeast Lithuania, where the playoffs were to take place. The players, coaches and luggage were barely squeezed inside for the 90-minute drive through twisty, mountainous roads. We arrived at the only hotel in town, not exactly the Ritz, but our home for two or three nights, depending on the results. I did not tell the players that about a half-mile from the field where we would be competing, 2,000 Jews were rounded up and murdered in the Rase Forest during the Holocaust.

I did not think that motivation was necessary at this stage, but the guys would learn of it later. Most of the players had roots in eastern Europe and some of their families had survived the Holocaust. I tried incorporating Jewish-heritage experiences for them in the countries we visited, but we did not always have free time to experience that.

We got to the field, and I saw that it was inside an abandoned horse racetrack, one that hadn't been used in perhaps 20 years. It had been upgraded as best as possible in the month since my conversations with the European baseball officials. Soccer benches and temporary fencing were added, and the fans were close to the field. The lights were pointed out from the baseball field and onto the horse track, but we'd be playing day games, so that didn't seem to matter. Many fans came out and enjoyed beer and bockwurst. It was a fun atmosphere, and at least they could enjoy the ambience

We swept the playoff's two games by a combined score of 27–2. In the first game, a 12–2 win, seven of our players tallied at least one RBI, led by Rob Paller's five to go with two homers. Four others went yard, including Rosenbaum, giving him and Paller dingers in back-to-back playoff games. Wagman bounced back from that line drive to his upper back to throw six innings of one-run ball, and Eric Brodkowitz closed it out with three perfect frames in relief.

In the second game, Lithuania's Olympic hopes ended in a five-inning, mercy-rule loss, 15–0. Gabe Cramer was the only pitcher we needed, going all five innings with two strikeouts against no walks. Rosenbaum homered for the third straight game and collected five RBI. The affair was such a laugher that three of our pitchers — Leichman, Lipetz and Pelman — logged innings playing in the infield, but our opponents could still only muster one hit for their only baserunner of the game.

It was so ugly that in that second game, in fact, someone in the crowd took a hat to cover the lone camera, which was streaming the action without audio. Our followers back in Israel were not amused. Had I known, I would have removed the hat.

By winning the first two games, we were able to leave our "Ritz" hotel in Utena and spend the last night at a Marriott in Vilnius. The guys were really thankful for that. We were limited in our sightseeing by overly protective Israeli security, but were still able to walk around downtown, enjoy the sites, cuisine and alcohol. I arranged a tour of the Jewish quarter. Vilnius was once a hub for Jewish learning and culture, and though the city's Jewish community was decimated in the Holocaust, evidence of its rich heritage remain.

I wanted the players to soak in some of the Jewish heritage, and most were appreciative of that. It was important for me to provide them with this opportunity for reflection and consideration of our roots, which was evident in the European cities we played in that summer. Vilnius was especially meaningful for some of the players, as their grandparents came from the area.

Our players and coaches ultimately left Lithuania for different destinations, knowing we would meet again in Europe in a few weeks. Our first appearance in the European championship's A pool was just ahead of us, but it was Japan in 2020 that we were shooting for.

We made it here and now added a few significant players who had just made *aliyah*: Danny Valencia, Nick Rickles, Ty Kelly and appearing later on, Jeremy Bleich. Danny and Ty were both solid major league players and greatly strengthened our hitting and fielding. We hoped to be one of the top five teams in this 16-team tournament to fly to Italy and, there, join South Africa in the Europe-African qualifiers. I figured that once there, any hot club with good pitching could win it – and we had good pitching. But other countries with similar aspirations were in our way, and they were not about to hand us a free pass.

The European championship A pool, Bonn, Germany

The opening game took place in Solingen and pitted us against a tough Czech Republic squad that featured an MLB prospect, catcher Martin Cervenka, and a two-way player, Martin Schneider, who pitched and played shortstop in the 2016 WBC qualifiers. This time, Radim Chroust was on the mound and he gave his team 5 2/3 gutsy innings, allowing three runs. But the Czech offense was no match for Joey Wagman and our bullpen. Wags surrendered an unearned run in 4 2/3 innings and our relievers gave up a big donut the rest of the way. We scored three more times off of their pen. Team Israel had begun its first European championship with a solid 6-1 victory.

For the next game, we were up against Sweden, and if you think that would have been an easy match up for us, guess again. The Swedes were either very lucky that day or they had a pitching staff to be reckoned with, because they held us in check for the first eight innings. Jon Moscot worked his way out of a jam in the top of the ninth, leaving runners stranded at second and third, but we trailed 3–2.

Nick Rickles led off the bottom of the ninth inning with a clutch single up the middle and Asaf Lowengart pinch-ran for him. Danny Valencia followed with an infield single that the Swedish third baseman threw into the first base dugout, giving us runners at second and third and no one out. Simon Rosenbaum walked for the third time, loading the bases and bringing Rob Paller to the plate. A wild pitch scored Lowengart to tie the score. Paller was intentionally walked and Zack Penprase struck out, bringing Jeremy Wolf to the plate. He was the only hitter in the lineup with two hits on the day. He drove in the winning run with his eye and not his bat, on a four-pitch walk.

The game was closer than it should have been and in spite of our late comeback, the celebration was subdued, as we knew we had to play better if we were going to beat Germany on its home turf the following day.

Playing Israel probably didn't mean as much to the undefeated German team as it was for us going up against them, even though we were both 2–0. Germany had a few U.S.-born players in their lineup and its starting pitcher, Ernorbal Marquez, was a 44-year-old Spanish veteran of European baseball. For our guys, it had a more sobering significance as we were the first Israeli national team to compete inside Germany since the Munich tragedy at the 1972 Olympics, and these days were the anniversary of that event. A few guys had grandparents who survived the Holocaust, and this game had extra significance for them. Jeremy Bleich was the grandson of two Auschwitz survivors. My grandfather was the lone survivor of his family in Auschwitz, losing his wife and two daughters, and many other members of my family perished in the Holocaust. We were pumped up to play Germany, which, as the home team, had a large contingent cheering them on. We had about 20 supporters on our side who sounded like a lot more than that.

If the Munich history wasn't resonant enough, the field in Bonn where we were slated to play was sponsored by and had an ad above the centerfield scoreboard that read, *Bonn Gas Company*. There were good facilities in Regensberg, which hosted the 2022 WBC qualifiers, and a field at the U.S. Air Force Base in Feltdstadt, where baseball's last-ever World Cup, in 2011, was held. In 2019, however, with Israel competing in Germany for the first time in 47 years, we found ourselves in a stadium in Bonn sponsored by the leading gas company in the country. Sometimes truth is stranger than fiction.

A pair of doubles by Mitch Glasser and Nick Rickles gave us a run in the top of first inning, and our starter, Gabe Cramer, worked out of a bases-loaded jam to preserve the lead. It didn't last long, and neither did Cramer, who left a tie game with the bases loaded and nobody out in the third. D.J. Sharabi relieved him and almost got out of it unscathed, but Glasser booted a double-play ball with one out, allowing a run to score. Sharabi then induced a second double-play ball, and that one got us out of the inning trailing by only one.

It stayed 2–1 through the seventh inning, and our frustration was growing, especially by our manager, Eric Holtz, over the quality of the umpiring. Officiating at this level is usually not of the highest caliber, and none of the umps were German, so I'm not accusing anyone of favoritism. However, every blown call seemed to go against us, which added to the tension as the game wore on.

Glasser led off the top of the eighth with a walk and Blake Gailen smacked a hard single to right. Danny Valencia popped out to shallow left, bringing up Nick Rickles. He would face the third pitcher of the inning for Germany, as they were clearly counting outs. Rickles struck out, leaving it up to Ty Kelly, if we were going to score for the first time since the opening inning. Batting left-handed, Kelly drilled a single to left field, tying the game and bringing some momentum back to our dugout. Jonathan deMarte came on in the bottom half and allowed two runners to reach base, but Rickles picked off the runner at first to end the threat.

We put runners at first and second with two out in the top of the ninth, but couldn't score them. The bottom half of the inning would start off about as badly as possible. with Marco Cardoso hitting a sinking liner to right that Jeremy Wolf played into a triple. With the winning run 90 feet away, the German fans were on their feet and we were on our heels. Holtz brought the infield in and left deMarte in the game to either get out of it or take the loss. He struck out the next batter and, rather than intentionally walking the following hitter to set up a potential double play, we kept the infield in. The risky call paid off huge as that hitter flew out to shallow left field, not nearly deep enough to score the run. The next batter, Sasha Lutz, ended a nine-pitch at-bat with a weak ground out to second, and we were on to extras as my heart temporarily stopped palpitating through each of those nine pitches.

Tournament rules had us beginning the 10th inning with runners at first and second: the last two batters of the top of the ninth, Glasser and Gailen. Danny Valencia was hit by an errant curveball and after being on the verge of a truly heartbreaking loss, we were sitting pretty with the bases loaded, nobody out and one of our biggest power threats at the plate. Rickles, after fouling off four two-strike pitches, stroked a single to center, scoring Glasser. Gailen was thrown out at the plate by a mile (getting the green light from Holtz, coaching third base)and after Ty Kelly became the second hit-by-pitch of the inning, a new arm was brought in. Simon Rosenbaum greeted Germany's sixth hurler of the night with a sac fly and we took a two run lead into the bottom of the inning.

What happened next had to be seen to be believed. Starting with runners at first and second, Germany was just one long ball away from winning the game. They opted to bunt with the first batter, Simon Gühring. Dean Pelman had taken over for deMarte and got ahead 0–2, forcing Gühring to swing away. He did and hit a ball that looked like the game winning, three-run dinger we feared. In what can only be described as uncommonly good fortune, the runner at second, Kevin Kotowski, was lined up directly behind leftfielder Rob Paller and the ball as it went over his head. Not only did the ball not clear the fence, but when Paller reached up for it, it disappeared from Kotowski's view behind Paller's glove, and his body blocked the view of it hitting the base of the outfield wall. Kotowski thought the ball was caught and ran back to second, only to realize it was still in play when he was met at the base by his teammate, Sasha Lutz. He turned around, ran through a stop sign at third base and was thrown out by 15 feet by Ty Kelly. What was less than six feet from a game-winning homer turned into the first out. It nearly was a double play, but the umps missed passing Lutz while rounding first.

The next batter grounded into a double play one pitch later, giving us a 4–2 win, the score appearing under the Bonn Gas Company sign as our players celebrated the wild, exhilarating victory. Germany, after failing to take advantage of that 9th inning leadoff triple, would lose to the Netherlands and the Czech Republic and have to square off against second-ranked Italy in the second round. We went on to beat Great Britain 7–4 on the strength of our bullpen's allowing only one run in five innings, while Blake Gailen led the offense with a pair of homers and three RBI. Having secured a spot in the championship round, we played a meaningless game against the Netherlands and lost 13–4. Not one player on our team gave that defeat a second thought.

After Belgium and Germany lost their first and only games of the next round to Italy and the Netherlands, respectively, we were one win from reaching the Olympic qualifiers. Standing in our way was France, whose baseball program was not very intimidating. Didier Semient, the president of the French baseball federation, was in the stands with me and we were trash talking one another. Joey Wagman, DJ Sharabi, Zach Weiss and Jonathan deMarte yielded no earned runs in nine innings and Danny Valencia's two-run homer in the first gave us a lead we would not relinquish. Nick Rickles added a two-run bomb in the fifth and we went on to win the game 8–2, securing our spot in the Europe-African Olympic qualifiers.

Reaching the A pool of the European championship had never before been accomplished by Israel baseball, and it was a true honor to compete at the tournament, our third in just eight weeks. Our main goal, however was to place in the top five so we could reach the qualifiers, and our staff debated whether we should try to reach the top three. Achieving that meant that Israel's sports ministry would award a higher bonus to the federation and the players.

While not throwing the next two games, Eric Holtz managed his pitching staff with an eye on the Olympic qualifiers, and we weren't exactly heartbroken to end the European championship with consecutive losses to Spain and Italy. The loss to the Italians was only disappointing in that the final score was 7–6; if we had eked out two more runs, we'd have secured at least a silver medal in the tournament. When Spain beat us 16–11, it took the bronze. We shed no tears, as we had a lot more meaningful baseball ahead of us

We had rested players and pitchers, while the Netherlands, Italy and Spain, who all understood what was at stake and had stacked their rosters accordingly, were not really concerned with us. That's exactly where we wanted them.

The top five teams from the European championship — the Netherlands, Italy, Spain, the Czech Republic and Israel — flew together on a chartered plane to Bologna from Bonn. It was quite a scene, seeing four teams together in their official travel outfits, and Team Israel, not identifiable at all, due to security considerations. The players mingled, as many knew each other from their playing days in the MLB, the minors, independent leagues and college.

The European African Olympic qualifiers, Bologna and Parma, Italy

In this tournament, each team would play five games against one another. Whoever held the best record at the end would reach the Tokyo Olympics. Unlike the four-team WBC qualifiers we had previously played in, there would not be a championship game.

The first three of our five games stacked us against all three countries that had just beaten us in Germany, meaning we would have to produce the exact opposite results if we were to have a shot at the Olympics. I was very concerned, but knew that we had excellent pitching and, in a short tournament, good pitching usually beats good hitting. It turned out we got both.

Our first matchup was against Spain in Bologna. We sent Joey Wagman to the mound, wearing uniform No. 14. His jersey number might as well have been 31 under Greg Maddux's name, because he gave a Greg Maddux-like performance. Wagman was phenomenal, pitching one of the best international performances you'll ever see. With a 3–0 lead, courtesy of Danny Valencia's two-run homer and Blake Gailen's sacrifice fly, he entered the ninth having not walked a man and throwing fewer than 10 pitches in each of the first eight innings. The two hits he had given up were a soft liner off shortstop Ty Kelly's glove and an infield single. The Spaniards were completely flummoxed.

Wags would give up a soft leadoff single to Spain's first batter, but Eric Holtz was so confident in his hurler's stuff that he did not visit the mound or have someone warming up in the bullpen. The next hitter bounced a ball off Ben Wanger's glove at first base, but Mitch Glasser, with his momentum going in the opposite direction, made a terrific play, turning to backhand it and complete the out at first. Spain's lone runner of the night had reached second base and Wagman finally had thrown 10 pitches in an inning. Spain looked to capitalize on its only legitimate threat. But Wagman was having none of it, and he got the next two batters on a meek ground out to third and a weak fly ball to right, completing the 3–0 shutout with 9 strikeouts and no walks. His complete game really boosted the team's confidence, and getting that first win without using any relievers was huge for our bullpen. The guys knew the significance of that as we prepared to face the top European teams on consecutive days.

That first game was played in Bologna, but the real bologna was that our Spanish opponents refused to shake our hands afterward. It was an appalling lack of class to turn their noses at one of the best traditions of international competition, and while few of Spain's players were Spanish, it was a blemish on the country's baseball federation, whose leaders didn't even try to get them to line up.

The Netherlands' team in the lovely city of Parma was next. The last two times we had squared off with the Dutch, they had given us the only two blowout losses in our history and we were anxious for that to not happen again. Our starter was former major league pitcher Jon Moscot, who knew coming into each game for us that every pitch could be his last. The trainers were working on him between innings, and I think he may have used more than 50 percent of the tape we'd brought for the team. He breezed through the top of the first inning, and our offense went immediately to work.

Catcher Nick Rickles, doing his best Johnny Bench impersonation, drilled a two-out, two-run homer to left. The Netherlands would put up back-to-back one-out doubles in the top of the second, but Moscot limited the damage to just a single run. We responded immediately, and loudly, in the bottom of the frame. With the bases loaded and one out, Mitch Glasser ripped a double into left-center and, with centerfielder Roger Bernadina shading him toward right, the ball rolled long enough for all three runners to score. Glasser would come home on a Valencia double and the Netherlands were well on their way to getting a taste of their own medicine.

With a five-run lead, Eric Holtz wisely decided to save whatever bullets Moscot had remaining and pulled him after four solid innings, replacing him with Jeremy Bleich. Bleich and other relievers continued our dominant pitching. Two more runs were knocked in by Rob Paller and Blake Gailen in the bottom of the fifth, and we cruised to a most satisfying 8–1 victory. After winning the European championship, the stunned Dutch team was expected to walk all over us again, but we showed them why we were here, having survived three qualifying rounds to get to this point. Unbelievably, miraculously, our guys were 2–0 and ready to face Italy, *in* Italy, for what was probably the most important game in the history of Israeli baseball.

We were clearly in the driver's seat heading into our matchup with the hosts, who were also undefeated after two games. The Italians are very prominent in the upper echelons of the WBSC, from the President, Ricardo Fraccari, on down, and there was no doubt in my mind that this Olympic qualifier was organized to give the host country a distinct advantage. They had a bye on the first day, giving them extra time to prepare even though the Netherlands had won the European championship. On top of that, they were scheduled to play the two lowest-ranked teams in the tournament in their first two games, allowing them to line up their pitchers for their matchup with the Dutch on the final day.

Gabe Cramer was our starter. He would only go 3 2/3 innings in a gutsy outing that he had to have been proud of and that we were lucky to get. Italy's Chris Colabello, who had played in 100 big league games, hit a first-inning double to put runners at second and third with one out. Cramer got out of that jam and quickly ran into another one faster than you could say *veal parmesan*. John Andreole, whose two-run single completed Italy's five-run ninth inning comeback win against Mexico in the 2017 WBC, tripled to lead off the second, but Cramer stranded him there.

In the top of the fourth, Rickles would start the scoring for us again with his second two-run bomb in as many days, both times following a Valencia walk. Then, in our first bullpen blip of the tournament, Zack Weiss gave up a two-run, fifth-inning double to Colabello to knot the game at two. Weiss stranded him at second and gutted his way through a tough, but scoreless, sixth inning, giving the rest of our bullpen a much-needed break after he replaced Cramer in the fourth. In the meantime, Italy's Luis Lugo was pitching a terrific game, holding us hitless after Rickles's homer.

If Mitch Glasser's bases-clearing double was the turning point of the Dutch game, the defining moment against Italy, and possibly the whole qualifier, occurred on defense. Jonathan deMarte came on to pitch in the bottom of the 7th and after walking the leadoff hitter, then drilled Colabello in the face. If not wanting to put two runners on base with no one out wasn't enough of a deterrent, deMarte's body language immediately following the pitch made it obvious he wasn't trying to do that. During a lengthy delay in which they tended to Colabello's bleeding nose, deMarte was pacing around the mound. I was very concerned that he would lose his focus and concentration at this most critical time, just as Josh Zeid had against Spain after our catcher's ejection in the 2012 WBC qualifier.

Colabello, Italy's hottest hitter, had to leave the game, but they still had runners at first and second and a prolific cleanup hitter, Giuseppe Mazzanti, at the plate. In a move that raised eyebrows in our dugout, Italy's manager, Marco Mazzieri, had Mazzanti bunt, something I have to believe he didn't want to do. To his credit, he laid it down perfectly to put runners on second and third. Mazzieri clearly knew his slugger was adept at bunting, but Mazzanti was also in the cleanup spot for a reason and you have to wonder why their manager would give our struggling pitcher a free out. Whatever the thought process, deMarte seemed to settle down after the gift and fanned the next two hitters to preserve the tie and send us into one of the weirdest half-innings I can ever remember.

Lugo started the eighth by hitting Ben Wanger, which was no more intentional than deMarte hitting Colabello. Lugo certainly did not want to put the lead runner on base this late in the game after having pitched so well for seven innings. He was replaced by a former big leaguer, the ambidextrous Pat Venditte, who wore a special glove so he could pitch left and right, which he did against us. If that wasn't weird looking enough, Venditte gave up the lead run and loaded the bases without giving up a hit, with the only ball to make it out of the infield being a shallow fly by Gailen.

It all started when Simon Rosenbaum bunted Wanger to second, and Wanger went to third on a wild pitch to Zach Penprase, who then walked. Glasser, the previous night's hero, laid down a perfect bunt as well. It earned him not only an RBI, but when Mazzanti, who took over at first for Colabello, bobbled the ball on the transfer, Glasser was safe at first base as well. After Gailen's flyout, Valencia reached on an infield error at short and the bases were loaded.

Venditte had to wonder what he had done to anger the baseball gods. Clearly, they weren't finished messing with him, as Nick Rickles hit a sharp grounder up the middle that ricocheted off Venditte's right foot, changing directions and rolling past the shortstop, who was heading in the opposite direction. Rob Paller became the second player in the inning to be hit by a pitch, loading the bases for a struggling Ty Kelly. Venditte's night was mercifully over and he was relieved by Michael Johnson, who gave up back to back singles to Kelly and Wanger, the latter having begun the inning with the hit-by-pitch from Lugo. Lugo had set down eleven men in a row, but after facing one batter in the eighth, he was now on the hook for the loss. After seven innings of clean, well-pitched, superbly defended baseball, we suddenly held an insurmountable lead and would go on to win, 8–2.

The Italians were shocked and quite upset at themselves, and never recovered. They lost their next game to Spain and were facing the possibility of a meaningless game on the final day of the tournament instead of playing for an Olympic berth in front of their home crowd. Team Israel, on the other hand, was in complete control, needing only one win in either of the next two games to qualify for the 2020 Tokyo Olympics. The first of the two games would be against the tough and dangerous Czech Republic team, managed by a former big league pitcher, Mike Griffin. (In 2022, Griffen would be replaced on the national team by Pavel Chadim, who brought in Czech coaches instead of U.S. transplants. His team would qualify for the 2023 and 2026 WBCs.) In spite of the Czechs' development, we were expected to beat them, but they had given us a tough game in the European final, so we were anything but over-confident. If they did defeat us, it would extend the chances of either Italy or the Netherlands overtaking us if were we to lose to South Africa on the final day.

The Czechs led 1–0 in the bottom of the fourth, when Danny Valencia blasted his second two-run homer of the qualifiers. The mood in the dugout was that this was just the beginning, that our offense was about to break out and would set up an Olympic celebration even before our last game. However, as I stated earlier, this was a tough opponent and they came roaring back with six runs in the top of the fifth. We scratched out two more runs and made great plays on defense, but our hitters just weren't clicking and we went out in the eighth and ninth innings to lose by a final of 7-4.

Not only was our final contest against South Africa now necessary, but if we lost, we would need Italy to bounce back after two straight losses and defeat the Netherlands, which had easily whipped Spain and South Africa.

On the team bus to the field for last game, Eric Holz addressed the players with a message he didn't think needed to be sent heading into our game with the Czech Republic. None of us was panicking, as we knew South Africa was the weakest country in the pool and we had Joey Wagman as our starter. Perhaps just as a reminder to anyone who might allow the slightest doubt to creep into their mind, Holtz said, "We left the hotel as a baseball team. If all we do is take care of business and control the baseball today, WE RETURN AS OLYMPIANS!"

Curiously, South Africa had chosen not to start Dylan Unsworth. He had pitched six innings of one-run ball against us in the 2012 qualifier and eight shutout innings against New Zealand in 2016, so he was no stranger to throwing a lot of pitches in international pool play. Given that he was accustomed to warming up as a starter, it didn't make a lot of sense for South Africa to use him as a reliever.

That's what they did, however and by the time he took the mound in the bottom of the third inning, we had already scored four runs, the first two without a hit, thanks to four walks and a hit batter. Blake Gailen drove in two more runs with a single up the middle. With Unsworth entering the game, we would be facing South Africa's best pitcher with a four-run lead in our back pocket. We scored two quick runs off him. Joey Wagman was pitching another gem, and we cruised into the top of the eighth with a 7–1 lead.

The mercy rule for the qualifier was that a 15 run advantage after five full innings or 10 runs after seven or eight full innings, meant the game would be called. When Gailen drove in his third run of the game in the top of the eighth with a single to right, we had runners at first and second to bring Danny Valencia to the plate. On a 1–0 pitch, he hit a towering, three-run homer over the left-centerfield wall, giving us an 11–1 lead for a 10-run margin and a chance to end the game in the bottom of the inning due to the mercy rule.

Several players from both the Czech Republic and the Netherlands sat in the stands, as the Czechs had not been mathematically eliminated from the qualifier when our game started. They had finished with a surprising 3–2 record. By virtue of beating us 7–4 after we beat the Netherlands 8–1, which came after the latter beat the Czechs 4–1, a Netherlands loss to Italy would have created a three-way tie. Since the head-to-head tiebreaker could not decide it, run differential would have to, which is why the Czechs were in the stands then. Valencia's homer all but ended their dreams and postponed those of the Netherlands, who would go on to qualify for the wild-card round. Both teams went silent when the homer cleared the fence, but Zack Raab and the rest of our fans were on their feet screaming, while Valencia's teammates couldn't wait to greet him in the dugout.

It was hard to fathom that now, after I'd served five years as IAB's president, eight as secretary general and 10 as the SNT general manager, we were about to reach the pinnacle of success. Our guys were three outs away from being the first athletes to represent Israel in a team sport in the Olympics since 1976 in Montreal, just four years after the Munich tragedy. September 22, 2019, would be a date that would live in infamy in the laurels of IAB's history.

In the bottom of the eighth inning, I did something very uncommon for me and went with Amit to the dugout to join in the eventual celebrations. I never go to the dugout during games, but this was different. Special. We had three outs to go. Zack Weiss retired the first two batters with relative ease. Holtz summoned Shlomo Lipetz to get the last out. It would be a very fitting tribute to his long and devoted service to Israeli baseball. I thought back to the first game of the 2012 WBC qualifier, when Brad Ausmus gave that honor to Lipetz as well, only to take him out when he struggled. Jerry Weinstein had put in Dean Kremer to close out the 2016 WBC qualifier in Brooklyn.

So, I was happy to see Shlomo, with whom I've probably shared the longest of all my relationships in Israeli baseball, get the call. He induced a grounder to third that was booted by Zach Penprase. That normally would have been of no concern, considering our 10-run lead with one out to go. But if South Africa were to push across a run now, we would have to play a ninth inning. Then, if South Africa rallied at all, the game would likely have to be finished by someone else, and no one wanted that honor taken away from Shlomo Lipetz.

I need not have worried. The next batter hit a fly ball to Simon Rosenbaum in right. He caught it, tucked the ball in his back pocket and charged to the infield to celebrate with his fellow Olympians. That ball soon found its way to Shlomo, and he selflessly gave it to me.

I was in tears as the game came to an end and hugged Amit, who was also very emotional. It was ideal to end this game in his arms.

The players celebrated on the field, and I hugged each and every person I could find. There were fireworks and a picture was taken of the team and the Olympics logo. Both Amit and I learned our lessons from the WBC, and he covertly bought and chilled the Champagne without anyone knowing and brought it on the field for the celebration. Too bad it was chilled because few players drank the bubbly, saving most of it to spray on each other.

"What we did is simply amazing, history for Israel. No one on this team has an ego. Everyone that came left it in their suitcase," Lipetz told *Yediot Aharonot*'s Oren Aharoni after the victory in the newspaper's two-page spread. "The story is the camaraderie that developed among the players: sabra's, players from the WBC and those that made aliyah this summer."

Aharoni asked Lipetz whether, given the American-heavy roster, if this was really the Israeli national team.

"I'm talking to you now in Hebrew, and every player is proud to have an Israeli passport," Shlomo replied. "Everyone belongs to the country, and that's what's unique about us. I mean, in the Olympics, athletes born in Ethiopia and Russia will represent Israel. Even if you grew up in the Diaspora, every Jew has the right to gain Israeli citizenship. Everyone on this team has a link to Israel."

Aharoni quote me as saying, "Now we are part of the Israeli Olympic delegation, and I still can't believe that. I have 10 months to plan, and I am sure that we will do some beautiful things that will help the team."

Blake Gailen was quoted by Ken Rosenthal in the NY Times: "I don't ever remember crying during a game. Even in the WBC, I only cried when it ended, when we got eliminated. But I was super emotional today. This is the Olympics. It hit me so hard. I saw how hard it was hitting guys around me also." Rosenthal's article quoted Lipetz: "Everyone in the room is shaking their head. We all have goosebumps."

Both my and Holtz's phones had exploded with texts and instant messages after the final out, but one person was conspicuously missing from the congratulators. Michael Ignagni, our fan in northern California, had sent us either a "Yeah, baby!" message within five minutes of every win since the first game in Bulgaria, or a "Get 'em tomorrow!" message after every loss. Eric noticed his absence first and sent him a message that read, "We did it! Where are you?" Ignagni, it turned out, had a horrible flu, had overslept and because of the game being moved up 90 minutes to avoid inclement weather, missed everything. He was elated, of course, that we had won, but told us how truly bummed he was to not have been watching our triumph as it happened. Eric and I assured him that he was with us the whole time.

Danny Grossman writing six months later in *The Jerusalem Report* (February 24, 2020), summed up the four tournaments and individual players' contributions:

> The boys of summer reeled off a string of consecutive victories, showing poise with come-from-behind as well as extra-inning victories, and beating teams like Russia (twice) and perennial European powerhouses the Netherlands and Italy. To a man, the players delivered timely hitting, sterling defense and clutch pitching. Blake Gailen was the slugging star of the first tournaments, and Valencia went on a tear in the last, hitting six home runs in seven games. Former Mets infielder Ty Kelly and catcher Nick Rickles combined great at bats with solid fielding, as did Zach Penprase, who also ran the bases like a thoroughbred. Yet in baseball, pitching is critical — especially in a short series — and the entire pitching staff stepped up its game. Red's pitcher Jon Moscot threw as hard as he had worked to make a comeback after undergoing Tommy John surgery. Ace Joey Wagman hurled a complete game and came back on short rest (a la Sandy Koufax in the 1965 World Series) to clinch the final victory over South Africa, which guaranteed a place in the Olympics. But

Wagman was the first to mention how his defense bailed him out, with Rob Paller making an acrobatic catch at a time of the game that could have taken a different course in the first inning

Doron Kramer of *Yisrael Hayom* summed things up this way:

Moments before Israeli sports become totally despondent about playing in any meaningful tournament, along comes the Israeli national baseball team, made up mostly of American Jews and one sabra (not correct) ... and says to everyone: Move over and make room on the map because we are here now, big time! With a bat in one hand and a hardball in the other, the Israeli-American team broke the glass ceiling and became one of six world powerhouses to reach the Olympics in Tokyo. The team showed that Jewish genes are not an obstacle to success, but the key is a healthy sports culture that breeds success...When you get a run in baseball, it happens when the player steps on home plate. Now, the "home plate" for the players is Israel, and their huge steps forward from this base will be remembered forever. Now it's time for Israel to be transformed into a place where baseball feels at home.

We also got great coverage in *Haaretz*, in an article by Itamar Katzir:

The Israel Olympic Committee and Elite Sports didn't see it coming. "This is an impressive sporting accomplishment, no doubt about that," says the head of Elite Sports, Danny Oren, although he also doesn't know what to make of this sporting achievement. Israel? Best in Baseball? Since when? The answer is: Since Peter Kurz decided to make it that. "I am in the clouds," says Kurz, president of the Israel Association of Baseball and the man behind the idea of developing the national team from zero and made it to the Olympics. "The feeling is incredible, seven years in the making, a dream I had that really began taking shape two years ago. I worked very hard and did a lot of public relations and fundraising and made huge efforts to speak with players and build the team, build baseball in Israel." Kurz's vision was simple and the execution was perfect. If you would have asked the Israel Olympic Committee a year ago, they would not have given baseball a chance to reach the Olympics. But in the interim, the IAB succeeded in convincing a group of Jewish-American baseball players to make *aliyah*, and this was exactly what was missing. Suddenly, Israel became one of the elite teams in Europe. Danny Oren explains: "The advantage of Israel is that most of their players are not from the top league, MLB, but from the lower leagues, so they are available. All the credit should go to Peter Kurz, and I tip my hat to him. In a sportsman's eyes: they performed as they needed to and beat the strongest European baseball powers, Holland and Italy.'

Kurz believed it all along, "If we can get to the Olympics, we can also reach 5,000 players in Israel and become the third largest team ball sport. It could be huge. It could be a real step up for our sport. Tal Brody didn't think it would take 30 years to get the first Israeli in the NBA. I hope it doesn't take 30 years to get the first Israeli in MLB."
Kurz continued, "We need to take advantage of this stage to grow baseball in Israel. We are going to build two new fields soon. Until the Olympics in 11 months, we need to leverage this and show the whole world what Israel baseball is about."
Kurz has one more hope that relates to what will happen in Los Angeles in 2028. "I am super proud of our U–18

team, totally made up of *sabras*, that won the qualifier this past summer and will play next year in the European championship. That proves the goal and the path is succeeding. ... I hope that in eight more years, when baseball returns to the Olympics, we will have a team made up of mostly *sabras*." And to that we say, "Amen."

Alon Leichman was quoted by Stav Ifergen in *Maariv* on January 19, 2020, about the claim of the "Americanization" of the team:

You are talking to a player who grew up in Israel and learned the game here. The baseball program in Israel gave me the tools to travel overseas and develop my career there. Yes, many of my teammates are Jewish-American players who made *aliyah*, but the main goal is to take advantage of them to raise the awareness of baseball in Israel and to eventually replace them with *sabras*. There is no reason to be anti-. The fact that Americans came and are representing us should not be discredited. They are Jews. My parents also came from America a long time ago and were not raised in Israel.

"In my eyes they are Israelis," said a Team Israel player, Asaf Lowengart. "They came here, went through the *aliyah* process which is long and not simple, and the fact that they did this shows their desire to give back to the country. In each tournament they fly to, they leave their families, children and careers behind. They didn't do military service, true, but I see this as doing *miluim* [reserve duty.]

Lowengart went on to say:

Just as judo was less well known until the Olympic medals of Arad, Smadja and Zeevi, that's what will happen with baseball. [The trio's] achievements led to many more kids in Israel doing judo, and today we see Olympians like [Sagi] Mukki and [Ori] Sasson. I hope the Israeli youth will see our athletes and will know that there are new fields in Raanana and Beit Shemesh. We want kids to have different options to try and see if they like baseball. If they like it, we all profit; if they don't like it, that's also okay, but at least they had the opportunity. I don't know if we'll ever be able to compete with soccer and basketball in this country, but we are the only Israeli national team to have reached this far in 50 years.

Years later, Nate Fish was quoted as saying the following:

The streak spanned over twenty games in five countries (he exaggerated a bit).Eric Holtz, the manager of the team who had been my roommate in the IBL all those years earlier, said if we had to play those games again, even if we had a thousand chances, we couldn't do it, we couldn't navigate the maze of transactions and travel and winning, errors, bloopers, walk-offs...We were going to the Olympics. The organization that had been started 30 years earlier so a group of kids could play in a real game was going to the Olympics!

Sixteen new players had joined across all four tournaments, with Team Israel going 17–4 and winning three of the four tournaments we played in. We won the games that counted and rested players for the games that didn't. Eight players joined us in Germany and Italy and were instrumental in leading us to victory.

In total, this accomplishment was made possible with the help of 32 players, five coaches, four trainers, one manager and yours truly, along with the moral and spiritual and financial support of the IAB, JNF and all our donors. All the IAB players of the last twenty years had a part. I want to take this opportunity to thank each and every one of them. We were going to the Olympic Games in Tokyo, and not even the Americans, the Dominicans, or the South Koreans, all of them baseball powerhouses, had yet qualified.

Reaching the Olympics was a perfect ending to a nearly perfect run, and now we had 10 months to prepare for the Tokyo Games, an athletic event that is the ultimate goal of every athlete.

But that would soon be 22 months, due to Covid.

Eighth Inning

Tokyo Olympics and Covid

"A ballplayer spends a good piece of his life gripping a baseball, and in the end, it turns out that it was the other way around all the time."
—Jim Bouton

The manager of the Japanese Olympic team, Inaba Atsunori, was at the qualifying tournament in Italy, along with members of his staff, scouting their first potential opponents to qualify. He said afterwards that they were "wary" of Team Israel, and that we were "a team with a fairly high level." Both were incredible compliments. I introduced myself to him during the tournament, and he graciously wished us good luck. I was riding high at that point. There were 7.3 million baseball players in Japan; by contrast, in Israel — this is where I'd usually stretch those numbers like a press agent — we had 1,000 players. That number, by the way, is .013 percent of our population. Team Israel was certainly an underdog, although in theory, we had a 50 percent chance of winning a medal. That's because, after all, only six teams would be competing in baseball.

One week after we qualified, on September 30, I, as president of the IAB, signed a document confirming that the Israeli baseball team would be using the spot allocated to the WBSC, under the qualification system for the XXXII Olympiad in Tokyo in 2020, as the winner of the Europe-Africa qualification event. Wow! It was now official. The presidents of the federations of Italy, the Netherlands, Spain, Russia, Bulgaria and others had dreams of signing that document, but I, Peter Kurz, was the one who did so. It was unbelievable!

July 24, 2020, it would all begin. Or so I thought........

The first family Shabbat dinner when I got home was dedicated to planning our trip to Tokyo. I wanted to take the entire family with me: Ronit, Maya, Amit and Adi with their significant others, Nimrod, Sandra and Itay, respectively, and my granddaughter Emilia, who would be 1½ years old by the summer of 2020. It would be a huge trip and very costly, but, hell, how often does one get to participate in an Olympics?

We looked at the schedule and started planning which events we wanted to get tickets for: opening ceremony, basketball finals, 100-meter races, gymnastics and, of course, all the baseball games. We started looking at maps of Tokyo and researching hotels. It would be a hugely expensive undertaking, as the Japanese were already gouging prices for even their tiny hotel rooms, but it was all very exciting to think about. I even contacted Beit Shalom, the pro-Israel organization that we stayed with our last time in Japan, which was very excited to host the Israeli baseball team's general manager and his family.

Upon my return to Israel, I immediately met with Gili Lustig and Danny Oren, the Israel Olympic Committee's secretary general, and the chairman of the Elite Sports Department, respectively, the same people who were highly skeptical of my proclamations just a few months before. They would be leading the Israeli delegation to the Tokyo Olympics and were full of congratulations and accolades for what we had just accomplished. It would be the first time in 44 years, since the 1976 Montreal Olympics, when our soccer team played, that a team sport with a ball would represent Israel at the Olympics. Both gentlemen came from team-sports backgrounds, and they were thrilled to get an Israeli team back in the Olympics, although neither was familiar with baseball.

They offered their complete support and a warm home, but soon realized the logistical, financial and social obstacles to overcome to get our team to Tokyo. They also liked the odds of us attaining a medal, with only six teams competing for three medals, whereas 12 to 16 countries vied for medals in other team sports.

Adding 24 male athletes to the Israeli delegation, which at the time had approximately 25 athletes qualify for Tokyo, meant the doubling of the athletes' delegation, which would soon be the largest the country had ever sent to the Olympic Games. The Israel Olympic Committee's stated goal had been to send a delegation that was gender equal, with the same number of men and women, but our team happily ruined those plans. But as I explained our excellent chances of reaching the medal round, they were quite excited about the prospects. After that, our regular meetings and updates were well attended.

At the first working meeting on September 26, 2019, I prepared a five-page document of subjects to discuss with them. The document, in both English and Hebrew, was entitled "Olympic Team Israel: The Roadmap to Gold." It set out our goals, a detailed timetable and what needed to be done in the 10 months between October 2019 and the Olympic Games:

It included IAB's three main goals for Tokyo and immediately after:

- to win a medal;

- to build two fields in Israel;

- to double the number of players by September 2020.

I presented the following items related to the Olympics
- Logistical issues: roster and delegation sizes, eligibility, families in Tokyo, the opening ceremony, training in Tokyo, accommodations, baseball uniforms, laundry in Tokyo and transporting our baseball equipment

- IAB issues: players, coaches, staff selection; a roster cut-off date; sponsorships and fundraising; public relations and social media; recruitment of players; growing local involvement and player numbers

Specifically, the following needed to be achieved and time was short:
- New player recruitment

- Fundraising – with the JNF, Jewcer, Jewish Federation, Maccabi, AIPAC and individual donors who we could turn to and helped us in the past.

- Sponsorships – SodaStream, Mizuno and others

- Events – both in Israel and the US to promote the team, to fundraise, to raise awareness and to get Israel baseball on the Israeli sports map.

- Visits to Israel to promote the team, the games, the IAB and get Israeli fans interested.

- Training camps to prepare the team.

- Staff to get on board.

- Merchandising and an IAB on-line store to sell our gear.

- Uniforms and other team swag

- Movie rights – *Heading Home* was so successful that we had to have a sequel to it.

- Hosting families in Tokyo and game tickets – this had the potential to be a huge headache.

- Flights to Tokyo.

- Player stipends so they can train on their own.

- Speaking engagements for me, for Holtz and for the players.

The budget I prepared was close to $350,000, plus stipends for the players and staff for 10 months until the Olympics.

All of this, and more, had to be done in 10 months, by myself, Holtz, the rest of the IAB's executive board, our coaches and players and the Olympic staff. It was an overwhelming task and let's not forget that I'd practically abandoned my paying job for the previous nine months in preparing to qualify for the Olympics. I never really thought through what would happen if we really did qualify.

The timetable heading to Tokyo was as follows:

- November 2019: Six new players will get citizenship. The Premier 12 tournament would be played, where, potentially, all five of the other Olympic teams would participate.

- January 2020: More than 20 players and staff will visit Israel. At that time, top MLB players not connected to Israel, were scheduled to visit the country: Carlos Santana, Sandy Alcantara and Amed Rosario.

- March 2020: American Israel Public Affairs Committee's conference in Washington, D.C, with fundraising opportunities and spring training appearances.

- July 2020: A two-week barnstorming mini-camp tour and fundraising opportunities.

- July 22, 2020: Leave for Tokyo

- July 25–28, 2020: Exhibition games in Japan

- July 29 to August 8, 2020: Baseball tournament at the Olympics

- February 2021: WBC tournament

With all the work that had to be done to prepare for Tokyo, I made the difficult decision to resign as IAB's president to focus 100 percent of my efforts on the team. There was so much to do, and a successful Olympic run could push Israeli baseball into the category of popular sports in this country, where soccer and basketball long resided. I was not happy to resign, as I still had a great deal to accomplish as president, but I also realized that I needed to focus all of my free time on the team and the impact it could have on Israeli baseball. I realized that my own job, as VP of Marketing and Exports would suffer, but I figured that it was only 10 months and could be overcome after the Olympics. I was confident that Jordy Alter, IAB's vice president at the time, could take over and capably run the operations. Indeed, he has succeeded through very troubled waters.

On the IAB's Website, Jordy wrote this back then:

> Peter dedicated himself to making the vision of sending a baseball team from Israel to the Olympic Games in 2020 a reality, and achieved what most would not believe possible. The task of Team Israel's general manager in the coming months will be immense, and we respect the decision that Peter has made to place his full focus on this crucial role and hopefully bring home the gold. His contributions to Israeli baseball over the past years have been innumerable, and he will continue to play a major role in his new position.

I chimed in there as follows:

> It has been my honor to have served over the past six years as president of the IAB. As president, I was able to expand Israeli baseball into the global arena, reaching number six in the world at the World Baseball Classic in 2017 and now, earning a place at the 2020 Olympic Games, which have been great accomplishments. I now look forward to fully investing my time and energy in ensuring that Israel is represented at the Tokyo Olympics by the best and most well-prepared baseball team possible.

In my regular meetings with the Israeli Olympic Committee through the fall, more and more of the committee's regulations regarding the team at Tokyo were uncovered and discussed.

Everything had to be negotiated. I originally asked for a staff of 15 people, in the end compromising on nine. The Israeli Olympic Committee wanted me to use its trainers who really knew nothing about baseball-related injuries, but in the end, I brought our trainers, Rootenberg and Rosenblatt. The committee didn't want the team to arrive for the opening ceremony, but in the end agreed to accommodate us. The committee agreed to purchase plane tickets from our U.S. mini-camp in July directly to Tokyo, but then offered to provide us with an amount per player and allow us to book the plane tickets on our own.

Everything was done in the spirit of cooperation and the desire to create the best conditions for the team, but I often felt like a kid at the Passover Seder who didn't even know what to ask for. The Israel Olympic Committee was unfamiliar with the process, too, as we were a "team" of 24 as yet unidentified athletes, not individual athletes they recognized and could connect to, since the experience for the previous 44 years was to not have a team representing Israel at the Olympics.

In November 2019, we brought five players on aliyah to join our ranks for the Olympics: Ryan Lavarnway, Josh Zeid, Scotty Burcham, Jared Lakind and Jake Fishman. Lavarnway was a catcher and powerful bat, and he and Burcham, at shortstop, would shore up our middle defense, while pitchers Fishman and Lakind would help support the bullpen. I wasn't entirely sure if Zeid could come back and pitch after three years away, but if anyone had the heart and desire to do it, it was he. Unfortunately, I was in Tokyo at the WBSC Congress and, by the time I returned, had only one day to spend with them, but Margo Sugarman, the IAB secretary general, arranged their whole stay in Israel. At one stage, one player's documents was questioned and there were trans-Atlantic calls and panic buttons set off with the parents, aunt and uncle to clarify matters, but it worked out in the end. The team was set, less one superstar who would join us the following year.

During my December visit to the US, I met with Elise Holman, Senior Vice President with the World Champion Washington Nationals, and we agreed upon an exhibition game in which they'd face Olympic Team Israel at the start of spring training. The Nationals are owned by the Lerner family, Jewish and Zionists, with whom we'd had many discussions over the years about supporting the IAB. What could be a more appropriate "coming out" for our team, and the National's Jewish ownership were very much in favor of this gesture.

My concern was fielding a competitive team that early in spring training, but since this would be the first game for the Nats, it was not that crucial. I just needed to get at least 20 players to West Palm Beach for three or four days, and was sure that whatever fundraising we did around that game would be substantial. We were discussing a golf tournament, a screening of the film *Heading Home*, inviting Israeli Ambassador Ron Dermer to meet owner Ted Lerner and even dreamt of Sandy Koufax showing up. The owner of Big League Chew bubble gum was even ready to launch "Hebrew Chew" for the event. Unfortunately, the game was never played due to the Covid crisis.

In January 2020, a visit to Israel was held for all the players and staff who could come to Tokyo. This was before we were sure what the final roster would be. We housed the team in a top-notch hotel on Rothschild Street in the center of Tel Aviv, and they had a blast. All the athletes had to have full medical check-ups in Israel at the Wingate Institute, the country's premier sports training center, so we shuttled them to nearby Netanya.

We also arranged for the Israel Olympic Committee to brief the players on what to expect in Tokyo, what the conditions in the Olympic Village would be like (dormitory rooms and suites, and not the five-star hotels the major leaguers were accustomed to), what their obligations were as Olympic athletes representing Israel, media and public-relations matters and security. They also partook in the Olympic Experience, a multimedia show at the committee's headquarters.

In Jerusalem, we organized for them a meeting with President Reuven Rivlin. At his official residence, we lined up on a stage in size order, and I was told to sit in the front row and found to my surprise that it was next to Rivlin. He was meeting with Sylvan Adams, a Canadian-Israeli billionaire who'd donated a bit to our cause and whom I hope to cultivate for a greater role, being that he's deeply involved in Israeli sports. I presented Rivlin with a jersey and a team-signed baseball. He asked a few questions of us, pictures were snapped and everything was over in 10 minutes. Rivlin is known to be a sports fan, but he knows nothing about baseball and did not express much of an interest in the sport, in our medal chances in Tokyo or in the group of primarily new immigrants he was meeting. It was really a photo-op for him and the team, and part of our obligations as Israeli Olympians.

Danny Grossman was able to arrange for Holtz, Lowengart, Moscot, Penprase, Glasser and myself to visit patients at Tel Hashomer Hospital and provide encouragement to them. There is a poignant scene in the documentary *Israel Goes for Gold* of Moscot meeting with an IDF soldier facing very difficult rehabilitation. Moscot is holding the soldier's hand

and giving him a team polo shirt, bringing some sunshine into his life. It is one of many emotional moments in the movie.

We arranged a press conference at the Israel Olympic Committee that was attended by over 20 Israeli journalists. Lustig and Oren sat on my left, while Holtz and the players were to my right. Watching the press vying for position in front of our Olympic team was a refreshing experience. We had finally succeeded in getting a forum for baseball with the Israeli press, and I was loving every minute of it. The journalists hung on every word. The Web site One ran the event live. The players and I were all in our Olympic polo shirts, made specifically for this visit and we couldn't have asked for a better cro wd.

I opened my words at the press conference in Hebrew with, "There is baseball in Israel and there is *good* baseball in Israel!" I said in my opening remarks. "We have more than 1,000 kids and adults playing baseball in Israel, and we want to double that number with the exposure of baseball in the Olympics. It's true that our Olympic team is composed of many new American *olim* [immigrants], but we also have *sabras* who grew up in our program. On top of that, our U–18 national team just won the European championship's B Pool, all with Israeli athletes who grew up in our program in Israel."

I spoke about building new fields, in Raanana and Beit Shemesh, that will bring out more players. I stated that when I told the committee two years before about foreseeing an Israeli baseball team playing in the Tokyo Olympics, they thought I was dreaming.

"I want to come back from Tokyo with a medal, and to bring a team to the Olympics in Los Angeles in 2028," I told the press. "I am optimistic that with this Olympics exposure, baseball will expand in Israel even more."

Lustig said, "The exposure of baseball is important. They did the unbelievable, and because of them, we will have the largest Olympic delegation ever: over 80 athletes. The Israeli athletes have proven that they can rise to the occasion. It is an unusual and dramatic event having a ball team make it to the Olympic Games. The team that sits here is one of the six best teams in the world and all the credit goes to the players and the staff, and especially Peter."

Importantly, Lustig added that "we have to take advantage of this to leverage the growth of baseball in Israel. I have no doubt that each of these athletes will represent us in the best possible manner."

Eric Holtz thanked everyone "who turned this dream into reality," including the players. "No one gave us a chance, but we did what we had to do and shocked the world. It doesn't matter who we play against. We will always play with the same attitude and approach. This is a once-in-a-lifetime opportunity."

Catcher Tal Erel, one of the few sabras on the team, spoke (in Hebrew) for the players: "We had a long road to reach this point. Our faces look towards Tokyo 2020, and we hope that we will succeed there. We have the ability to do something very special."

I told the Israeli journalists what I'd told them and the foreign press before, about naysayers like ESPN, which compared Team Israel to the 1988 Jamaican bobsled team, had underestimated us. Yet, we went 4–2 and finished in sixth place at the 2017 WBC. I talked about being in the "B" Pool of European Baseball in 2019, and people looked at me like I was a crazy man, talking about making the Olympic qualifiers. We had a good and complete squad of players, all pulling for one another, all egos left behind with a powerful mix of Israeli confidence and Jewish *kop*. We had MLB veterans, alongside college players and career minor leaguers playing with independent-league ballplayers. We had strong pitching, and that's always the first requirement in short tournaments. We were a smart team that talked about stock trading and world strategy on bus rides, and baseball statistics like OPS, WAR and WHIP in the dugout.

At the Olympic committee's headquarters, Lustig provided the players a complete briefing on what to expect in the Olympic Village. I had prepared them already, but they appeared shocked at his words. On one hand, they appreciated the opportunity to be in the select cohort of Olympic athletes to walk on this earth. On the other hand, they were used to much better conditions and settings, and to hear they would be housed in dormitories, sleeping on carton beds, eating in a glorified lunch room, exercising in a crowded gym, waiting for buses to go everywhere and washing their own laundry and carry their own equipment – that quickly brought them all down to earth. But those were the conditions in the Olympic Village.

There was some bitching and I tried to make improvements where I could, but most took it in stride and understood that this was what the Olympics were about. With the later covid restrictions making life even more difficult, this was certainly not the experience many of us expected.

The players held clinics throughout the country, making appearances in front of almost all the IAB youth players in Israel.

As Danny Grossman reported in *The Jerusalem Report*: : "During a 16-hour trip up North, players joined Israeli kids from Jewish and Arab backgrounds in playing catch – perhaps the most psychologically rewarding activity based on sharing an equal exchange. In Raanana, the kids were thrilled when Valencia spontaneously Face Timed his buddy, Manny Machado who last year became the MLB's first $300 million free agent. Not only did Machado graciously mention that he was traded for one of the Israeli players (Dean Kremer), but he took great delight when a 16-year-old Israeli shortstop cockily announced that he was gunning for Machado's position. Machado later tweeted his good-natured offer to slide over and play Third Base to make room for our young hopeful."

The event in Raanana was supposed to be at the Baptist Village, but due to inclement weather, we had to move it indoors at a local gym. It was a huge success, with more than 300 kids attending. The players were arranged in stations, and we rotated the kids to let them talk to each player, get autographs and take selfies. The kids were thrilled to be with Israeli Olympians, and our players were exhilarated to meet them and feel their adoration. It was quite successful on all fronts.

The visit to Israel gave our Olympians the opportunity to once again feel the country, see what a glorious place Israel is and to reach out to their ardent fans. It solidified their commitment to the Holy Land and justified the steps they would be taking. Some were in the midst of their baseball careers, and this commitment had some adverse effect by interrupting their offseason, a time to recover from the beating their bodies normally took. For others, it was the pinnacle of their careers. For the Israeli kids, it was a chance to meet future Olympians, superstars in a sport they knew very little about but would hopefully learn to love in the coming months. The media was mostly sympathetic, although there were pockets of resistance. Mostly, I felt confident that if the team could bring home a medal, they would be even more warmly embraced.

The players were concerned at this stage where the funding would come from. They saw our difficulties in dealing with the Israeli Olympic Committee. They expected to be treated as they were by MLB in the WBC: business-class plane tickets, five-star hotels, generous per diems. I did my best to dampen those expectations, but these were professional ballplayers, and they had certain standards, unlike the amateur Olympians in sports where budgets were much smaller and expectations lower. There were some miscommunications, and this led to some bad feelings on both sides, but those were also quickly forgotten.

For a final polish of the Olympic roster, I really wanted to enlist Ian Kinsler. He had just retired from a 14-year MLB career, and I was hoping that this was the right opportunity to finish his playing career. Kinsler would be our most decorated player, having been an All-Star four times and two-time Gold Glove winner at second base. He won a World Series and a WBC championship. I was convinced that a player of his pedigree would substantially increase our chances for an Olympic medal. Once I got to know him, I was even more certain of that, and he has become an integral part of our organization.

I contacted Ian in January 2020 after he announced his retirement. He was all-in. He filled out the paperwork for making *aliyah* and we planned on him visiting Israel in April. Then in the beginning of March, I realized that some dreaded virus, the virus that became Covid-19, started to spread in China and the western United States. Fearing that the crisis might ruin those travel plans, we arranged for him and his wife, Tess, to come the following week. We spoke when they landed in transit in New York. The Kinslers were concerned that they wouldn't be allowed into Israel, but, without thinking twice, I allayed their concerns and told them to come. On March 9, the eve of Purim, they landed. That was at 4:00 p.m. Two hours later, Prime Minister Benjamin Netanyahu announced that anyone arriving after 8:00 p.m. had to be in quarantine. The Kinslers, fortunately, missed by four hours having to be in quarantine! Unreal. The planning was perfect.

They were great travelers, staying in the Dan Tel Aviv, along with maybe 10 other guests. The city's streets were filled with Purim revelers, the last hurrah before Covid-19 hit in full force. We all went out to dinner that evening with Emily Rosuck, a close friend of theirs from Dallas, the Kinslers' home. Rosuck was living in Israel at the time, and she made them feel much more comfortable about the situation. Amit joined us and connected right away with the Kinslers. We went to Jerusalem with Danny Grossman, who acted as the tour guide on visits to Yad Vashem, the Western Wall, the Old City and got the full tour of Jerusalem.

The next day, we were scheduled to go to the interior ministry so Ian could be issued his Israeli passport. I was called that morning and was asked if he had arrived from the United States recently. I answered in the affirmative and was told that their doors would be closed to him and unfortunately, they could not be received at the ministry. I was in shock and tried to convince the ministry official that we had no other opportunity, that he was be an Olympian for Team Israel here on a short visit. The official acquiesced on one condition: that he wear a surgical mask and gloves, which today seems natural, but at that time was unheard of. Ian laughed and said it was not a problem.

We bundled him up to go, dressed for the part. He received his passport on the spot, a lot quicker than those before him, as the ministry wanted him out of the office as quickly as possible. He took his physical at Wingate, then we went to the Baptist Village field to make a short video to reveal that he was now an Israeli Olympian. While there, he spent four hours running a clinic and working with our youth athletes, loving every minute of it.

The next day was stormy, so instead of a baseball field, Ian came to a school to speak to two classes of kids. We could barely drag him away to go to the airport to fly home. It was a whirlwind visit, but "Kins" is a very impressive guy and would be a huge addition to the team. I loved our defense up the middle, with Lavarnway behind the plate, Kinsler and Burcham at second and shortstop, and Gailen in center.

This is what I texted to the Kinsler's as they left Israel:

Dear Ian and Tess,   Your visit to Israel has come to an end and you have made a lot of wonderful friends here and truly impressed a lot of people. I thank you both for coming this distance, for being such great troopers, for being so flexible and accommodating, for just being truly good people. I had a wonderful time hosting you and showing you this amazing country through our eyes, and I know you appreciate Israel much, much more now because of that. I have made two wonderful new friends, and together we will be in Tokyo and the U.S. barnstorming. I really look forward to all our adventures together as a team with you two now on board. Have a great trip home, warmest regards to your kids and your dad Ian, and I do hope to see you both in Dallas in May at the fundraiser. Safe travels, guys!

They replied: "Thank you, thank you, thank you, Peter! Our trip was a true lighthouse moment, and we plan on coming back again and again. The different things and people that we have encountered have changed our life! Talk soon!"

Kinsler was quoted as follows by reporter Adi Rubenstein in *Yisrael Hayom* on April 8, 2020: "Every athlete dreams of playing in the Olympics and I am very happy that I now have the opportunity to do so for Team Israel. It is quite emotional for me to wear the blue-and-white colors of Israel, way beyond the game itself. The opportunity to represent this county, as well as my roots, is very meaningful for me. I can't wait for the games to begin!"

Kinsler was later quoted by *JTA*: "Medaling for Team Israel would create that buzz and obviously bring more attention to the sport. So, it's exciting to think about all that."

Covid-19

And then, Covid hit, and hit hard. At first, in March, we thought it would pass quickly, or at least we hoped so. But life in Israel kept shutting down, and then came the quarantine, and quickly afterwards we were limited to being within 100 meters from home and the world became a much different place. Although it had hit the West Coast of the United States, there was still hope, as it had not spread further and seemed to be waning even in the Far East.

Those first few weeks with Covid were very traumatic for everyone who went through it — really, anyone on this planet. So much was unknown and mysterious, and the terrible pictures — coffins piling up in the churches in Italy, people dropping dead in the streets of China, refrigerated trucks outside a New York hospital — made everyone wonder how insignificant their lives had become. Wiping down the outside of groceries before bringing them into your home was just one of the precautions that people took, myself included, until we realized that Covid does not spread that way. I stayed home for weeks at a time, and the only exercise that I got was walking 100 meters outside of my apartment building, back and forth on the same street, making sure to avoid anyone who was walking their dog or was also out for exercise. The streets were deserted, there were no cars, and you could drive to the Tel Aviv beach in less than five minutes —but no one wanted to go there. At one point, for my sanity's sake and to exercise prior to going to Tokyo in July (or so I thought), I walked up and down flights of stairs, reaching 200 floors (100 each way) in my four-floor apartment house. Neighbors thought I was crazy. Ronit and I would cook food for the kids, then pack it all up in our car and make the run to all three of their homes in Tel Aviv, to at least see them for a few fleeting moments and make sure all was okay. Of course, all of this was done with gloves and surgical masks squarely in place. The Passover holiday was conducted over video rather than in person, so it was a very sad holiday, indeed.

For the first few months, I had little communication with the players, as everyone, of course, was concerned for themselves and their families. Guys were trying to work out on their own as best as they could. On May 7, we held the first of many team zoom calls on video, and the players would relate their experiences, how they were coping and what kind of remedies they were suggesting to overcome the burden and loneliness. These were important sessions for me and, I am sure, for the players and staff, because they kept us going and hopeful that soon we would all be together in Tokyo.

I knew that I would be the first person to get a vaccine. I was never afraid of shots or needles and, being over 60, considered a vulnerable age group, I wanted to make 100 percent sure that I was protected from that destructive virus. On December 22, 2020, I was among the first people in Israel, after the medical emergency teams, to get the Covid vaccine, and I have gotten all the boosters since then. I was not going to take any chances, and I certainly did not believe the doomsday predictions of the terrible consequences of the vaccines. My family and I trusted modern medicine and especially this new vaccine. I did come down with Covid much later, in February 2022, and was bed-ridden for a few days, but, knock on wood, that was the only time I got it. Let's hope it stays that way .

On March 24, after New York was hit very hard and Israel was just starting to recover, the International Olympic Committee announced that the Olympics would be postponed for one year. That was like a knife in my gut, but it was the right thing to do. Looking back now, although our team was one year older, and many guys did not play during the layoff, we got stronger and were focused more on the result and not just the process. On every zoom call we had (Who even heard of Zoom before?), the guys were psyched to play, ready to advance and win a medal. One video call centered on who was doing what in the spring, with guys like Gailen speaking from a hotel room in Sydney, where he was in quarantine for the upcoming Australian baseball season and where he stayed in shape for the Olympics. I looked forward to the challenges of the next 250 days to get the team ready and raise funds and awareness.

On our web site, Margo Sugarman, the IAB secretary general, highlights the date the Olympics should have started (July 24, 2020) by extensively quoting our players and myself:

> Today was the day that every Team Israel baseball player had marked on his calendar since September 22, 2019, when they danced off the field at Nino Cavalli Stadium in Parma, Italy, having clinched a berth at the 2020 Olympic Games. On Friday night, the 24 men on the Team Israel roster were to march into Tokyo's Olympic Stadium for the opening ceremony, thus experiencing another dream come true in their collective Cinderella story. Days later, they would take the field for the first time and challenge for their ultimate goal, winning an Olympic medal.

Alas, the Covid-19 pandemic put those dreams on hold. The Summer Games were postponed by one year and will now begin on July 23, 2021. It has created an interesting dynamic for Team Israel's players. The group is still tight and gets together for regular zoom calls, while each pursues his baseball path to ensure they will be in peak form when they get to Tokyo, which is no easy task in the wake of the virus, with lockdowns and league and team closures around the world. But they all know that baseball is secondary in the battle against the pandemic. "At this time, my thoughts are that I'm happy that everyone is safe and healthy," Coach Eric Holtz shared earlier this week. "It's an incredible shame that we will not be leaving for Tokyo as planned, but everyone will continue to train and remain ready for the first time the umpire screams, 'Play Ball!'

Coach Holtz's players echoed their leader's sentiments, though each reflects on the fact that the games were scheduled to start now in his own way. "It's crazy to think we should be in Tokyo right now," said Danny Valencia, who with nine seasons in the major leagues is one of Team Israel's most accomplished players. "I try to envision what I'd feel like over there both in sport and with my family. I know we were all doing our part in being as prepared as possible to compete for a gold medal. I was feeling really good in a baseball sense. Hopefully we can get past this pandemic and reset with clear minds and figure out how to be better than what we are today, come this time next July."

"It doesn't feel real that today would have been the opening ceremony. We're so far removed and so much has happened. The thing I keep coming back to is that everyone all over the world has their own 'would have been' or 'supposed to,' so I try to keep perspective and be thankful for the things we do have," the team's ace pitcher Joey Wagman said. "I cannot wait for next summer. It just adds another challenge for this team, which has already overcome so many. It gives us another year to prepare in every way and represent Israel to the best of our abilities."

Blake Gailen: "It's going to be one of the greatest experiences of all of our lifetimes and I can't think of a better group to share that with." Gailen is one of the few who has already put the 2020 Games out of his mind and is only looking forward. "It's crazy how quickly we adapt because the notion of going to the Olympics this year slipped my mind once we knew for sure it was postponed. ... As surreal as it's been to qualify for the Olympics, it's hard to imagine that a year from now we are going to be at the opening ceremony," he said. "I'm fairly certain that I can speak for everyone in saying that there aren't really words to describe the excitement and anticipation that are leading up to next year's Olympic Games. It's not just about playing; it's going to be one of the greatest experiences of all of our lifetimes and I can't think of a better group to share that with."

The postponement of the Games has been bittersweet for three of the best players Israel's local leagues have ever produced. Alon Leichman, a pitching coach in the Seattle Mariners system; and college baseball players Tal Erel and Asaf Lowengart, who had their respective 2020 seasons in the United States taken away. However, that has opened the door for them to take on integral roles with the Israel Association of Baseball by playing in the local premier league while coaching and mentoring the next generation of stars.   Alon Leichman: "I prefer to focus on the positives. ... I know that the one-year delay will only make the fire in our team burn stronger.   I imagine that walking into the Olympic Stadium for the opening ceremony will be one of the greatest moments of my athletic career," Leichman said. "I have an uneasy feeling when I think about the fact that we would be in Tokyo now under normal circumstances. However, I prefer to focus on the positives. I embrace the time I get to spend at home with my family and the time coaching and playing with the guys in Israel. I view this time as a unique opportunity to train in Israel and at the same time help get more exposure to the sport. It's been amazing. And I know that the one-year delay will only make the fire in our team burn stronger before we go to Japan next year."

No man has a deeper perspective on how far Israel baseball has come to be in the position it is now than team Israel GM Peter Kurz. "Its been a long road to reach where we are today as Olympians, starting with the IBL in 2007 and continuing on to our three appearances in the World Baseball Classic and our frequent appearances in European championships B- and C-pool tournaments. The guys have played under insurmountable baseball conditions, and to play in four tournaments last summer in a span of 10 weeks and come out as one of six Olympic teams was the highlight of my 20-year career with the IAB so far.   I look forward to the next chapter, and although it's frustrating to wait an additional year, it's something all Olympic athletes need to deal with. Our players are keyed up and aiming towards July 2021, and I have no doubt they will be ready. It's also given us an opportunity to improve the team, adding Ian Kinsler; WBC Team Israel alumnus Ryan Lavarnway, who was our MVP in South Korea in 2017; and Scotty Burcham, who got the winning hit against South Korea in that tournament and played a stellar shortstop. It has also given us an extra year of fundraising for the IAB and our goal of developing fields all over Israel and increasing the number of players in Israel two-, three- and four-fold. It is for them that we are playing in the Olympics, and I do hope that today there are kids playing in Beit Shemesh, Raanana and Tel Aviv who will be on the roster of the Israeli Olympic team in Los Angeles in 2028."

As March, April and May rolled along, the preparations for the Olympics and the two-week minicamp became much more intense. I was working with the Israel Olympic Committee — Lustig, Oren, Kobi Solomon, Lihi — in making all the incredibly complex arrangements. They included Covid testing procedures, 96 and 72 hours before flights; downloading apps for contact tracing and recording temperature and god knew what else; ordering uniforms; securing accommodations in the Olympic Village; arranging funding from Israel's sports ministry; and countless other tasks needing to be done.

I worked with Adam Gladstone and his team in preparing the mini-camp and barnstorming tour: venues, protocols, merchandising, equipment, staff, budget — and it was all money, money and more money. I was coordinating with Lou Rosenberg from the JNF's Los Angeles office to raise funds for Project Baseball: from video calls with donors, to shmoozing people and getting the players to come on board.

Stuart, our travel agent, was helping me make all the plane reservations to Tokyo and back, dealing with the idiosyncrasies of the players, trying to make sure that any changes could be made easily and inexpensively — and always staying within budget.

With the players, I needed to meet their needs, but also balance them against the good of the team.

I worked with Jordy Alter, Yaron Erel, Amit and the IAB's board to make sure everything was done transparently and legitimately and would not come back to haunt the IAB. Everything was done to pave the way to growing baseball in Israel, the goal we all had.

It was a 48/7 job, and I did it all and somehow kept my sanity. Barely, and continued my work as the VP of Exports of Hamat............

In June, one month before the Games, a very moving ceremony was held with many of Israel's Olympic athletes at the Tel Aviv memorial site to the 11 Israelis murdered in a terrorist attack at the 1972 Olympic Games. I attended as the lone baseball representative. Many of the family members of the Munich 11 were there as well. The gathering was held prior to every Olympics, and in addition to telling the story again and again, they told us how proud they were of the accomplishments of our Olympians, and wished us luck in the games.

Some context: Munich was the first Olympics held in Germany since the Berlin Games in 1936, famous for the four gold medals won by African-American sprinter Jesse Owens, embarrassing Hitler and his Aryan-supremacy principle in his own capital. Little known is that standing to Owens's right on the Olympic podium, having earned a silver medal, was another black athlete named Mack Robinson, brother of Jackie.

At 4:30 a.m. on September 5, 1972, more than a week into the Munich Games, a Palestinian terrorist group, affiliated with the Black September terrorists, entered the Olympic village disguised as athletes. Using stolen keys, they forced their way into the Israeli team's quarters, murdered Yossef Romano, a weightlifter, and Moshe Weinberg, a wrestling coach. Nine other members of Israel's team were taken hostage, and the terrorists demanded the release of more than 200 Palestinians from Israeli prisons and of Andreas Baeder and Ulrike Meinhof, the leaders of the Red Army Faction terrorist group, from German prisons.

The German authorities' handling of the Munich crisis was flawed and tragic. As if heavily armed terrorists' infiltration of the Olympic Village wasn't negligent enough, the security forces' attempt to raid the quarters and rescue the hostages had to be called off when the terrorists were alerted of the plan by TV news coverage. A second attempt, at the Fürstenfeldbruck Air Base after the athletes had been transferred there via helicopter, was so incompetent as to stagger the mind and begged the question: Just how serious were the German authorities about any rescue scenario? Members of a SWAT team, waiting inside the passenger jet that was supposed to take the terrorists and hostages to an undisclosed destination in the Middle East, decided they weren't qualified for such an operation and abandoned the plane. They were probably right about their abilities, but for reasons that defy explanation, they did so without informing anyone.

During the firefight after the terrorists realized the plane had no pilot, a German sniper was shot by a fellow sniper because the two had been positioned facing each other on opposite sides of the strip on which the helicopters from the Olympic Village had landed. Grenades were thrown into the helicopters before anyone could get to them, killing eight of the nine hostages. David Berger, the ninth, died of smoke inhalation.

That is how the 11 Olympians — athletes, coaches and referees — were killed. After a brief postponement, the Olympics continued. Some of the victims' family members would be attending the Tokyo Games, and there was hope that for the first time after 49 years, the IOC would a minute of silence to honor the Munich 11 at the opening ceremony. Hope, but no assurance.

* * *

On July 1, 2021, Ronit and I boarded the United Airlines flight to Newark Airport for the start of a journey that I had no idea what the end would be, but I was excited for it to begin. We drove on to upstate New York for some much-needed R&R prior to the craziness I knew I would face for six weeks. We had planned a team training camp in the Rockland County town of Pomona for a few days, and then a barnstorming tour that would take us up and down the East Coast to play against minor league and amateur teams. The intention was for the players to practice and compete in preparation for the Tokyo Olympics and to galvanize American Jewish baseball fans behind Team Israel's efforts, thereby raising funds for Israeli baseball. We succeeded in both.

Our original roster for Tokyo contained 44 potential names, which we'd have to cut to 24 for the final travel roster. We included some players on the expanded roster to honor what they had done in the past for Israel baseball and preserve pride in their role. We took 28 players with us to the United States, knowing that four would have to be left behind. Of the final squad, nine were ex-MLB players, 12 played on the 2017

WBC team, six came from the 2019 U–18 qualifying team and four were *sportaim* (classified in Israel as elite athletes). We had our team.

On July 7, I arrived with Ronit at the Boulders stadium, at Palisades Credit Union Park, in Pomona. Anticipation was felt in the air as Gladstone and his staff were getting the clubhouse ready for the players' arrival the next day. Seeing uniforms hanging in lockers, boxes of baseballs prepared for signing and players coming into the clubhouse, were all sights to be beholden. I stepped onto the concourse of the stadium and the fresh green grass of the field laid out in front of me (OK, it's actually artificial turf), really made me feel at home, knowing that the show was about to begin. It was great to see Shawn Reilly, the manager of the facility and a man who treated us like royalty during our stay there. It was great seeing all the players later, at the Sheraton in nearby Mahwah, after such a long and unplanned break.

We all had a lot of catching up to do. We held practices the next three days, and everyone projected enthusiasm and excitement.

And then, Covid hit........

Jordy organized Shabbat *kiddush* and dinner on Friday, July 9. Everyone wore their nicest clothes, some coming with spouses and kids. My friends Andy and Julie Sandor were due to arrive, and we were going out to have dinner together, following the kiddush.

Then the call came from Tal Erel, who was waiting outside the hotel. He informed me that he just tested positive for Covid. Oyyyy.... He felt fine, but this was only the start of what would weigh heavily on us over the next few weeks.

I went out to meet him, making sure to stay 50 meters away. We talked, I verified his story, and consulted with Gladstone, Rootenberg and Weinberg. First thing we did was call Assaf Lowengart, Erel's roommate, to tell him to move his luggage to another room. He was understandably in shock by the news. We said he needed to get tested and stay in isolation for now. I then called Zach Penprase so that he and his family, the only ones unvaccinated, could leave the dinner and temporarily quarantine in their room (The Penprase' s were the only ones in camp who were not vaccinated).

We then went into the dinner, and I made an announcement and told everyone what had just happened and cautioned that we all needed to be extra-careful now. There was an eerie silence as everyone soaked up what was just said and slowly began to understand the repercussions – that we might not be travelling to Tokyo at all, or at least not when we'd planned. I assured everyone that we still had two weeks until the flight, and emphasized that now was the time to watch over each other and protect ourselves. We began a series of rapid Covid tests that we purchased for hundreds of dollars in drugstores all over the northeast, including at the local CVS, where we walked out with 100 such kits, depleting the store's stock. We could have been an advertisement for rapid testing.

The next morning, Jordy conducted the testing in our team's hotel lounge, and all the results came out negative. Erel and Lowengart also tested negative, and we hoped we were over the hump. Everyone wore masks at all times outside the playing field and things were starting to look more optimistic. We would rapid test at least two more times, and each time, all the results were negative. Erel stayed behind in Pomona for two more days, just to be on the safe side, but joined us after receiving two more negative PCR tests. Unlike the test results, things were looking positive.

We continued the barnstorming tour with games in Pomona and Brooklyn. It was great getting on the field and into game action, seeing the guys jelling in the clubhouse. I made my rounds throughout the sold-out stands in Coney Island, shmoozing and mingling with the crowd of JNF supporters (its leaders, Russell Robinson and Mitch Rosenzweig, were in attendance), meeting the South Korean pitching coach who'd came to scout us and talking with Steve Cohen (the manager of the stadium, the Mets' A facility – and not THAT Steve Cohen); watching the police out in full force to deal with potential protestors. (None came.) We ate all the food brought to us in the clubhouse (including Nathan's Famous hot dogs). I soaked in the love and adulation of the very positive, supportive Jewish community, our 25th Player, as it were. As part of our fund-raising campaign, we asked our fans to be the "2 5th player" – our roster consisted of 24 players, and we used that expression to generate moral and financial support. It succeeded, as Jewish organizations sent fans by the busloads to watch us play, and the players got a kick out of hearing their names serenaded. They autographed balls, caps, *kippot* and programs — whatever the fans could get their hands on.

In Pomona, despite the pouring rain, a crowd of over 3,000 people remained enthusiastic, even when the weather shortened the game. The pregame ceremony, in which Shawn Reilly honored the 11 Israeli Olympic athletes murdered in Munich, was very moving. I was proud to be at the microphone, speaking on behalf of the team about the meaning of the sacrifice of those athletes. There was a protest outside the stadium, the only one we saw, with five Palestinians and five Netura Kartei anti-Israel *haredim*, that most people ignored. After a few minutes in the rain, the protestors left.

The next day, Amit left for Manhattan to meet Ronit, while I went to the USA office of my employer, Hamat, to meet with Peter Raleigh and the team. (I did occasionally work during these hectic months!) The three of us met for dinner in Chinatown, where by chance another, unrelated Kurz, Austrian Chancellor Sebastian Kurz, sat at the next table. I met the team in Hartford, Connecticut, where we'd be playing two games against the Class AA Yard Goats, hosted by the owner, Josh Solomon. The crowds were sparser, but no less enthusiastic, drawn to the games by the fundraisers of the JNF New England office, Sarah and Dar. Solomon and Tim Restall, the team's president, were the perfect hosts in the excellent facility.

After the second game, it was on to the next venue, Harrisburg PA, a 4-hour bus trip. We played the next morning at FNB field, home to the AA Nationals team, against the Cal Ripken All-Stars. We also played games in Harrisburg, Pennsylvania, where I met Mary Anne Schmitt, the chief executive officer of the Carey Health Solutions test lab, who were testing on behalf of Mt Sinai Hospital. She administered the first coronavirus testing, 96-hour tests, to be done of the players and staff on behalf of the Japanese authorities. All the players duly spit into their test tubes, the first of many tests and saliva swabs we would all go through, and submitted them. We also had to go through a long session on how to download the apps required by the Japanese authorities, how to fill them in and what to do. The players were cooperative, and really anxious to get to Tokyo. The test results for the 96-hour saliva test were all negative, and there was a collective sigh of relief as we passed the first hurdle after the scare from the week before.

The next day was Shabbat. We played a game in Lancaster at the home field of Blake Gailen, who played for them. From there, we drove to

Bethesda Maryland, outside Washington, D.C. Amit and I had a lovely evening at the home of my sister Ester, her husband John and their son David. John is a true baseball and Nats fan and always interested in how Team Israel is faring.

The next morning, we took a 72-hour Covid test. The guys came into the hotel's conference room prepared, their mouths full and loaded with saliva. We made our way later to the smallest facility we would play in, Shirley Povich Field, (capacity 800), named for a great sportswriter, to play the Bethesda Big Train, named for the great Washington Senators pitcher, Walter Johnson, who had lived in the area. We were hosted royally by their owner Bruce Adams, who has always been extremely supportive. The game started at 9:14 p.m., to allow for the fast day of Tisha B'Av to conclude. Our catcher, Ryan Lavarnway, rejoined the team, which made a big difference for our pitchers. A sold-out crowd watched, including the Washington Nationals owner Mark Lerner, who talked with Jordy and me until he left in the third inning. It was a great place to play ball, and the players had a lot of fun there. I felt that things were coming together and we would land in Tokyo ready to play.

Little did I know then how mistaken I was.......

Just before the team left the hotel the next morning, Mary Anne called to report that everyone but Andrew Lorraine had tested negative on the 72-hour Covid test. Ughhh. In the interim we had a meeting with players who would not make the travel team, and as soon as that was over, I informed Andrew and the coaching staff and told him that he would have to stay in Bethesda until we decided what to do. He and I were shocked and were unsure of how to proceed.

We drove to our eighth game, in nearby Aberdeen, stopping along the way for lunch at Jimmy's Famous seafood. On the bus, I updated the players about Lorraine. They were visibly upset due to the uncertainty that now surrounded the team. No one knew if the virus was spreading on the team and if we would be able to fly to Tokyo or not. We decided to keep this under wraps for the moment and immediately went to another CVS to buy more rapid tests. Everyone was tested and the results were all negative.   It was a very stressful time for the players and staff, and especially for me.

That was not enough for me, so I asked someone from the test lab to come to the field that evening and conduct an additional PCR test on everyone for our own internal use. I wanted to know if we had more infected people, rather than find out after we arrived in Tokyo and have to be in quarantine for two weeks. I was extremely anxious about that, as were the players, and we could neither enjoy the game nor the crowd that came. They included Marshall Einhorn of the Maccabi USA sports organization; Peter Raleigh and Ben Alliker with customers from Hamat USA; and ex-IAB players Justin Peedin and Alejandro Eskanazi. It was great to see them all, but I was preoccupied with the tests we were taking.

After the game, we drove to Long Island, arriving late at night. Visions of cancelling all the Tokyo-bound plane tickets were on my mind, as well as dealing with the repercussions of not making it to the Olympics. I barely slept.

Jordy was in touch with Lorraine (who subsequently tested negative on a rapid test) but the lab testers said that a false-positive reading was absolutely impossible, as his test had been checked twice. I asked Lorraine to drive to New York the next day to be retested. No one outside the team had a clue as to the storm within. We even heard rumors of more and more positive Covid cases in Tokyo and threats of cancelling the Olympics four days before the opening ceremony. The tension was high.

Cancellation was a real possibility. Less than 30 percent of the Japanese population was vaccinated. Many of the athletes were not, as it was not a requirement.

We were due to arrive at the field at 4:00 p.m. that afternoon. In the morning, I heard back from the test lab on the additional testing that we did, that everyone came out negative, except for one person, Danny Valencia. I felt my entire world collapsing, that everything I had worked so hard for over the last four years was being destroyed by the coronavirus. If Valencia had Covid, who would be next? I consulted with Jordy, Rootenberg and Gladstone and called Valencia, who was getting coffee with Jeremy Bleich, and asked them to rush back to the hotel. When I broke the news to Danny, his shoulders sagged and his confusion was apparent, his eyes anxious. That's just as I had felt. This could not be. I told him to go back to his room until we decided how to proceed.

We were all due to fly to Tokyo the next day. I was sure that all was lost now............

Jordy arrived and we went to speak to Valencia as everyone else left for the ballpark for our final game that evening. I will never forget the situation, not wanting to go into his room due to our own Covid concerns, and standing with him in the hallway, trying to decide together how to proceed. We spoke for close to an hour, and Valencia just wanted to return home to Miami while we tried to convince him otherwise. Eventually, we decided together that Valencia would join Lorraine in doing another PCR test at Mt. Sinai Hospital in Manhattan. We held out a sliver of hope that they were both false positive tests and we could make the flight that was coming up in less than 24 hours.

Jordy took Valencia to do the test and then to his hotel next to the airport, while I joined the team at the evening's game. The guys were depressed and concerned, but decided they had done enough testing, and what was to be was to be. We would fly to Tokyo with trepidation and concern but with the hope that a miracle could happen.

Amit and Adi came to the game on Long Island, and when I saw them both all my emotions came pouring out, and I cried on their shoulders as they hugged me and tried to reassure me. They brought me a lovely bobblehead doll of GM Peter Kurz and it really moved me, especially when I read the card that accompanied it from all three of my kids. It was a beautiful moment and I was very happy to have them with me, as it really helped me to rise above the situation. I cannot possibly thank them enough for that. It meant the world to me. I still had to cope with the situation at hand, but knowing I had the complete support of Ronit and my kids behind me was calming.

I went to bed after 2:00 a.m., exhausted, frustrated while at the same time, concerned and anxious.

At 5:00, I was awake. A miracle indeed happened. I had message from Michael Shahbaz from the test lab , an Iranian immigrant who was incredibly helpful to us (thank you Michael) but who also claimed that a false-positive test, now two of them, was impossible. Well, it was possible and it did happen. There are indeed, miracles and Team Israel was about to see one, as both Lorraine and Valencia now had negative test results.

We were all going to Tokyo!!!!

From the depths of despair to the heights of optimism, Team Israel was going to the Olympics with heads held high, without any Covid worries (there were some, but the players were very positive in themselves) and confident that if we could get through this, we could gain a gold medal.

We boarded the plane for our long flight to Tokyo. I had all the team's paperwork prepared in a folder and was prepared for any questions whatsoever. We flew together with members of the Dominican Republic and U.S. teams, and all of us were in a pensive mood.

Tokyo Olympics

We arrived in Tokyo and were met by staffers wearing gowns, surgical masks and gloves. There were signs all over, in Japanese, English and Spanish, directing us to different areas, warning us about violating protocol, and discussing the dangers of Covid, getting infected and passing it to others, and god knows what else. The Japanese love their signs. The scene was scary, eerie and quite unnerving, but we were in Tokyo, and that's what counted.

We were herded from place to place, told to wait for hours at a time. People stuck cotton swabs up our noses and in our mouths. After more than four hours in the airport, we were taken outside, asked to identify our bags that were transported directly to the Olympic Village and put on buses for the trip through Tokyo. This was not the same Tokyo that I remembered from previous visits. The streets were barren, except for small groups of people waving to us and those who greeted us as we entered the city, and the feeling was creepy and unearthly, like a science-fiction movie in which society was rebuilt after a near-apocalypse.

Arriving at the Olympic Village, we were taken to the Israeli delegation's building. The 14-story high rise also housed the Finnish delegation. The Israelis were relegated to the top four floors. In order to reach our floor (the baseball team was assigned the top floor), one had to take the elevator to the 11th floor (it was locked to prevent it rising any further), where Israeli security personnel were waiting. We had to pass through a facial-recognition system, which did not always work well, just to be able to go through the turnstiles. Only official members of the delegation were allowed to enter. The first floor of the delegation was made up of offices, clinics and some of the management staff's living quarters. The baseball team had to walk up three flights of stairs to reach our suites. It was a good thing I had done stair-walking during the pandemic, because now I was in shape for the three-story hike, made more than 20 times a day. It kept us all in shape but was also a great big pain in the ass.

We were provided dorm rooms, and I had carefully planned out a rooming list. We had multiple six- and eight-person suites, all with small rooms, two players per room, Japanese bathrooms, and a small, central seating area. The Japanese were very proud of their heavy carton beds that were recyclable. Each player had a small closet and nightstand. That was it. This was the Olympics, after all.

Kinsler, Valencia, and Holtz were assigned the only single rooms we had, while all the other members of the Israeli delegation had to double up, including Jordy and myself, who lived together in the same room for two weeks. Our view was of the dorms across the way, and a sliver of the Sea of Japan could be seen in the distance. The players were not thrilled, to say the least, but they had been warned about it, so they accepted it as the price of playing in the Olympic Games.

We were right across the street from the huge dining facility: two floors with hundreds of tables and plastic dividers to protect against the spread of Covid, making conversation or socializing impossible. It was all cafeteria-style, with a huge selection of Western, Eastern, Indian, South American, meat, vegetarian, vegan, kosher and God-knows-what-else types of food. The cafeteria was open 24/7 and you could come any time and as often as you liked and just eat. It wasn't always the most appetizing food, but certainly plentiful. There were all manner of drinks and desserts, and one had to wear disposable gloves before taking a tray. As was the case everywhere in the Olympic Village, there were plenty of Japanese hosts to herd you from place to place, explain what to do and help those who got lost. There were food deliveries that could be ordered from outside the Olympic Village, but not much of a need unless you got tired and fed up with all the Japanese sterility. The gym was a large facility with free weights, treadmills, stepping machines, mats and other equipment, but I barely used it. Athletes who were stronger, faster and more developed than I would ever hope to be were the primary users. I definitely felt out of place among them, unless they added stair climbing as an event.

There wasn't much to do in the Olympic Village if you weren't doing your sport or resting. You could walk around and see the other athletes, visit the waterfront to watch the boats, play ping pong, or go to the wildly overpriced store to buy souvenirs. You could watch the lone TV in the lobby of our building, which was almost always tuned to the Olympic channel, and the Israelis would gather around the set when their countrymen were competing. Avishag Samberg brought great cheers when she became the youngest Israeli medal winner by taking the bronze in taekwondo, and we watched gymnast Artem Dolgopyat win a gold medal in the men's floor exercise. Linoy Ashram won her gold medal on the last day of the tournament, when I was already home watching on my TV.

You could not attend other events or matches at all and were dissuaded from leaving the Olympic Village. There were guards at the gates to both keep the public out and us in. Athletes were trading pins with each other, but since contact was dissuaded, that didn't amount to very much. I did not collect any.

I guess boredom may have been behind what was eventually called Bedgate. Many delegations were uploading videos related to the Olympic Village and the carton beds. Some had people jumping on them to show how springy they were, while others focused on their strength. Ben Wanger sent me the video our players made, and my first impression was how professional it was done, with the voice-over fitting in perfectly to the action shown. The video showed how it took nine Team Israel baseball players to collapse a Tokyo Olympics carton bed. The video went viral. I saw it as a cute prank, done without malice and done well.

I was soon subjected to immense criticism from the Israeli press, the Japanese media and the Israeli Olympic committee, much of it I felt was totally unjustified and exaggerated. But it had to be dealt with, quashed and eliminated quickly from the conversations emanating from the Olympic Village. Of course, there was talk of these "immature Americans" dressed up as Israeli athletes, and I needed to show that they were indeed professionals who were serious about preparation and achievement in the Games. Our own media was particularly concerned with it and Lustig was irritated that in light of how tense everyone was from the strain of Covid, that this was what was being covered. Wanger recorded an apology that he uploaded to TikTok and started a fundraising campaign for Japanese mudslide victims. I apologized to the Japanese and Israeli Olympic committees; and the issue died, but it hasn't been forgotten.

Every morning, as we woke up, before even drinking anything, each delegation member had to spit his saliva into a test tube and wrap his identification sticker around it. By 10:00 a.m., the test tubes were taken for processing. Only once did Gili Lustig call me into his office to tell me that someone might have tested positive. It was Andrew Lorraine. I laughed and told him about what happened to us in the United States and said that I would bet on Lorraine's test coming out negative. He did need to immediately go to the isolated medical facilities to have more extensive testing, but returned a few hours later with a clean bill of health. That was our only real scare the whole time, and I was relieved that the ultimate responsibility was removed from my hands.

We bought a TV screen and a printer so that we could show the players videos of other teams and print pages of scouting reports. Alex Jacobs did a great job of providing the players with complete breakdowns on the opposing hitters and pitchers we would face, and we held daily strategy meetings in our suite.

Laundry was a huge problem. We used the Olympic Village's service the first few days, but had to wait two days for our clothing to return — but only 75 percent of the items submitted came back. We needed an alternative for the daily cleaning of our team's uniforms. Luckily, there was a public laundromat 500 meters outside the Olympic Village, and almost every day Jordy, Yaron and I were able to leave and wash the laundry for the team. It gave us something to occupy our time, provided an opportunity to see how the outside world was surviving and we could run to the supermarket for supplies. It was truly a psychological lifesaver for us, as it broke the oppressive monotony of being stuck inside our quarters.

The day after we arrived was the Opening Ceremony and as the guys tried to get over their jet lag, they also tried to fit into the outfits to be worn that evening, which were brought directly from Israel to Tokyo for them without being fitted in advance. These outfits were provided by Israel's largest retailer and fashion design house, Castro. My daughter Maya, the head of women's design for the company, led the Olympics-outfit project, and I was very proud to wear mine. Some were tight and some were loose, some were long and some were short, but we all more or less fit into them. Only players were allowed to march in the Opening Ceremony, but Lustig requested that I also join them and I was thrilled to do so. He wanted me marching in front, next to him and the two flag bearers: Hana Minenko, Israel's top triple jumper, and Yakov Toumarkin, Israel's top backstroke swimmer. I was provided special credentials to get in. The rest of the staff stayed back and watched on TV as the Israeli delegation loaded onto a bus to the Olympic stadium.

Who did I happen to see right behind me? Nate Fish was on the bus! Assisted by team members to avoid the prying eyes of the Japanese officials who checked all the credentials, he succeeded in joining us, to the amusement of everyone. It was Israeli determination and *chutzpah* at its best.

At the stadium, we were led into the bowels of the facility — deep bowels, for sure. The teams lined up in alphabetical order, so we were close to the Iranians, who evidently were under strict orders not to socialize with us, but also next to the Iraqis, whom we mingled with, and the Italians, who were lots of fun. At least here I did not have to hide my affiliation as I did at the first WBSC meeting in Tunisia. We waited for hours, with no place to sit and no food, but I knew that would happen from my experience at the Maccabiah Games' opening ceremonies. Finally, we moved forward and, upon entry, photographers' bulbs flashed in our faces. It took me a while to realize that we were in a 68,000-capacity facility, but with only a few thousand people in attendance due to Covid restrictions. This was mostly a made-for-television event, after all. Despite that, I felt enormous pride and gratification, marching at the head of the Israeli delegation, smiling and waving and making my own video of the ceremony. I looked behind me and saw Valencia, Lipetz, Bleich, Kinsler and others waving to imaginary people, smiling and laughing. Seeing them brought me great satisfaction. Walking next to Toumarkin and Minenko gave me an amazing feeling of elation and delight.

We rounded the stadium in procession and came to a stop as the official ceremony began. I don't remember much of it, but I do clearly recall I was moved by the minute of silence for the 11 Israeli athletes murdered at the Munich Olympic Games 49 years earlier. Allowing 49 years to pass without the murders ever being recognized at an Olympics was shameful. But the wrong was righted at "my" ceremony, and I was proud to be on hand. Thomas Bach, the International Olympic Committee's president *and a German* deserves credit for agreeing to this request, one made prior to every previous Olympics since the tragedy.

Only later did I learn that next to him stood Ankie Spitzer and Ilana Romano, the widows of two of the athletes, women who had been tirelessly working all that time toward this moment. The women later said in a joint statement: "Finally there is justice for the husbands, sons and fathers murdered at Munich. We went through 49 years of struggle and never gave up. We cannot hold back our tears. This is the moment we have waited for."

Until the very last minute, it was not known if the committee would agree to the latest request. The Israeli delegation knew only that it *might* happen. When that minute of silence was announced, my mind returned to the square in Tel Aviv where, just a month before, these same, strong women had told us to boldly go forth and live our dream and bring back Olympic medals, ensuring that the Munich 11 would always live on in our memories and hopes.

* * *

It would seem odd to call our opening game against South Korea a rematch of the opening game of the 2017 WBC. For one thing, South Korea only had two players from that Classic on their Olympic roster-catcher Euiji Yang and shortstop Jae-won Oh, teammates on the Korea Baseball Organization's Doonsan Bears. By contrast, our Olympic squad had 10 players who also played in that WBC, notably Ryan Lavarnway, Scott Burcham and Josh Zeid. Our significant additions included Kinsler and Valencia.

On the mound we had Jon Moscot, who had told Eric Holtz before joining the team that he had no idea how many more pitches he had left in his right arm, but he would throw them all for Israel if asked. After he did a stellar job in the qualifiers, we were confident that he was our ace, so Holtz tapped him as his opening-game starter. Moscot was looking to get back to the major leagues, and his performance on this world stage was a crucial first step in that direction. He was a true *mensch* and team leader, and I realized that my intuition about bringing him to Israel with the WBC players in 2017 and again in 2019, when making *aliyah*, was paying off. The man was a fighter, and I knew he would fight for Team Israel for as long as his arm would let him.

On the second hitter he faced in the bottom of the first inning, we found out exactly how many pitches he had left and the fight came to a shocking end.

After giving up a leadoff single, Moscot seized his elbow in pain and a collective gasp could be heard in the entire stadium, which was only me and Danny Grossman. He jumped around the mound in obvious agony and the training staff and Holtz immediately went to the mound.

Moscot tried to throw another pitch, but he could barely extend his arm, and Dan Rootenberg accompanied him off the field. After only a handful of pitches, our ace had again torn the ulnar collateral ligament in his right elbow, ending both his Olympic dreams and his playing career. And, without having collected an out, we were already into our bullpen. Our Olympic hopes disintegrated quickly.

I immediately went down to the clubhouse, greatly concerned not about Moscot's elbow – it was obvious that he was not coming back for this tournament – but about his psyche. I found Rootenberg sitting next to him as he was tightly holding his arm, in great pain, tears of frustration, anger and disappointment flowing down his cheeks. I gave him a big hug and told him that he helped get us this far and that he was a hero in my book. I reminded him that he gave his all on the field, and there was nothing he could do about the result, that he was loved by all the players, and we all appreciated his attitude and leadership. He looked up at me, with a very sad and dispirited look, but also a touch of hope and optimism. I then pointed out that he could at least go home and be with his wife, who was due to give birth to their first child any day. He appreciated that. The next day, he told me that he had spoken to his wife and that she told him she would kill him if he came back early. She said the team needed him, even if was only to pinch-run, and not to worry about her. A real trooper and she did the right thing for Moscot, and he made it home in time for the birth of their son, who will always be remembered for waiting to be born till his dad came home from the Olym pics.

Both teams traded runs throughout the contest and in the top of the ninth, we were trailing 5–4, having used five pitchers to get this far. In Tokyo, a golf cart shaped like a baseball mitt brought relievers in from the bullpen, and the guys loved coming in on it, feeling like knights entering the fray. Of course, they would have preferred coming in to protect a lead instead of trying to keep us close, as was the case here.

Ryan Lavarnway, who began the Olympics where he left off in the WBC, hit his second homer of the game to tie the game, bringing every-one in the entire dugout to their feet. Standing tallest was Moscot, whose right armed was bundled up like a baby Eskimo but who cheered like a player whose career had just begun rather than ended. Josh Zeid set down the South Koreans in the bottom of the ninth, completing 2 2/3 scoreless innings of relief. Our winning WBC battery was doing it again. We headed to extra innings.

Seunghwan Oh, who had given up Lavarnway's homer, stayed on to pitch the 10th and kept us off the board in spite of extra inning rules giving us a man on first and second to start the top of the frame. Jeremy Bleich entered under the same arrangement, and the result was decidedly different. He hit the only two batters he faced, giving South Korea a walk-off win, 6–5, and putting us in the loser's bracket.

It was a tough loss in every respect, but the team tried to focus on the positives, as our offense had belted out three homers, came back in the ninth to tie it and saw Zeid keep us in the game, just as he did every time he took the mound in 2017. It was an impressive performance for Josh, whom I was reluctant to bring to Tokyo because he had not pitched for three years, but he proved his mettle. In spite of that, it was a still a loss that cost us our best starter and forced us deep into our bullpen before the second game had begun. Even if we could battle our way into the medal round, it was likely we would run out of pitching before we ran out of games.

Our next match up was the next day against Team USA, who crushed us, 8–1. Although we did not have to endure extra innings, we used up more pitchers (seven) than the day before (six), and five of them gave up runs. Ian Kinsler homered in the opener, but was 1 for 9 overall at the top of the order. The only player who seemed to be taking consistently good swings at the plate was Lavarnway, who added two more hits, giving him four of our 14 total hits in the first 19 innings. The only other positive was the two scoreless innings of relief from D.J. Sharabi that kept us in the ballgame until the Americans added on against the arms that followed.

The games were played in Yokohama Stadium, capacity 34,000 seats — 34,000 empty seats. More like 33,980 empty seats. I would occupying one of those seats (that's one at any one time – during a game, I would often seat in at least 10 different places), then there were a few reporters from Israel and our opponent and occasionally some people from the Israel Olympic Committee and Israel's sports ministry would appear, as they were the only ones allowed to attend games. I often sat alone, because that's the way I like to watch Team Israel games, but I also needed to schmooze with these visitors, explain to them the finer points of the game (such as what a strike or ball is), give suitable quotes and lobby for more funding. Danny Grossman was at every game (he seems to be the IAB's Forrest Gump), covering it for *The Jerusalem Post*, and journalist Oren Aharoni attended often.

Under the rules at Tokyo, we had a chance at winning at least one Olympic game and also still had a chance of earning a medal. Mexico, also at 0–2, was next on the schedule; the loser of that game would be eliminated, while the winner advanced to what was called the knockout stage. The last thing we wanted to do was to go home after three consecutive losses, so our guys were as focused as lasers.

The Mexican squad had qualified for Tokyo by finishing third in the Premier 12, ahead of the United States, which was a major accomplishment. In spite of Mexico's having a lengthy baseball history, it wasn't one rich with international titles. Cuba had long been the dominant Latin American country in men's play, while Japan and the United States had won the majority of Little League World Series. Mexico had beaten the Americans twice in the WBC, but neither got them into the semifinals. After making the huge leap to the Olympic Games, Mexico fired its general manager, Kundy Gutierrez, and manager, Juan Castro, less than two months before Tokyo, and there was a lot of dissension in the ranks of Mexican baseball. Both men made public remarks about their country's governing sports body not supporting them enough financially, but those comments did not lead to more funding, just their dismissal. Former major leaguer Benji Gil was asked to take over as the team's manager, and he was not off to a flying start as he was one loss away from being the lone baseball team to leave Tokyo winless.

We took a 6–0 lead into the bottom of the third and hoped to continue generating enough offense so we could use our pitchers judiciously with an eye to preparing the pen for the next game. When Mexico scored four runs, Eric Holtz had no choice but to abandon that plan and manage for this game instead. We led just 6–5 after six innings, and the game was eerily similar to our WBC contest with Taiwan in which we let them back into the game after building an early, six-run lead. But, like that affair, we took the momentum back in the top of the seventh inning, scoring five runs and taking back control of the game. We won 12–5. and the positives were that six different players drove in runs and we didn't need to win our next game to reach the knockout stage. The negative was that we'd used five more pitchers, which is at least two more than you should have to when scoring 12 runs in any victory.

We were exhilarated by the victory and staving off relegation. When we returned to the Olympic Village we were greeted by the Israeli delegation and a congratulatory sign at the entrance to our floor. After all, this was the first victory, in Olympic history, for an Israeli ball team, and still is to this day. But we had more work to do and were still in the running for a gold medal.

Our next game may not have had us facing elimination, but it was our last chance to compete for a gold medal. South Korea was our opponent, and this time they handled us like the Yankees playing Syracuse. We were mercy-ruled after seven innings, 11–1. We'd scratched out only three hits, one by Lavarnway, of course. He was batting .350 after four games. What was killing our offense was that the batters at the top of the order were not getting on base to set the table for the power hitters. They were putting too much pressure on themselves, knowing that our bullpen had already been stretched about as far as it could go.

We still had one more shot at getting into the bronze-medal game if we could bounce back against our next opponent, the Dominican Republic. Its reputation as a baseball powerhouse was largely earned by its current major leaguers and an undefeated run in the 2013 WBC. This squad, however, was not unbeatable, having needed the wild card round just to qualify. If we still hoped to win a medal, they were the right team for us to play an elimination game against.

Josh Zeid did his best, giving us four innings of two-run ball, both runs unearned after uncharacteristic errors by Lavarnway and Scotty Burcham. We were down 5–4 in the eighth when Danny Valencia, looking like his old major-league self, drilled a two-run homer into the empty leftfield bleachers. Danny Grossman went scurrying out there to find the ball for him. We would carry that lead into the ninth, our medal hopes still alive but hanging by the thread of our overextended bullpen arms. Zach Weiss, who had already given up a run, was asked to stay on for his third inning of work because we just didn't have any viable alternatives.

Johan Mieses led off the inning by launching a no-doubt-about-it homer to tie the score, and we were running on fumes. The Dominicans put runners at first and second, then Burcham bobbled a would-be inning-ending double play to load the bases and out us 90 feet from disappointment. Jose Bautista came to the plate. Nicknamed Joey Batz, he was no longer a major leaguer, but he had some career as a power hitter, primarily for the Toronto Blue Jays. As the saying goes; "If he has a bat in his hands, he's dangerous." Bautista did not have a hit the whole tournament and had been benched for the game until this at bat. He came up as a pinch-hitter at the most crucial time and ripped a game-winning single to left-center, ending our Olympic dreams.

That we came within three outs of reaching the bronze-medal game was a testament to our players' hearts and the ingenuity of our manager and coaching staff. Unlike the classless Spanish team that refused to shake our hands in the Olympic qualifier, the Dominican team paused their celebration and headed toward our dugout. Holtz was the first to receive a hug from one of the opposing players as both teams gathered near the first base line. We were, of course, heartbroken not to get a medal, but in the middle of the pandemic, there was something profoundly hopeful in watching these Olympians embracing on a ballfield inside an otherwise empty stadium. Players were not allowed to even touch each other in Tokyo, let alone embrace, and this gesture from the Dominican team was heartfelt and spontaneous, the beginning of a relationship that has since blossomed between the Israeli and Dominican baseball federations. A memorandum of understanding was even signed by the two federations' presidents at the 2023 WBC in Miami.

Mitch Glasser sums up his experience playing for Team Israel:

> In the Olympics, I was playing right field, and it was eerie, because you are playing in a 40,000-seat stadium, but because of Covid, it was empty. And you can say you felt like you are alone, and it's a weird feeling, but I never felt alone. I felt the support of my family and the Jewish people, like, I wasn't playing for myself. I felt that my wife was there with me, my family, and not just living people, but my grandparents were above watching, something like I never felt before and it was like an out-of-body experience....And I hope everyone will experience that feeling that you're performing for something greater than you.

We returned to the Olympic Village dispirited and defeated, and everyone just wanted to head home after our long, four-week journey. I had to scramble, together with Jordy and Stuart, the travel agent, to change all of our plane tickets so players could leave Tokyo within 48 hours. Guys packed and bought last-minute souvenirs, and we left with mixed feelings. After all, we were Olympians and had achieved Israel's first Olympic victory in a team sport ever! Losing Moscot the first inning of the opener and being walked off by both South Korea and the Dominican Republic made things even more painful, as we were so close to victory each time. But an accomplishment that hadn't been done in nearly 50 years, an Israeli team's reaching the Olympics, made things hopeful and satisfying.

The Dominicans would come back to defeat South Korea to take the bronze, while Japan claimed gold in a 2–0 thriller against the United States. In what was probably the strangest Olympics ever due to the pandemic and the empty venues, the Israeli baseball team would go home empty-handed, but only in the medal count. Unofficially, we had put our country firmly on the international-baseball map and our guys had demonstrated once again that you may beat Israel, but they we will always come back for more.

Ninth Inning

The Olympic Aftermath

"Life is like a baseball game. When you think a fastball is coming, you gotta be ready to hit the curve."
— Jaja Q.

Six weeks after the Olympic Games, we had to go to the European championships in September in Italy. I was hoping that they would be postponed, as a new outbreak of Covid was taking over Europe, but unfortunately, the organizers pressed forward. Once again, we had to be tested for covid often, show proof of our vaccinations, stay more or less isolated and be as cautious as possible. That can be draining.

I was burned out by the Olympics and all that I had gone through before then, but we could not withdraw from the tournament. Most of the staff and players were also pretty spent and no one really had much desire to leave their families and go to Italy for 10 days after the disappointment in Tokyo.

Teams in Europe were gunning for us, as we were the European representatives to the Olympics, and we felt the target on our backs. Almost everyone amongst our players and staff gave me excuses for why they couldn't participate, mostly work-related, but family also was a major concern. I know that Holtz had to attend to his academy and could not make it, so Nate Fish stepped up as the team manager. Many of our top players bowed out, but I was glad to have Kelly, Glasser, Wagman, Paller and Wanger as the backbone of the team. Bubby Rossman was playing for us for the first time, as only two weeks before he had received his Israeli citizenship. He had just missed the Olympics, and we could have used him there. Lipetz, Lowengart and Erel were our veteran sabras. But this current roster would be known for its large *sabra* presence: 11 of the 17 players were Hebrew speaking.

2021 European championship, Piemonte Region, Italy

At team meetings, in our meal area and on our bus, Hebrew was the common language, and it was a true pleasure to be on an adult Israel National team with Hebrew as the dominant language. This is exactly what I had been striving to achieve all these years, and it was coming to fruition. On the other hand, I didn't want to make anyone aware of my feelings, but as I was putting this roster together, I was quite concerned that we may end up being relegated to the B pool. Little did I realize how wrong I could be, and how elated I was for these players who went beyond their capabilities to — well, I'll tell you.

We were slotted in pool C with Great Britain, Russia and France, with the top two teams advancing to the quarterfinals. While the rest of the countries in the tournament could bring a full, 24-man roster, Team Israel only had 17 guys. We were so shorthanded that one of our coaches, Natan Bash, registered as a player in case we needed someone to play to avoid a forfeit by running out of bodies.

With all that going against us to begin the 2021 European Championship, our opener against Russia, naturally went into extra innings. Joey Wagman gave up one run in eight stellar innings and left with the score 1–1. D.J. Sharabi replaced him in the ninth, got into trouble and Bubby Rossman was called in and escaped the jam. We failed to score in the bottom half. After nine innings, we'd amassed only five hits, none for extra bases. Rossman pitched a scoreless top of the 10th, with Russia unable to take advantage of the extra inning base runners on first and second.

We'd lost the Olympics opener to South Korea without giving up a hit, when back-to-back hit batsmen did us in. Well, we won this ballgame similarly, scoring the winning run on a balk without recording a hit. The victory was a huge sigh of relief for us and thanks to Wagman going deep into the game, our bullpen only had to convert six outs, including the extra inning. I always feel fortunate to win a game if our offense isn't there, and we carried that good feeling into the next game, against France.

Team Israel had beaten France just two years earlier in this event. It was a one-sided affair that clinched our spot in the Olympic qualifiers. As often happens after winning a low-scoring game that you could have easily lost, we came out relaxed and scored two quick runs in the top of the first. We tacked on four more in the sixth, three on Asaf Lowengart's homer, his first of two dingers on the night, and another four in the ninth to complete a 10–0 shutout. Ben Wanger, who played first base for us in the Olympic Qualifiers, gave up one hit and struck out seven in five and two-thirds innings of relief to record the easy W.

After doubling our hit total and using one fewer pitcher in the regulation nine innings, we were 2–0 entering our last pool contest, against Great Britain. Historically, they were usually lacking in offense, but they had scored 13 runs in their first two games against France and Russia. When we opened up a 5-0 lead after only three innings of play, it was looking a lot like the last time we played them in the 2016 WBC qualifiers where we almost no hit them en route to 9-1 victory. The final score was 11–4, with Lowengart and Jordan Petrushka leading the way with a homer apiece and five RBIs between them. Fish used six pitchers, but that was because we had already clinched a spot in the next round and wanted some guys to pitch rather than rust.

Officially, our next match-up, against the Czech Republic, was called a quarterfinal, but everyone on Team Israel will remember it as the Joey Wagman Game. Wagman, who played spring and summer ball in the Czech Republic prior to the Olympics, had actually pitched for and against most of the players on this Czech roster. He hurled seven terrific innings, giving up only one earned run, but left the mound behind 2–1 due to an error at third by Lowengart. Wagman stayed in the game to play left field, and he tied it with a single in the bottom of the seventh. Ben Wanger gave up only a walk in two innings of relief, setting up Wags for a chance at further heroics when he came to the plate in the bottom of the ninth, with the winning run on second and two outs. Unflappable as always, he ripped a single to center, driving in Itai Goldner and sending us to the semifinals. I normally watch the team celebrate from the stands and then go into the dugout to congratulate the coaches, but this time I charged out onto the field to be with the players. I could not quite believe that this team was 4–0, having defeated Russia and the Czech Republic on blood, sweat and tears. Gutsy performances.

Due to Covid, we weren't allowed to leave the hotel's grounds and had to eat all of our meals at the hotel. We more or less kept to that for the first few days, and only Yaron and I were allowed to go out for the purpose of doing the team laundry daily. I turned a blind eye to the players who went to the supermarket for supplies, as long as they did it discreetly. I knew that they needed a release from the claustrophobic bubble we were in.

Our opponent in the semifinal game was Italy, managed by Hall of Fame catcher Mike Piazza. I am a lifelong Mets fan, and Piazza had provided many memorable moments, none more so than his game-winning home run in the first New York sporting event after the September 11 terrorist attack of 2001. That blast lifted an entire city up off the ground. It made Piazza both a Mets legend and a New York legend but when he managed against Team Israel, I saw a side of him that was anything but heroic. I introduced myself during batting practice, but, although he acknowledged me, he had little interest in the small talk that characterizes opposing staffs before games. In the stands for this contest were also my Italian counterparts from the WBSC, anxious to see Team Israel get its comeuppance and expecting Piazza to deliver exactly that.

Italy would break out to an early 4–1 lead against Shlomo Lipetz, and I was beginning to worry that our team had finally met its match. Silly Peter. Our guys roared back with 10 runs, sparked by Lowengart's two-run double that tied the game in the bottom of the second. We tacked on three more in the bottom of the third when Mitch Glasser, reminiscent of his key hit against the Netherlands in the Olympic qualifiers, cleared the bases with a double. We never looked back. After adding another three runs in the fifth, Team Israel took a seven-run lead into the eighth.

Fish decided to save our bullpen for the championship game, bringing in utility infielder Ty Kelly to pitch the last inning and two-thirds. When Kelly stepped onto the mound, Mike Piazza began riding him, yelling that he was trying to embarrass his players. and *'who did he think he was?'* You would think that as a manager, he knew how few people we had in uniform in the dugout and the bullpen, but I guess he was still learning that part of the game. It was the first time I saw Kelly get riled, and afterward he was muttering out loud, even though his pitching was largely successful. Piazza even had the audacity to sit in the dugout in the middle innings smoking a cigar, and that motivated our players to bury

Team Italy even more. It made our lopsided victory, 11–5, that much sweeter.

With Joey Wagman on the mound against the Netherlands in the championship game and a day off prior, things were looking about as good as possible for our undermanned team. Then, just as our Olympic medal hopes were dealt a severe blow when Jon Moscot blew his arm out in the first inning of the opener, disaster struck again, this time on the last day of the tournament.

While warming up in the bullpen prior to the game, Wagman experienced severe shoulder discomfort. No one saw it coming. He gutted his way through one scoreless inning before having to come out. Starting the contest with only two-thirds of a roster, we were now forced to play for a gold medal with a bullpen game. To quote Tevye in *Fiddler on the Roof*, "Dear Lord! I know we are the chosen people, but once in a while, couldn't you choose someone else?"

Ben Wanger gave us five heroic innings of one-run ball and Asaf Lowengart hit a two-run homer in the sixth to provide a 4–1 lead. With our pitching options thin, we had no choice but to stretch Wanger as far as he could go. Unfortunately, after allowing back-to-back singles in the bottom of the seventh, it would prove to be two batters too many. Bubby Rossman, who was huge against Russia, just didn't have it and allowed four runs in the inning.   We lost to the Netherlands, 9–4, and the tournament was over, Cinderella again coming up just short of the glass slipper fitting. I was overwhelmed with admiration and respect for all of our guys, for the *sabras* who played well beyond their capabilities, and for the Israeli *olim* (new immigrants) who were the glue keeping the team together, who left their egos at home and played their hearts out. I was most happy for and proud of Nate Fish, who once again rose to the occasion to save Israeli Baseball, just as he has been doing since his playing days in the IBL. I use this team as an example for what I have said all along: that we need the American-Israeli players to raise the level of our organization, to be role models, to serve as catalysts and gurus to the sabras and to eventually give way to them. This version of Team Israel was a definite first step in that direction, and although my game plan was for it to happen in four to six years, I am thrilled that it started this early.

<u>2023 World Baseball Classic, Miami</u>

The rumors of 2017 being the last WBC were put to rest by a tournament for the ages. One out of every four games was decided by a single run (including both semifinal games) and seven of those went into extra innings, including a thriller between Puerto Rico and the Netherlands. Israel was the feel-good story, but we shared the spotlight with Japan and Puerto Rico, both of whom finished pool play with undefeated records.

Though I wasn't rooting for Team USA to win, in hindsight, it may have been the best thing that could have happened to the tournament, as American baseball fans finally bought in after lackluster support for the previous three events. It was the Americans' first title, and the WBC needed it as much as they did. Attendance rose 23 percent to reach one million for the first time, while the TV ratings went up 32 percent. By the time the United States and Puerto Rico matched up for the 2017 championship game, the WBC had become a marquee sporting event. This was not only great for baseball, but for Israel as well, as we reached sixth place and could ride that momentum into our next challenge: qualifying for the 2020 Olympic Games.

Obviously, our run to the Olympics was glorious, but our performance was a letdown, so we were looking forward to competing in the WBC in 2023. Israel had proven we could get there, but we hadn't proven yet that we could stay. Our homegrown talent was still in our future, so the present was more about competing, winning games, earning prize money and drawing more and more interest in Israel baseball, especially back home. The International Olympic Committee had decided that baseball would not be played at the Paris Olympics in 2024, and that exclusion amplified the importance of the 2023 WBC.

When big names like Mike Trout, Clayton Kershaw, Bryce Harper and Shohei Ohtani committed to playing in the WBC in 2023 after the enormous success of 2017, it was obvious that the WBC was the most important international event for the sport. Kershaw had to pull out because he couldn't get insured for the tourney, while Harper was recovering from an injury that kept him in spring training. But after Adam Jones robbed his former Orioles teammate, Many Machado, of a homer in 2017, the baseball world was buzzing about the possibility of Ohtani pitching to Trout with the championship on the line in the ninth. The odds of that actually happening were very slim, of course, and even a Hollywood script writer would think it farfetched.

There were still naysayers who questioned the validity of the tournament, mostly based on the fear of injuries that could sideline a player, especially a high-priced one, from his MLB team's starting lineup for a long stretch. On the other side, WBC proponents touted the importance of globalizing the game while pointing out that mishaps happen in spring training, too.

While some of the sports talk-show hardliners still had their doubts, the momentum was definitely on the side of the Classic, especially among players who admitted they had made a mistake by not playing in the last one. When Fox Sports bought the exclusive rights to telecast the event, which included committing pool games to their prime-time lineup along with the semifinals and championship game, it was obvious the tournament was not only here to stay, but was now eagerly anticipated on the international sporting calendar. Team Israel, having qualified already, definitely had it marked on ours.

The planned Apollo 13 moon mission was called a "successful failure": a failure in that it didn't reach the moon and a success in that the crew, facing enormous adversity due to a serious malfunction, returned alive. That makes me think of our 2023 WBC flight.

I had previously lobbied Jim Small and the WBC's management to place Israel in a North America pool so that active major leaguers might play for us, knowing they wouldn't *schlepp* to the Far East during spring training. I also played up the Jewish fanbase attending our "home" games, in such areas as southern Florida and Brooklyn, where we'd played in those two qualifiers. Little did I realize that in the end, many of the big-league stars we hoped for opted out for varying reasons, and that our fan base would be overwhelmed by what felt like the entire Latin population of Florida. Jim and his team there, primarily Nelson Gonzalez and Chris Haydock, ran a very efficient operation and always supported Team Israel throughout the years we worked closely together. They are true professionals.

Ian Kinsler managed and assembled the team, and his coaching staff was top-notch: Brad Ausmus was back, this time as bench coach; first-timer Kevin Youkilis; returnee Jerry Narron; Josh Zeid, not as a pitcher but pitching coach; Tyger Pederson, Joc's younger brother, first base coach; Blake Gailen as third-base coach; reliable Nate Fish, manning the bullpen; and Simon Rosenbaum as our scout. Some of those guys were in such good shape, they seemed they could have suited up to play.

"I was very excited when I was asked to manage Team Israel at the WBC, and it didn't take long for me to accept the position. I enjoyed my time playing in the tournament and now that I know Israel Baseball well from my time in the Olympics, I am convinced that we will have a very competitive squad that will go far," Kinsler said. "I can't wait to visit Israel this summer and see the young talent that will be on display at the Maccabiah Games. We are already hard at work putting together a winning roster for Israel at the WBC and I look forward to making all of our fans proud."

The potential to put together a powerhouse team when we set out to make up our WBC roster was definitely in front of us. Jewish major league players were proliferating, and our roster could have been filled with the likes of Max Fried, Alex Bregman, Rowdy Tellez, Harrison Bader, Dylan Cease, Kevin Pillar, Jake Bird and Eli Morgan. I was in touch at one stage or another with all of them. Some were injured, others were fighting for spots, one decided to join the team representing his patriarchal heritage, but in the end, all remain potential players for 2026. The big leaguers who did join the team and contributed were Joc Pederson, Garrett Stubbs, Dean Kremer, Richard Bleier, and players who reached "the show" during the 2023 season: Zack Gelof, Matt Mervis, and Spencer Horwitz, Zach Weiss, and Bubby Rossman. The ex-major leaguers were Ryan Lavarnway, Danny Valencia, Ty Kelly, Jake Fishman, Rob Kaminsky, Robert Stock and Alex Dickerson. We had a very good roster, but thoughts of what could have been made my mouth water. I want to take this opportunity to thank all those players who did take off from their spring training to join Team Israel in our WBC quest.

I was quoted on the IAB website as saying, "Ian has enthusiastically taken on the dialogue with the Major League players, and I have no doubt those conversations will be fruitful. We are also getting many queries from outstanding young Jewish minor leaguers to play for Team Israel, and we have the roster of Israeli players from the Olympics who are still active. We also have a strong contingent of native-born Israeli players who are now playing in American colleges and our domestic league, who will be eligible as well. There is a potential pool of hundreds of players to choose from."

Unfortunately, we were placed in what would be dubbed "The Death Pool" with the three Latin American powerhouses Puerto Rico, Venezuela and the Dominican Republic. A fifth team was the newly-qualified Nicaragua. You might very well have counted the Latin fans as a sixth country, as they made their presence felt from the first pitch to the last. With this round taking place in Miami, the Jewish contingent almost disappeared inside a sea of Latino team colors, but they were definitely there, led by Zack Raab and Michael Ignagni. Eric Holtz and two of his three children were also in attendance. Mike Sosa, who helped create a WBC forum on Facebook that has over 200,000 members, has been a good friend and supporter of Israel and was rooting for us against everyone but his home country of Nicaragua.

In spite of all the big-league talent that would take the field, the most common name on the backs of jerseys in the stands was not Trout's or Ohtani's. It was Clemente's, for the late, great Pittsburgh Pirates right fielder. It makes you wonder what the WBC would have been like had it been conceived much earlier. Along with Roberto, one could imagine Juan Marichal pitching against Reggie Jackson, or Tom Seaver facing Rod Carew. Luis Aparicio could have turned a double play with a toss to Joe Morgan, while Pete Rose could break one up by taking out his Reds teammate Dave Concepcion. Or, Willie Mays robbing a home run from Orlando Cepeda, or Luis Tiant putting a fastball under the chin of Carlton Fisk. Oh, well. We're lucky that Bud Selig spearheaded the idea when he did.

Israel opened our 2023 WBC play against Nicaragua. They led 1–0 in the eighth inning and brought in one of the Yankees' top relievers, Jonathan Loaisiga, to finish us off. In spite of how many big-league stars we didn't have, we mounted a come-from-behind rally against Loaisiga to win 3–1, highlighted by a two-out, bases loaded double off the bat of the Philadelphia Phillies' catcher, Garrett Stubbs. Unfortunately, it was Stubbs's last at bat, as he was injured and replaced on our roster by his brother, C.J., who hadn't yet reached the major leagues. After that win over Nicaragua, we lost the next three games and missed the quarterfinals, a far cry from the sixth-place finish we attained in 2017.

But this pool was so daunting that the Dominican Republic, which won the 2013 WBC, failed to advance.

In sports, success is not always measured in victories. Hell, even the Yankees fail to a win the championship more than 75 percent of the time. In coming from behind against Nicaragua, we secured a spot in a third consecutive WBC. Mexico, Panama, Australia and Taiwan, each with far deeper baseball roots and richer infrastructures for the sport than Israel, have all had to requalify for the tournament. We haven't. Six countries have never made it out of the first round, something we accomplished in our very first try, and eight more will be left behind after the next WBC qualifiers. The other four European teams had at least one victory and will compete with us in 2026, so surely they have to look at that as a partial success as well.

The rest of the tournament turned out to be another smashing success, filled with upset victories and high-drama moments that would be permanently etched into WBC lore. Great Britain, who had played a surprisingly competitive game against the US, upset Colombia to qualify for 2026, while the Czech Republic did the same by beating China in their first ever game in the main event. Australia stunned South Korea and made it out of round one for the first time in their history while Mexico and Cuba outdid the three Latin powerhouses by qualifying for the Semifinals. Team USA's Trea Turner tied a tournament record with five home runs, including an unforgettable, game winning grand slam that knocked Venezuela out in the Quarterfinals.

The United States would beat Cuba handily in the semis, while Japan came from behind in the bottom of the ninth against Mexico, setting up a championship game between the two biggest baseball countries in the world. Turner homered in that game, too but in the top of the ninth, his team was trailing by a run and it would take a rally to reach his spot in the order. And if they were to mount such a rally, it would have to be against Shohei Ohtani, who was called in for the save and already having an MVP caliber tournament.

Japan was one out away from winning its third WBC championship and had Ohtani, the modern-day Babe Ruth who is a star as a hitter and pitcher, on the mound. Standing in his way was the batter, his Los Angeles Angels teammate and friend, Mike Trout. In a tournament that seems to offer indelible moments, this was the best it gets: Ohtani versus

Trout for all the marbles. Who needs a script writer when you have baseball, specifically the WBC?

Ohtani had a full count before his wicked slider struck out Trout. Japan once again asserted its dominance of the international game. Meanwhile, Ohtani had added the 2023 WBC's MVP trophy to his growing legend, while fans and players all around the world were already looking at the calendar with an eye on March 2026. No one can predict which All-Stars will suit up and what incredible moments will unfold going forward, but one thing is for sure: Team Israel will be a part of it.

2023 European championship, Czech Republic

Nate Fish returned as manager for our team in this tournament, bringing along former Team Israel players Josh Zeid as pitching coach and Mitch Glasser as bench coach. Richard Kania was our hitting coach and Alex Jacobs was coaching and scouting for us again. I was happy to have a staff of Team Israel veterans. This tournament was held in the Czech Republic for the first time, and from the outset, you could tell this would be a different tournament. We had larger crowds, more attractions, better food, fireworks, mascots and lots of fun for all. The atmosphere was electric, the best European Championship tournament to date.

If one player stands out for his contributions to Israeli baseball and what he has faced over the years, that would be Mitch Glasser. He has a heart the size of Texas. Mitch helped us win the 2016 WBC qualifiers but was not selected for the 2017 travel team that went to South Korea, one of my biggest blunders as general manager. Mitch helped us win all those games in the legendary summer of 2019 that qualified us for the Olympics. In Tokyo, he manned right field and led the team in batting average and on-base percentage. He played in the 2021 Euros, leading the team, and coached in the 2023 and 2025 Euros. He is intimately involved with the IAB, mentoring our Israeli coaches, and I am confident he will be a major contributor to Israeli baseball in the years ahead. Although we had the *mensch* on the bench with us in South Korea and Japan in 2017, the real Team Israel *mensch*, Mitch Glasser, was missing that time.

Our 2023 tournament got off to a flying start with a 14–1 mercy–rule victory against Switzerland. Team Israel veteran Rob Paller led the way with the game's only homer to go with his three RBIs, while Brett Holtz, Eric's son, had a hit, two walks, two RBIs and a couple of runs scored. Brett would go on to have a solid tournament for us; it was a shame his father had to watch from home while recovering from hip-replacement surgery. The fact that the games were broadcast on-line in the middle of the night in the United States didn't stop Eric from tuning in, as he seems to rarely sleep.

Unfortunately, we may have been too loose. Our bats fell silent against a German team that had just beaten Belgium 15–4 the previous day. Germany held us to six hits and no runs, including an uncharacteristic 0 for 5 for Ryan Lavarnway, the only starter to have gone hitless against Switzerland. What made the loss particularly frustrating was that our pitching was solid, allowing only two runs to a tough team that would reach the bronze-medal game. In spite of giving up only four hits, Fish had to use five pitchers because we had no actual starters on the roster. That loss set the stage for a second-place finish in our pool and an early, second-round match-up against the Netherlands, something we wanted to avoid.

We bounced back against Belgium with an 11–8 victory, but that game was not nearly as close as the final score suggested. We entered the top of the ninth with a seven-run lead on the strength of a 3–4 performance by Holtz (he also walked), and two RBIs each by Ty Kelly, Rob Paller and Lavarnway. Though he was still a great team leader for us, Ryan was really struggling with the bat, and, after three games, remained hitless, while driving in two runs with sacrifice flies.

Our next match-up was against the Netherlands, which beat us in the gold-medal game in the previous European championship. The Dutch scored six times in the top of the first inning off Alex Katz, who only lasted a third of an inning. We knew that going too early to the bullpen every game in the entire tournament would be our downfall. In spite of three good innings by Shlomo Lipetz, we fell 12–2 in eight innings and were out of contention for a medal, though we still had games to play and hoped for a fifth-place finish.

We were marginally buoyed by a 6–4 victory against Sweden the following day, a game marred by a hamstring injury to Holtz that took him out of the tournament. Lavarnway's bat showed signs of life with a pair of base hits, while Zev Moore and Rob Paller each collected two

RBIs. Justin Alintoff went 4 1/3 innings, the longest outing by any of our starters, while Bubby Rossman delivered our best relief outing with three perfect frames to close it out.

Our last game was against the Czech Republic, which had briefly postponed our Olympic celebration by handing us our only loss in the 2019 qualifiers. The Czechs were now led by Pavel Chadim, who had replaced Mike Griffin as manager and taken them to the 2023 WBC, where they beat China to qualify for 2026. The Czechs had always played us tough, and this game was no exception. We lost, 5–1, with three Czech pitchers holding us to four hits. I was not overly disappointed about losing to them, as this was their last game of the tournament in front of their home crowd, and some of their legendary players would be retiring after the game.

We had finished sixth out of 16 teams, and while it was clear that our homegrown talent was up and coming, it was also clear that we still needed more experienced American players to succeed during this phase of our development.

Epilogue

What's next for Israel baseball?

After the tournament, I decided to take a needed vacation with Ronit. We drove to Austria and really enjoyed travelling around the country and seeing the mountains, rivers, streams, waterfalls and plenty of nature. We were due to return on October 8 and found ourselves the morning of October 7 in a lovely inn overlooking Lake Hallstatt. Ronit was the first to wake up in the morning and look at her cell phone, and she saw the difficult-to-believe videos of Hamas terrorists in Sderot.

I was certain what she showed me was a fabrication, scarcely believing that thousands of terrorists were overrunning Israel. It just couldn't be. I watched more and more what was going on in total shock, and Amit, who was vacationing with his family in Japan and already awake, was sending us most of the news. We were concerned for Maya, Adi and their families back in Tel Aviv, especially when we saw videos, later known to be fake, purporting to show terrorists on the streets of Tel Aviv.

For hours that morning, we couldn't put down our phones or turn off the TV. I immediately told Ronit that Austrian Airlines would probably cancel its flights, so I reserved a spot on El Al, but could get seats only for Thursday, five days later. The kids told us there was no reason to rush home, that we should stay overseas until the situation was clearer, as Amit decided to do, but I wanted to get back to my family and country. This was something different, something traumatic and I needed to be with my fellow Israelis.

Israel was a very divided country up until October 7, with the systematic attempt at destroying the judicial system by the current government in an effort to save Prime Minister Benjamin Netanyahu from prison.

After Hamas's attack and massacre of 1,200 Israelis, *everyone* came together in one mission: to destroy Hamas, get the hostages back and wipe out this national trauma and shock. Israelis all around the globe scurried to get home, some flying on El Al in jump seats, anxious to reunite with family and friends, and to join the fight, be it in the army against Hamas and Hezbollah or as rear guard support.

Those first days were devastating, and at our airbnb in Vienna, it was difficult to deal with the dichotomy of the scenes from Israel shown on social media, and the normal life Austrians were living around us. We received a lot of sympathy and kindness from our Austrian hosts, with not a hint of the antisemitism that would soon sweep across the world just a few weeks later. If I had been in the United States or Europe during this hateful groundswell, I surely would have been confronted by it head-on. My gentile friend in California was receiving dirty looks and endured antisemitic remarks while wearing some of the Team Israel merchandise I had sent him as thanks for his continued support.

We also had our share of anguish. Two people connected to Israeli baseball were taken hostage: Keith Siegel, the brother of long-time IAB board member Lee Siegel, was kidnapped from his home in Kibbutz Beeri; and Sagui Dekel-Chen, who played on our national team as a 15-year-old 20 years previous, was taken hostage from his home in Kibbutz Nir-Oz. The son of my work colleague was killed in battle in the days following the attack. Every morning during the war, I woke with great trepidation at the 6:00 a.m. radio and TV announcement of any soldiers killed the previous day.

Today, more than two years into the war, as these words are being written, the trauma continues. Keith and Sagui came back in Israel's negotiations with Hamas, as did all the others who survived, but their lives will never be the same after the trauma they went through. 41 hostages never made it back alive. With the return of the final body from Gaza, there are now no Israeli hostages there in more than a decade. The destruction rained on the Gaza Strip, both physical and emotional, is heartbreaking, but as a person on the left side of the political map, it was totally justified in my mind. Destroying Hamas, a military organization able to wreak the same type of destruction on my country, with all means necessary is simply a no-brainer. Innocent civilians should not be put in danger, but, unfortunately, there are few innocent civilians in Gaza, as

Hamas has completely infiltrated the hearts and minds of two million people, using them for their own destructive needs. Israel could do a much better public-relations job in letting the world know what is truly going on here, but public relations and marketing have never been my people's strength.

That same friend in California sent me back in October 2025 the results of a CNN poll of Democrats in the United States. It showed that sympathy for Israel, which had peaked at +48 in 2023, was now +1 for Palestinians. After freed Israeli hostages spoke of sexual violence they had suffered at the hands of Hamas, many Hollywood celebrities were quick to post on social media that we should not jump to the conclusion that these reports were accurate. These were the same liberals who, during the #metoo movement, insisted that we should always believe women's allegations of rape and sexual harassment. Some celebrities — David Schwimmer, Scarlett Johansson, Jerry Seinfeld, Michael Rapaport, Gal Gadot and a few others of the Jewish faith — called out the hypocrisy of anti-Jewish protestors. So did non-Jewish celebrities, like actress Patricia Heaton and Jon Voigt.

Now the rebuilding must start, in Gaza and in Israel as well. A new government will be elected this year who will oversee the healing process, unite our nation, and work optimistically toward a better future for my grandchildren. Antisemitism across the planet will crawl back into its shell. I immigrated to Israel close to 40 years ago to build a better homeland and will continue in that endeavor. Things always get better in Israel (they can't get much worse...). That's what the lives of the Jewish people have been like for over 2,000 years.

On the personal front, these years were full of rapid expansion in our immediate family. Our five-person nuclear family for more than 20 years (Ronit, Maya, Amit, Adi and yours truly) is now a 12-person (and growing) unit. The difference is easy to notice when one sets the table — my job — for our Friday-night family dinners. Adding our three children's significant others (Nimrod, Sandra and Itay) and our four grandchildren (Emilia, Dylan, Mayer and Neri) means never a dull moment in the Kurz household. Ronit and I often find ourselves overwhelmed, but truly contented. Emilia wanted to be in Papa's book, so here she is, along with my other musketeers.

Four grandchildren are still one short of an NBA starting line-up, and reaching an MLB opening-nine seems ambitious — but we are game. Each grandchild received a Mets baby overall or t-shirt at birth. Emilia and Dylan proudly display Lavarnway's children's book with the illustration of Papa. Mayer goes around swinging his plastic bat and is joining us at the WBC. Neri, a year old, has a wicked curve ball when he rolls it to me. I am not sure how many of them will grow up playing or loving baseball, but I'm doing my best to indoctrinate them all. Having them living in Tel Aviv today means grandpa and *savta* have babysitting duty half the week, and we gladly spend quality time with our grandchildren anytime. The role is a true pleasure and satisfaction of mine.

Baseball-wise, following the setbacks from the coronavirus, the war has been a huge blow to our organization, and the IAB is always scurrying around to find coaches and managers who can work our teams and leagues, with many of our older players and coaches now in military reserve duty. Because of the twin crises, I left Jordy with the huge, unenviable task of twice having to lead the IAB and pick up the pieces to move this organization forward, and he has done a commendable job of meeting the challenge.

On December 2, 2024, I was awarded the Bonei Zion Prize, an award given annually by Nefesh B'Nefesh to inspiring Anglo *olim*, immigrants from English-speaking countries, who have made exceptional contributions to Israeli life. It was a true honor and public acknowledgement of what I have done over the years for Israel baseball. I was awarded the prize in the category of culture, arts and sports. Other honorees that year included founders and presidents of academic institutions, such as Ben Gurion University of the Negev, Herzog Medical Center and Reichman College; Eylon Levy and Fleur Hassan-Nahoum for their contributions in the field of global impact and Israel advocacy; Natan Sharansky, human rights advocate imprisoned for nine years in the Soviet Union; and my good friend Danny Grossman for his work dealing with trauma, especially in the aftermath of October 7.

Minister of Aliyah Ofir Sofer said this at the event:

> The Bonei Zion Prize is an important opportunity to express our gratitude to *olim* who contribute in extraordinary ways to Israeli society and have led significant changes in every field they have been involved in. These *olim*, each of whom represents an inspiring life story, embody the spirit of Zionism and demonstrate that making *aliyah* is not just a personal act, but an immense contribution to the resilience and future of the State of Israel. I congratulate the esteemed recipients and thank them for their exceptional contributions, which strengthen Israeli society.

I was truly honored to receive the prize, although I felt that it was given prematurely, before I had a chance to complete my mission for the IAB. I was proud that Jordy and other close friends of the IAB were in attendance, as well as Ronit, Adi and Itay. (Maya and Amit were overseas on that date.)

Jordy approached me in May 2024 to return to the IAB as chief executive officer. He needed my administrative skills to help get the IAB out of the quicksand that it was in, due to corona and the war. We worked together on a plan, the centerpiece being the establishment of a cadre of professional coaches working full-time for the IAB, that would provide stability, uniformity and consistency to the organization. I began working on this project. I made progress through the year in finalizing contracts, building new programs, expanding cooperation with Israeli partners and putting the IAB back on the right track. I worked on improving the professionalism of the organization, using my management skills to improve the flow of work and tradformation within the IAB, getting out to the fields and meeting with all of those stakeholders involved (coaches, parents, players, volunteers), getting everyone on board to push in the same direction. I established clear working procedures, funding processes and set clear priorities.

After one year on the job, huge improvements were made, and the IAB was in good position to face the 2025–26 baseball season with expanded enrollment, greater stability, professional coaches in place, regional directors who knew what the expectations were and an optimistic future.

Unfortunately, all of this hard work was blown out of the water, when in the spring of 2025 we saw the first inklings of revolt among the peripheral areas of the IAB, a revolt that snowballed before Jordy or I could understand where it was coming from. I was too involved in the day-to-day running of the organization and Jordy was blindsided by this opposition and unable to stem the tide. In July, Jordy was voted out as president, and Ari Varon and his new administrative team, were elected. I was let go as CEO, told that my assistance was no longer required.

Till today, a few months later, I don't quite understand how it evolved or why, but I think that those who were behind this change never imagined that it would occur with such finality and with such devastating results. The work I put in for the previous year was tossed aside, yet no new plans were enacted. To my sincere regret, now, six months later, the legacy that I left to the IAB is coming unraveled and I do not know what the future holds for Israeli baseball. I hope the new powers that be will find their footing because if they don't, the future of the IAB remains in jeopardy.

The International Olympic Committee announced that baseball will be back again for the 2028 Olympic Games, in Los Angeles. The qualification process will be similar to that in 2019, although details and venues have not yet been made public. Despite my not being part of the decision-making process today, the gears are beginning to turn, my brain is starting to focus, and a plan is slowly developing: How do we perform a second miracle and gain an Olympic baseball berth for Team Israel?

The IAB first has to tackle the 2026 national team season, with multiple teams at the U-23, U-18, U-15 and U-12 levels, and prepare for the 2027 European championships, which will be the qualifiers for the Olympic qualifiers, just as in 2019. The next Premier 12 tournament, which Israel has never competed in, will be in 2027. It is expanding to 16 teams and adding a qualifying round, which includes the 17th- and 18th-ranked teams plus two invitations to additional countries. It's highly unlikely that we'll be invited, although we are currently ranked 20th, due to the political nature of the selection process, but, given that we are the top-ranked country in the Middle East region, it is not inconceivable. In addition, the IAB will compete in the March 2026 WBC tournament, and I hope that Israel's team can maintain at least fourth place and not need to requalify for 2029.

Alas, I will not have any part to play in all of this, as I find myself on the outside looking in. I'm not at all sure which of these projects will even be considered or reach any level of fruition. The dreams that I turned into facts on the ground were realized by a small cadre of believers and doers, who no longer play any role in the IAB. That may bring this story to an end. But who knows? Maybe there will be extra innings...........

The story of baseball in Israel, from the first IAB days through the IBL, WBCs and Olympic Games, is not yet over, and just as David defeated Goliath in ancient Israel, this David is holding his own on the playing fields with the Goliaths of the baseball world. From my first memories growing up in New York to my last days on this earth, baseball has always been the great equalizer. But an Olympic gold medal would look very pretty on my wall.

Stay tuned for more.............

About the author

Peter Kurz has truly been a pivotal figure in the world of baseball in Israel. Under his leadership, the Israel Association of Baseball experienced remarkable growth, fostering international cooperation and exposure, developing stronger ties with the American Jewish community, and culminating in Israel Baseball's participation in the Tokyo Olympic Games. As general manager of the Olympic team, Peter meticulously recruited players, many of whom made aliyah from North America to join this journey.

Peter has voluntarily served as both president and secretary general of the association, dedicating over 25 years to the development of baseball in Israel. He has managed ten national teams abroad and has taken on various roles as a coach, manager, and board member. His tireless efforts have transformed the Israel Association of Baseball from a small group of passionate olim into a national movement, establishing elite academies and little leagues that focus on teaching children teamwork and sportsmanship through the joy of the game, as well as training future coaches for these children. Today, more than 1,000 Israeli sabras proudly play baseball across the country.

In addition to his contributions to baseball, Peter works as a marketing and export consultant, collaborating with numerous Israeli and international companies to enhance their exports, particularly to North American markets. Previously, he served as senior vice president of the Hamat Group.

Peter made aliyah from New York 35 years ago, and he lives in Givatayim with his sabra wife, Ronit, close to their three children and four grandchildren in Tel Aviv.

Two formative events from his youth have shaped his journey: in 1967, at the age of ten, he visited Israel just weeks after the Six-Day War and felt the vibrant energy, electricity, and enthusiasm of the society; and in 1969, as a 12-year-old, he celebrated as the Amazing New York Mets won the World Series.

As the Israel Association of Baseball's tagline states, "Israel Baseball... where traditions meet..." Peter embodies this spirit, bridging cultures and creating a legacy for baseball in Israel. Peter has written his story – the story of Israel baseball, entitled "Where Traditions Meet".

9 789655 977943